TWELVE AGAINST EMPIRE

The Anti-Imperialists
1898–1900

Robert L. Beisner

With a new Foreword

Imprint Publications, Inc.
Chicago

To my history colleagues at The American University

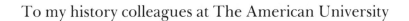

Published by Imprint Publications, Inc., Chicago, Illinois.
© 1968, 1985, 1992 by Robert L. Beisner. All rights reserved.
Imprint Publications edition, 1992.
Printed in the United States of America

Library of Congress Catalog Card Number: 92-073359
ISBN 1-879176-10-6 (paper)

Originally published in 1968 by McGraw-Hill, New York.

CONTENTS

Foreword, 1992   v

Preface, 1985   vii

Introduction   xxi

Part I: *The Mugwump Assault on Imperialism*

1 The American Mugwump   5

2 Carl Schurz: The Law and the Prophet   18

3 William James: Paradise Lost   35

4 E. L. Godkin and Charles Eliot Norton: The Last Straw   53

5 Edward Atkinson: The Informal Empire   84

6 Charles Francis Adams and the Election of 1900   107

Part II: *Republicans Out of Step*

7 George F. Hoar: The Trials of Dissent   139

8 Andrew Carnegie: The Primacy of the Philippines   165

9 Old Chiefs and Stalwarts: The Impotent Protest   186

The Anti-Imperialists and America:
A Conclusion   215

Note on Sources   241

   Addendum, 1985   247

Reference Notes   251

Index   295

FOREWORD, 1992

Since the appearance of this book's most recent edition (1985), history has been none too tender to the world's empires. The late 1980s and early 1990s have shown that centralizing powers attempting to control distant regions or unsympathetic peoples faced a daunting task running contrary to contemporary historical forces. The Soviet—and imperial Russian—empires collapsed, and Tibetan resistance to amalgamation with China continues. Yugoslavia falls to pieces, Azerbaijanis fight with Armenians, Moldovans with Rumanians. The struggles for ethnic self-determination in eastern Europe and the unraveled Soviet colossus testify dramatically to the superiority of the *national* over the *imperial* idea. Woodrow Wilson has turned out to be a far better world prophet than Theodore Roosevelt. Empires appear to be obsolete and imperialism completely discredited.

Or are they? A look at the remnant of America's formal imperial acquisitions of 1898 suggests an ambiguous answer. On the one hand, with its abandonment of naval and air bases in the Philippines, Washington has apparently separated itself from the main bone of contention in the 1898–1900 debate featured in *Twelve Against Empire*. Earlier in 1946 the United States had forsaken its formal imperial control over the archipelago. By surrendering its Philippine bases in 1991–92 in response to resurgent anti-Americanism and the breakdown of the Soviet "threat," the United States has now abandoned an outpost of the post–World War II national security empire and the Philippines undergone a second stage of de-imperialization. In contrast, Puerto Rico carries on as a U.S. dependency, half in and half out of the American republic.

Another mixed story appears in areas dominated but never annexed by the United States. In one form or other, many Caribbean and Central American states subjected early in the century to various degrees of U.S. hegemony remain in place. United States power, though often unexercised, remains overwhelmingly dominant in the Western hemisphere. Many Latin Americans worry (ambivalently) that with the end of the Cold War the United States will exercise more untrammeled power than ever in the region yet without the old urgency to give economic help in the name of maintaining the orbit of "peace-loving" nations. Both worries appear justified. Thus the United States carried out the 1989 invasion of Panama—the equivalent of a ghetto drug raid—with barely a nod to *anyone's* anti-imperialist scruples, at home or abroad. Sometimes overbearingly, it has pressed Colombia and Peru to liquidate the cocoa to which so many U.S. consumers have become addicted, even deploying armed forces in patterns echoing failed Vietnam counterinsurgency tactics. In contrast, Washington now shrugs off former cockpits of Cold War contention like Nicaragua and El Salvador: insurgencies have ended, external "threats" vanished. Wobbly left-right regimes stagger toward reconstruction, now with Washington neither monitoring leftist excesses a là Cold War days nor offering anxiety-generated financial assistance. At this writing Washington still hopes for Fidel Castro's fall in Cuba but does nothing new to hasten the process. Moreover, nearly all important developments in U.S. relations with the other American republics occur in a public opinion vacuum. Anti-imperialist criticism remains as toothless as ever (see the 1985 preface), having practically no influence in shaping the American empire as it stands in the last decade of the twentieth century.

Their attention directed elsewhere, historians have recently added little to earlier scholarship on American anti-imperialism in the 1890s. When they return to the subject, two fresh analytical perspectives—the almost bloodless fall of the Soviet empire and insights drawn from gender analysis—should produce original conclusions. Both challenge our traditional conceptions of authority. Today not only is *imperial* authority in trouble but so too are many other hierarchically organized systems of power. Scholars who reexamine American anti-imperialism in the 1890s will probably not find much resembling feminist social criticism in the arguments of an Andrew Carnegie or Charles Francis Adams, Jr.; but they should find abundant evidence of gendered language in the 1898–1900 debate, especially in the attacks by what William James called the "party of red blood" on womanish anti-imperialists. More basic are such issues as the traditional dependence of empires on a sense of hierarchical order drawn from the patriarchal family. To what degree did the builders of empire invest their own masculinity in the symbols and armies of *imperium?* How much have anti-traditional critiques of hierarchical power structures contributed to the erosion of imperialism in our time? Is any empire—familial, local, or international—safe once ordinary people, whether in trim American suburbs or crowded Chinese dormitories, reject the traditional paradigm of "father knows best"?

Robert L. Beisner
Washington, D.C.
June 1992

PREFACE, 1985

The publication of this new edition allows me to reexamine some of my original views and profit from other writings on American anti-imperialism. More speculatively, I now see the failure of the *fin de siècle* anti-imperialists in light of a longer perspective, a view of the past and present offering scant solace about the future.

Today I might handle the selection of the Twelve Against Empire differently. Concerned with the intellectual foundations of anti-imperialism, and too quick to equate partisanship with insincerity, I disregarded as tainted the protest of such Democrats as William Jennings Bryan, Grover Cleveland, and Ben Tillman. Although Richard E. Welch, Jr., who took me gently to task for this error, concedes that the Democrats' "institutional response" to imperialism was "selective" and "neither emphatic nor consistent,"[1] nonetheless, these men represented a significant dimension of the anti-imperialist campaign.

I should also have stated more clearly why I focused on this particular dozen mugwumps and Republicans. Having confessed to some arbitrariness in the choice (connected in part to availability of evidence), I should have specified that I was writing about leaders, not followers. And I should have made a case for the representativeness of the leaders selected; substituting Moorfield Storey or David Starr Jordan for Carl Schurz or William James, or Eugene Hale for Benjamin Harrison, would not have altered the basic argument.

Many studies published since 1968 support the arguments made in this book. Although James Zimmerman demonstrates that the young and middle-aged spearheaded anti-imperialism in Chicago,[2] most historians depict a campaign led by old men with conspicuously few youthful followers; Rough Rider Theodore Roosevelt saw the anti-imperialists as "men of a by-gone age having to deal with the facts of the present. . . ."[3] Allowing for small disagreements, recent scholarship continues to view anti-imperialists as elitists past their prime, infatuated with an idealized past. Historians writing since 1968 have also confirmed the proclivity of McKinley's critics to lament imperialism's impact only on Americans, rather than on Filipinos or Puerto Ricans, a parochialism of spirit discussed further below. Finally, major works published on the anti-imperialist movement since 1968, while confirming my picture of anti-imperialists quarreling among themselves over various issues, reject the view that the dominant purpose of the anti-imperialist movement was to chart a cheaper and less blatant path to empire.[4] Principles were at stake, and, as Ambrose Bierce wrote in June 1898, "The conquest and retention of distant colonies is a matter of magnitude. It is not done while you smoke a cigarette."[5]

Some new biographical works have refined the portraits in this book. Richard Welch's splendid biography confirms George F. Hoar's power to deny inconvenient political facts. It also suggests that I exaggerated his flirtation with jingoism in the early nineties.[6] Works by Gay Wilson Allen and Jacques Barzun enrich our understanding of William James's zest "for change, new experiences, new scenery, new faces, novelties of almost any kind."[7] But I could no longer describe James, whose life was "a struggle to overcome crippling neuroses," as a "sanguine" man.[8] It is unlikely, moreover, that anti-imperialism could have been at the head of James's agenda, for through 1898 – 1900 other projects kept him out of the country much of the time, he suffered persistently from heart disease, and other personal and family problems wrapped him in anxiety. Finally, Paul C. Nagel's sensitive study of the Adams clan confirms my view of a man of "impatience, bad temper, and abrasiveness. . . ." My account of his crotchety behavior as an anti-imperialist would now profit from Nagel's devastating portrait of Adams's perennial sourness, financial recklessness, "hunger for attention," and "need to dominate."[9]

Disagreement persists about the gap between Republicans and Democrats in the election of 1900 on the issues of imperialism and the Philippines. Richard Welch describes their platforms as sharply at odds, while Walter LaFeber views the parties as rapidly converging on foreign policy issues during the months before the election. If historians used numbers to describe the parties' positions, with 1 representing hostility to imperialism and 10 enthusiasm, Welch appears to see the Republicans and Democrats at about 7 and 3, respectively, LaFeber more like 6 and 4. They do not disagree about the facts of the matter. A synthesis suggests itself. Welch shows that Bryan and the Democrats were never at peace with a policy of imperialism, while the Republicans, though not without furrowed brows, were. Yet he also describes how Democrats waffled on the future of the Philippines and strove to appear loyal to the American "boys" fighting the U.S.-Philippines war. The anti-imperialists' electoral gymnastics (discussed in chapter six) and vain efforts to mold Bryan into an acceptable candidate[10] reinforce LaFeber's thesis of convergence between Republicans and disgruntled but vote-hungry Democrats.[11]

Arguments also persist about the severity of anti-imperialist racism. E. Berkeley Tompkins's thorough narrative of the anti-imperialists' campaign, in line with his rosy exaggeration of their liberal activism, defends them against the charge.[12] Stuart C. Miller takes a darker view, comparing the imperialists and anti-imperialists to the latters' disadvantage. Although most expansionists were racists, he agrees, they tended to adopt a benign, fatherly outlook, consistent with an image of a duty-bound United States watching over the "lesser breeds." In contrast, many anti-imperialists (especially in the south and west) were virulent "race haters," aghast at the thought of tainting America through contact with the "natives."[13] No compromise can be found between such clashing interpretations. While the ubiquity of racism in American society at the turn of the century is evident, so too are the varieties in which it was packaged, suggesting the wisdom of focusing on individuals and small groups instead of trying to generalize about all anti-imperialists' racism.

Although in 1968 I suggested that racism was less a flaw of the anti-imperialists individually than of their era, I drew from shallow pools of charity in explaining the broad failure of their movement. Except for crediting McKinley's skill at parrying anti-imperialist thrusts and stressing the disadvantage of old age over which they had no control, I laid the blame for the movement's failure directly at their feet. Their public displays of internecine disputes, their tendency to applaud expansion in Hawaii but find it morally intolerable in the Philippines, and their shortage of forward-looking proposals, made the anti-imperialists repellent to partisan opponents and unattractive to interested spectators. So did their self-righteousness and an occasionally waspish, mean, and brittle spirit.

But blaming a particular group of men for the barren results of the anti-imperialist movement no longer seems fitting. For—warts and all—they quickly passed from the scene, while American imperialism persisted. Americans may still admire anti-imperialist doctrines, except for the racist baggage, resting as they do on mythic memories of the Revolution and values of freedom and equality. Yet, while American doctrines have no doubt encouraged generosity and prevented the United States from committing crimes and excesses common in the histories of other empires, these values were not strong enough to halt the creation of American empires and an imperial tradition. The failure of the movement of 1898 – 1900 is a chapter in the longer, and continuing, story of the weakness of the anti-imperialist tradition in America.

Here readers may object that I have already convicted the United States of imperialism without a trial. But "imperialism," which displays as many facets as it enjoys definitions, is amply illustrated in the American past: continental expansion from the seventeenth century to the end of the Indian wars; expansion beyond continental boundaries, as in the annexation of the Philippines, Hawaii, and Puerto Rico; *de facto* protectorates over *de jure* sovereign states within the American "sphere of influence," as with Cuba, Haiti, and the Dominican Republic; acquisition of unreciprocated, extraterritorial privileges within the boundaries of other nations, as in China, Japan, and Turkey; and, arguably, assumption of the mantle of "free world" leadership at the end of World War II. Nor can American imperialism be dismissed as an aberration of the distant past while the Pentagon still leases new bases in faraway lands, its men and women often protected by partial immunity from the laws of host nations. The United States embargoes Cuba, filibusters against Nicaragua, twists arms of NATO allies on nuclear and trade issues, maintains troops by the tens of thousands overseas, and worries about the fate of outposts as distant as South Africa and (again) the Philippines.

The anti-imperialist protest at the turn of the century provoked second thoughts about the joys of empire, but did not stay Theodore Roosevelt from "taking" Panama, or prevent a decade of interventions in Mexico, the Caribbean, and along the crescent from Venezuela to Central America. Two of the greatest professed idealists ever to manage American foreign policy, Woodrow Wilson and William Jennings Bryan, launched the most presumptuous intrusions of *Yanqui* power, which ebbed in the 1920s. Anti-imperialist protests rarely dented these assertions of American power. Presidents Herbert Hoover and Franklin Roosevelt finally restored the marines to their barracks in behalf of a "good neighbor" policy, not because anti-imperialists had produced a public uproar but because the United States had discerned more sophisticated means to accomplish national objectives. Less subtle chiefs-of-state would later revive the resort to arms, by proxy in Cuba and unabashedly in the Dominican Republic and Grenada.

The Vietnam war, I now believe, further demonstrates the impotence of American anti-imperialism. *Twelve Against Empire* appeared in book stores weeks after the climactic Tet offensive. By choice, I had omitted the word "Vietnam" from the book to focus attention on the neglected anti-imperialists, but parallels with the struggle in southeast Asia were evident on more than one page. In the summer and fall of that year, I researched and wrote the paper, "1898 and 1968: The Anti-Imperialists and the Doves," wanting to take a direct look at the similarities and differences between the two movements.[14] I found more of the latter than the former, particularly the radical dissimilarity in international context. I also highlighted the vast difference in the *dramatis personae,* young student protestors playing a role in the 1960s not dreamed of seventy years earlier. Methods, too, differed—genteel essays on the one hand, obscene graffiti and street demonstrations on the other. I noted parallels as well, expecially in ideology; Arkansas Senator J. William Fulbright would have provoked no dissent from George Hoar or William James when he attributed the motives of the "Doves" to "a feeling that America has betrayed its own past and its own promise . . . most of all, the promise of the American Revolution, of free men building a society that would be an example for the world. Now the world sees that heritage being betrayed; it sees a nation that seemed to represent something new and hopeful reverting to the vanity of past empires. . . ."[15]

But I overlooked the correspondence of failures in the two movements, largely by assuming that an American exit from Vietnam was imminent. Critics had not prevented American intervention in the mid-sixties, and after 1969 they found themselves effectively disarmed by President Nixon's "secret" plan for peace, his troop-withdrawal announcements, and the abolition of the draft. Thus he gained breathing room to fight and talk four more years before throwing in the towel in 1973.

Congressional hostility to a Watergate-weakened administration outweighed popular opposition to imperial American behavior in causing his final surrender.

Americans' decade-long tolerance for such a poorly-conceived war is puzzling. So, too, in the summer of 1984, is the gap separating certain indicators of public opinion and national policy in Central America. Polls show that most Americans fear military intervention in the area and have found the idea alarming for several years. But Washington arms and bankrolls El Salvador against guerrilla rebels and, with barely a wink at the United Nations or World Court, channels weapons and strategy to counterrevolutionaries in next door Nicaragua, all without provoking major protest. These events seem less puzzling, however, in the context of one thing they have in common: an ineffectual critical response to imperialism. The anti-imperialists' failure in 1898 – 1900, the paltry domestic opposition to twentieth-century gunboat diplomacy, the anti-war movement's susceptibility to neutralization in the Vietnam war, the people's ambivalence about Central America—even their tendency to ignore or misinterpret the erosion of ties between the United States and its allies—are all associated with the weakness of the anti-imperialist tradition. At issue are not the evils of American imperialism—empires can be more or less enlightened, and the record of the United States compares favorably with that of Rome, Spain, Britain, France, or the Soviet Union. What needs explanation is the squeamishness of Americans in recognizing their imperialism and ineptness in criticizing it.

Americans' lack of immediate experience with social revolution has left them uninterested in Marxist or Leninist social analysis and criticism, one reason for the absence of a strong anti-imperialist tradition. More important, however, is the powerful myth of national virtue and, among most Americans, a strikingly provincial outlook on the world; both the myth and American insularity work against the development of an effective idiom of anti-imperialism.

First, the theme of virtue. Most Americans (including statesmen) see their country as innocent and altruistic. Wont to equate the Old World with sin and tyranny and the New with innocence and justice, they applaud the American record in world affairs, seeing in it the superiority of values, not the supremacy of military and economic power. Most believe the United States disdained imperialism until the aberrations of 1898, after which she turned her back on distant colonies and returned to the true faith. She entered World War I for a "peace without victory," hoping to save the planet for democracy and social progress. In the next world war, she gave billions in Lend-Lease aid to Britain and Russia and, with a little of their help, whipped the Axis Powers. After both wars, she nursed the defeated enemies to renewed health and sponsored their return to the community of nations. With the Marshall Plan, she opened her purse to Europeans, so they could rebuild after war's destruction. Today, thousands of her volunteers in the Peace Corps toil anonymously, trying to improve the lives of millions in poorer nations.

This sunny summary overlooks how often American good works served Washington's definitions of national self-interest, just as it fails to explain why the United States felt free to act on values of charity, liberty, fair play, self-determination, human rights. Early freedom from the common caustics of war and oppression permitted Americans to transcend cynicism and pessimism. Remarkably good luck also helps explain their optimism and generosity. Nature began by setting their table with material abundance, while for generations geopolitics ignored Americans as inconsequential, and geography immunized them from dangerous enemies. Today, however, most Americans are either unconscious of the gifts received from Circumstance, or choose to dismiss them. Ignoring the grays common to any nation's history, they prefer instead a picture of America drawn in primary colors: the United States is simply too virtuous to be imperialistic.

Another source of this inadequate understanding of the

world—and thus of the weakness of the anti-imperialist tradition—is American parochialism, which promotes self-preoccupation without enhancing self-knowledge. Constantly reexamining themselves to see how they're doing, Americans excel at eliminating lice from the body politic, but not at drawing insight from other societies. Just as nineteenth-century Britons carried along afternoon tea throughout an empire over which the sun never set, so Americans now expect to encounter their own values and language in any latitude. Even Americans dissenting from their own government's policies often seem parochial. Most of the anti-imperialists described in this book neglected the wishes and future hopes of Cubans and Puerto Ricans while agonizing about the Philippines. And with few exceptions, they feared not so much what U.S. imperialism would do to the various peoples of the Philippines, about whom they knew precious little, but to American ideals and institutions. In retrospect, most of the leading critics of the Vietnam war appear no more cosmopolitan. If not racism, a large dose of ethnocentrism informed liberal economist John Kenneth Galbraith's 1966 crack that, were it not for the United States's foolish intervention in Southeast Asia, "all of that part of the world would be enjoying the obscurity that it richly deserves."[16]

Another facet of American provincialism is a failure of historical memory, which stems from the belief in a special American mission. Typically assuming that the future will bring better times and more interesting things than the past, Americans are unlikely to know anything about how the marines suppressed a Nicaraguan uprising sixty years ago, the one for which today's "Sandinistas" are named. The United States is a fundamentally ahistorical nation, consciously scorning the past as a place to look for information or good judgment. Its people know little either of other nations or of their own involvement with them.

Thus, U.S. intervention in Central America is executed by policymakers and meekly resisted by critics who know little and understand less about El Salvador and Nicaragua, not to mention Miskitos and the Soccer War. A 1983 poll found only one in sixteen Americans able to identify correctly which side their government backed in *both* El Salvador and Nicaragua, poorer results than random guessing should produce. Critics who themselves are unaware of El Salvador's centuries-old domination by oligarchs and their pliant armed forces are ill-equipped to contest the issue in the public arena against a determined and resourceful administration. Public ignorance, undoubtedly worse about Honduras and Guatemala, let alone Chad or Zimbabwe, makes the people sitting ducks for either deception or co-optation.

The weakness of the anti-imperialist tradition, then, results from having inadequate and inappropriate tools of criticism. Most Americans simply are not qualified to judge whether the U.S. has been "imperialistic" in, say, Guatemala or Liberia, given their ignorance of these nations. And, given their belief in American innocence, few of them would even consider the question. Blind faith in a unique national morality (and for-getfulness of the past) renders people unable to recognize the enormities in their own history, or, more generally, to face honestly the role of power in human affairs; the myth of inno-cence causes them to forget three centuries of slavery, the massacres of Native Americans, the suppression of the Filipino insurrectionists, the shooting of striking Anglo-Saxon work-ingmen; and it makes them blind to American imperialism even when it stares them in the face. The myth of innocence means that Americans are constantly being surprised, repeat-edly losing their innocence despite empirical evidence that, past a certain point, it is impossible to remain a virgin.

Naïveté about America's imperial role strips critics of the power to marshal persuasive arguments against it. Lack of knowledge about other nations, and reluctance to admit that states and groups deploy raw power in pursuing national and class interests, make both past and putative critics look soft in describing international foes, unworldly in offering policy alternatives, inaccurate in forecasting future outcomes. Thus, the anti-imperialists of the turn of the century overrated Emilio Aguinaldo and the support he received from other Filipinos;[17] anti-Vietnam activists often depicted the intrepid revolutionaries and nationalists of the north as quasi-liberal victims of southern recalcitrance; critics today, in their repeated calls for compromises, coalitions, and "power-sharing," underrate the revolutionary zeal and determination of Sandinistas in Nicaragua and the guerrillas in El Salvador; and for nearly seventy years one variety of American dissenter has specialized in naïve manifestos about the good intentions of the Soviet Union.

Contemporary anti-imperialists cannot afford this mental sludge—a precipitate of parochialism and the myth of inno-cence. They must deal in truths and realistic alternatives, not peddle reassuring nostrums about how the guerrillas and the oligarchs in El Salvador will unite to write a happy ending if only Uncle Sam will stay out of it. A true policy of non-intervention in these contests, especially if other governments act less diffidently, may lead to radical, anti-American victo-ries. If anti-imperialist critics view such outcomes as an intol-erable threat to the security of the United States, they would be feckless to advocate hands-off policies in the name of prin-ciple. If, on the other hand, they see a preferable course in abiding the consequences of revolution, anti-imperialist critics should say so openly. What they should not do, is provoke contempt by shallow analysis and jejeune proposals.

A retreat by the American eagle from its imperial perch, or outright molting of its "responsibilities," appears unlikely in the forseeable future. Equally improbable is the imminent rise of anti-imperialism as a significant platform of criticism, a development that would require Americans to employ tougher social analysis, entertain fewer illusions, and acquire far more knowledge about not only the "third" world, but the "first" and "second." In the absence of such radical changes, critics of the excesses of American imperialism will probably follow

the path of the anti-imperialists of 1898 – 1900. In the hope
of sparing American ideals and institutions from corrosive
damage, they will exercise the conservator's role in protecting
the myth of American innocence. This is better than nothing,
for, however given to myths, anti-imperialists do not share the
illusion that a republic can prosper in a career of empire.

In originally writing this book, I was especially indebted to
Colgate University and The American University, for providing financial support; to the staffs of the University of Chicago
Libraries, Colgate University Library, the Manuscript Divi-
sion of the Library of Congress, the Massachusetts Historical
Society, Houghton Library of Harvard University, and New
York Public Library, for their unfailing skill and courtesy in
leading me to research materials; to Daniel Aaron, Mary
Beisner, Walter Clemons, Walter Johnson, Eric McKitrick,
and Bernard Weisberger, for reading the entire manuscript
and offering valuable criticisms and suggestions; and to Roger
Brown, Will Inman, the late Arcadius Kahan, and Herman
Sinaiko, for the stimulating conversations that helped far more
than they were able to know. For this edition, I am also grateful to the remarkable staff of the Bender Library of The American University Library, for its brisk acquisition or borrowing
of necessary materials; to my department colleagues Valerie
French and Allan Lichtman, for their penetrating criticism of
the first edition and patience with a "seat-of-the-pants" historian; to Walter LaFeber, for his helpful critique of the new
preface; and to colleagues in diplomatic history too numerous
to name, for encouraging the University of Chicago Press to
bring this book back into print.

Notes

1. Richard E. Welch, Jr., *Response to Imperialism: The United States and the Philippine-American War, 1899–1902* (Chapel Hill: University of North Carolina Press, 1979), p. 61; for his criticism, see "Motives and Policy Objectives of Anti-Imperialists, 1898," *Mid-America* 51 (April 1969): 121.

2. James A. Zimmerman, "Who Were the Anti-Imperialists of 1898 and 1899? A Chicago Perspective," *Pacific Historical Review* 46 (November 1977): 589–601.

3. Quoted in E. Berkeley Tompkins, "The Old Guard: A Study of Anti-Imperialist Leadership," *Historian* 30 (May 1968): 387.

4. I refer to the book by Welch cited in note 1; E. Berkeley Tompkins, *Anti-Imperialism in the United States: The Great Debate, 1890–1920* (Philadelphia: University of Pennsylvania Press, 1970); Stuart Creighton Miller, *"Benevolent Assimilation": The American Conquest of the Philippines, 1899–1903* (New Haven: Yale University Press, 1982); and Daniel B. Schirmer, *Republic or Empire: American Resistance to the Philippines War* (Cambridge: Schenkman Publishing Co., 1972). Identifiable ideological stances of these authors range from Welch's moderately conservative to Schirmer's avowedly radical.

5. Ambrose Bierce, *Skepticism and Dissent: Selected Journalism from 1898–1901*, ed. Lawrence I. Berkove (Ann Arbor: Delmas, 1980).

6. Richard E. Welch, Jr., *George Frisbie Hoar and the Half-Breed Republicans* (Cambridge: Harvard University Press, 1971). On the other hand, I may have underestimated how low Hoar stooped to appease Republican leaders in 1900 and how strenuously he wooed anti-imperialist voters to McKinley's ticket. Schirmer, *Republic or Empire*, pp. 210–11.

7. Gay Wilson Allen, *William James: A Biography* (New York: The Viking Press, 1967), p. x. Barzun's book is *A Stroll with William James* (New York: Harper & Row, 1983. Paper reprint. Chicago: University of Chicago Press, 1984.)

8. The quotation is from Allen, *William James*, p. xii.

9. Paul C. Nagel, *Descent from Glory: Four Generations of the John Adams Family* (New York: Oxford University Press, 1983), pp. 245, 214–15.

10. In Göran Rystad, *Ambiguous Imperialism: American Foreign Policy and Domestic Politics at the Turn of the Century* (Lund: Scandinavian University Books, 1975).

11. Welch, *Response to Imperialism*, pp. 58–74; Walter LaFeber, "The Election of 1900," in Arthur M. Schlesinger, Jr., and Fred L. Israel, eds., *History of American Presidential Elections* (New York: Chelsea House Publishers, 1971), 3:1877–1964.

12. Especially *Anti-Imperialism in the United States*, passim. Richard Welch distinguishes between imperialists who believed in a "master race" and most anti-imperialists, who "did not want the Filipino as a fellow citizen," but who also did not "wish him as a vassal." He has also suggested that, while they may

have resonated as racists while still trying to dissuade color-conscious senators from ratifying the Treaty of Paris, anti-imperialists "emphasize[d] the rights of the Filipinos" after switching to a campaign for Philippine independence. "Motives and Policy Objectives of Anti-Imperialists," pp. 119, 123–24; *Response to Imperialism*, p. 106.

13. *"Benevolent Assimilation"*, Chapter Seven, passim.

14. Originally delivered in November 1968 at a meeting of the Southern Historical Association, it was published in the *Political Science Quarterly* 85 (June 1970): 187–216.

15. J. William Fulbright, "For a New Order of Priorities at Home and Abroad," *Playboy* (July 1968), quoted in "1898 and 1968," pp. 191–92.

16. "The Importance of Obscurity," *Time*, 6 March 1966, p. 27.

17. Glenn A. May, "Why the United States Won the Philippine-American War, 1899–1902," *Pacific Historical Review* 52 (Nov. 1983): 353–77.

INTRODUCTION

Wherever the standard of freedom and independence has been unfurled, there will [America's] heart, her benedictions, and her prayers be. But she goes not abroad in search of monsters to destroy. She is the well-wisher to the freedom and independence of all. She is the champion and vindicator only of her own. She will recommend the general cause by the countenance of her voice and the benignant sympathy of her example. She well knows that, by once enlisting under other banners than her own, were they even the banners of foreign independence, she would involve herself, beyond the power of extrication, in all the wars of interest and intrigue, of individual avarice, envy, and ambition, which assume the color and usurp the standard of freedom. The fundamental maxims of her policy would insensibly change from liberty to force. The frontlet upon her brows would no longer beam with the ineffable splendor of freedom and independence; but in its stead would soon be substituted an imperial diadem, flashing in false and tarnished lustre the murky radiance of dominion and power. She might become the dictatress of the world; she would no longer be the ruler of her own spirit.

JOHN QUINCY ADAMS, *July 4, 1821*

On May 1, 1898, an American fleet commanded by Commodore George Dewey opened fire on Spanish ships in the harbor of Manila and within a few short hours sent them to the bottom. Half a year later in Paris American negotiators demanded and received formal possession of the Philippines from a defeated Spain. And several months thereafter American soldiers were fighting Filipino patriots who had wanted complete independence instead of a mere exchange of colonial masters. In less than a year a strong but largely self-contained America had changed into a far-flung empire already harassed by a colonial rebellion.

Such vast changes do not go unopposed. Americans who feared the implications and consequences of empire—who believed that colonial expansion would propel the United States into the vortex of international power politics, contradict its democratic principles, and reverse the whole thrust of its history—launched the anti-imperialist movement, a campaign of opposition that flourished for two years before losing momentum after the election of 1900. In the course of these two years, 1898–1900, hundreds of prominent politicians and private citizens denounced American imperialism in newspapers, magazines, and pamphlets, made countless speeches on the subject, fought the acquisition of Puerto Rico, Hawaii, and the Philippines in Congress, organized anti-imperialist leagues and associations, and even waged factional warfare among themselves, all in the name of restoring the United States to the haven of safety and rectitude from which it had been rudely dislodged by Dewey's eight-inch guns, the Rough Riders, and the expansionist policymakers in Washington.

This campaign against expansion attracted a diverse group of people. Because they "lost" and time has dimmed our recollection of them and their cause, it is worthwhile to note the identity of some of them. Ex-Presidents Benjamin Harrison and Grover Cleveland were anti-imperialists, as were many active politicians of both major political parties. Among the Democratic anti-imperialists were Presidential aspirant William Jennings Bryan, Representative Champ Clark, Senators Ben Tillman and Arthur Gorman, and former cabinet officers Richard Olney and J. Sterling Morton. Republican anti-imperialists included three New England senators, George F. Hoar, Eugene Hale, and Justin Morrill, House Speaker Thomas Brackett Reed, and John Sherman, who served as Secretary of State in 1897–1898 before retiring and entering the ranks of the opposition. Some Republicans who were no longer active in politics joined the anti-imperialist movement, among them former senators George F. Edmunds and John B. Henderson and former state governor, senator, and cabinet officer George S. Boutwell. The many reformers and political independents who flocked to the banner of anti-imperialism included in their numbers Carl Schurz, E. L. Godkin, Charles Francis Adams, Jr., Moorfield Storey, Gamaliel Bradford, Henry Demarest Lloyd, Jane Addams, and Horace White.

In an age when the general public paid respectful attention to the sayings and doings of university presidents, David Starr Jordan of Stanford lent substantial aid to the anti-imperialists while a more erratic and lukewarm attitude was expressed by Cornell's Jacob G. Schurman, Michigan's James B. Angell, Northwestern's Henry Wade Rogers, and Charles W. Eliot of Harvard. Other academic figures in the movement included Yale's William Graham Sumner, William James and Charles Eliot Norton of Harvard, Hermann von Holst of the University of Chicago, Graham Taylor, Thorstein Veblen, and Bliss Perry. Representing the clergy were Edward Everett Hale, Henry Codman Potter, Henry Van Dyke, Charles H. Parkhurst, Theodore Cuyler, and John Lancaster Spalding.

A few labor leaders joined anti-imperialist leagues, notably Samuel Gompers. Steelmaster Andrew Carnegie was the most prominent anti-imperialist businessman, but he was in the company of Edward Atkinson, George F. Peabody, and Henry Villard.

Former abolitionists like Thomas Wentworth Higginson discovered a new moral cause in anti-imperialism, as did sons of Ralph Waldo Emerson, William Lloyd Garrison, and James Birney. Finally, a host of writers became anti-imperialists, among them Mark Twain, William Dean Howells, William Vaughn Moody, Edgar Lee Masters, Edwin Arlington Robinson, Hamlin Garland, Henry Blake Fuller,

Thomas Bailey Aldrich, Finley Peter Dunne, George Washington Cable, and Ambrose Bierce.

It would be no mean task to think of another issue that has united such a collection of Democrats and Republicans, progressives and conservatives, party stalwarts and independents, businessmen and labor-union chiefs.

This book is not a comprehensive study of all the participants just mentioned, nor is it a history of the organizations they established to combat expansion or a detailed study of the anti-expansionists in Congress. I have been more interested in ideas, sentiments, and prejudices than in votes and maneuvers. For this reason this work is concerned with men who had no obvious partisan reasons for opposing the expansionist developments that marked the close of the nineteenth century. I have somewhat arbitrarily decided not to discuss the part played by members of the Democratic Party even though they provided all but a handful of the votes cast against the Treaty of Paris in the Senate in February, 1899. The convoluted tactics of William Jennings Bryan—who first volunteered to fight in Cuba, then declared himself an opponent of expansion, and finally urged Senate approval of the peace treaty—make a fascinating story, but they belong in a history of political tactics. The purpose of this book is to discover the emotional and intellectual wellsprings of the anti-imperialist movement. Bryan and many other Democrats were doubtless sincere in their opposition to the expansionism of McKinley's Republican administration, but it is a fact that outside the halls of Congress and the speeches of the campaign trail they restricted themselves for the most part to rather perfunctory expressions of dissent and added little strength to the anti-imperialist movement as a whole.[1] An even smaller role was played by labor leaders like Samuel Gompers and progressives like Henry Demarest Lloyd and Jane Addams.

A comprehensive history of the anti-imperialist movement would have to deal with all of these Democrats, labor leaders, and progressive reformers. But in the pages that follow I have focused attention upon leaders from the two groups that really spearheaded the cause: the "mugwumps" Carl Schurz, William James, E. L. Godkin, Charles Eliot Norton, Edward Atkinson, and Charles Francis Adams, Jr., and the dissident Republicans George F. Hoar, Andrew Carnegie, Benjamin Harrison, George S. Boutwell, John Sherman, and Thomas Brackett Reed. The newspapers, magazines, pamphlets, and private correspondence of the day show clearly that the anti-imperialists who were most vocal in the speaking halls, most prolific in the public prints, and most energetic in the anti-imperialist leagues of 1898–1900 came from these two groups. These are the men who furnish a key to an understanding of the spirit of the anti-imperialist movement, for it was their energy and their sense of commitment which provided whatever strength and vitality the movement had.

The mugwump and Republican leaders of the movement had a long record of criticizing American expansion. Many of them in fact had fired their first salvoes against an expansionist foreign policy in the 1860s during the administration of Andrew Johnson. Some had begun their protest even earlier during the agitation for the acquisition of Cuba in the 1850s. Opposed to a belligerent diplomacy in general as well as actual annexationist projects, men like Godkin, Schurz, Hoar, and Justin Morrill, although not always in agreement among themselves, fought against the expansionist tendencies of one administration after another. Some of them were alarmed by the tone of American relations with Britain and France in the years after the Civil War, and a few were disturbed by the annexation of Alaska in 1867. Adamantly disapproving the Grant administration's attempt to annex Santo Domingo, they helped turn the public tide against it.

In the seventies and eighties, even though the course of American expansion seemed momentarily halted, anti-imperialists continued their warnings against deepening involve-

ment in the Caribbean and in Hawaii. With the advent of
the nineties, they saw dangers at every turn—in the establishment of an Anglo-German-American protectorate over
Samoa in 1889, in the war scare with Chile in 1891–1892, in
the attempt to annex Hawaii in 1893, and in the conflict
with Britain over the boundary of Venezuela and British
Guiana in 1895–1896. As expansionist efforts multiplied,
anti-imperialist sentiment increased correspondingly. The
anti-imperialists were prepared for the full flowering of
imperialism in 1898. They had seen it coming for thirty
years.

Nonetheless, just as the death of a friend comes as a shock
even when the fatal decline has long been apparent, the
events of 1898 stunned the anti-imperialists even though
they were not taken by surprise. In their eyes the very purpose and destiny of the nation was at stake. As an anti-
imperialist put it with deceptive lightheartedness: "Dewey
took Manila with the loss of one man—and all our institutions." [2] The movement was for its adherents far more than
simply a critique of American diplomacy in 1898.

The roots of social and political movements normally go
far beyond the immediate issues to which they are addressed.
We know, for instance, that the Populist farmers who
wanted to "raise less corn and more hell" cannot be fully
explained in terms of grain prices or railroad rates in the
nineties. Much more was at stake, some of it hard to define.
Similarly, the emotional reformism of the Progressive Era
stemmed from far more than just dislike of monopoly and
the stuffed ballot box. So it was in 1898. The Spanish-
American War provoked a major crisis of belief and attitude
that caused men not only to wrestle with the problems directly raised by the war, but also to inquire into more general questions about the makeup of American society, the
future of American democratic institutions, and the nation's
future role in international affairs. The debates and arguments that swirled through the country in 1898, 1899, and

1900 dealt with issues of party loyalty, self-government, race, and national character as well as the question of whether to embrace or resist imperialism. The anti-imperialists touched off one of the most exacting and thorough examinations of the basic principles of American government and society in our history.

Americans never again fought another war like the "splendid little war" of 1898. But it would be foolish to dismiss the years of the Spanish-American War, the Philippine insurrection, and the anti-imperialist movement as an aberration, a meaningless sport in the evolution of American history. It was during this period that Americans first committed themselves to a major role in the international politics of the Far East, first found themselves policing the affairs of the Caribbean, and first fought men of a different color in an Asian guerrilla war. The conflict with Spain and the acquisition of an empire did not in themselves draw the United States into the treacherous stream of power politics. But they heralded the approaching end of a century of "free security" and the beginning of a new epoch of war and international crisis. Since 1898 and especially since the First and Second World Wars Americans have wondered what effect these wars and crises will have on their democratic society and its underlying principles. They would still do well to consider the arguments of the anti-imperialists of 1898–1900. Although some of the anti-imperialist credo seems irrelevant, prejudiced, or shortsighted today, there are lessons to be learned that are as pertinent as ever for a people who profess to regard freedom, justice, and a regard for humanity as the most cherished objects of their national existence.*

---

* A word about terminology is appropriate here. People on both sides of the debate of 1898–1900 held widely differing views about the issue of imperialism. There was no such thing as *the* "anti-imperialist" point of view or *the* "imperialist" point of view. I see no useful purpose in attempting to make a rigid and structured definition of these terms or in distinguishing them from such words as "expansionist," "colonialist," "anti-expansionist," and so forth. Instead, I have followed the usage that prevailed at the time

and employed these various terms in their broad connotations. Thus, for general purposes, "anti-imperialist" and "anti-expansionist" are considered synonymous terms, as are "imperialism" and "expansionism," and "imperialist" and "expansionist." It will be evident in the following pages that men who accepted the term "anti-imperialist" as descriptive of their views differed sharply among themselves on particular issues; this great range of opinion is, in fact, one of the themes of this book.

Part One

The Mugwump Assault on Imperialism

On February 6, 1899, the United States Senate ratified the Treaty of Paris, which brought to an end America's first foreign war in half a century. Although the actual hostilities of this war lasted a mere four months, the results were momentous: the destruction of the last vestiges of Spanish imperial glory and the acquisition of an American overseas empire. Cuba, the original bone of contention in the conflict that led to the outbreak of the Spanish-American War, was left in a state of nominal independence under American supervision; in the Teller Amendment to the war resolutions of April, 1898, the United States had explicitly forsworn any intention of annexing the island. Citing the war as justification, Congress did approve the annexation of Hawaii by joint resolution in July, 1898, and, as a result of the peace treaty itself, the United States acquired the island of Guam in the Marianas, the Caribbean island of Puerto Rico, and—most portentously—the distant Philippine Islands. Opponents of expansion had in most cases resisted the drift toward this war, fearing that it would bring empire in its wake. Many of these men were mugwumps, the genteel gadflies of the era who were to lead the anti-imperialist movement of 1898–1900.

CHAPTER ONE

The American Mugwump

A few days after the United States Senate ratified the Treaty of Paris, the old abolitionist Thomas Wentworth Higginson attended a local meeting of the Anti-Imperialist League and returned home to note in his diary that it had "seemed like an old Mugwump gathering." [1] Higginson's observation was both accurate and obvious, for a striking parallel did exist between mugwumpery and anti-imperialism. In June, 1884, for instance, when Boston newspapers had printed a "Call" publicizing the unwillingness of a number of local Brahmins to support James G. Blaine, the Republican candidate for President, the signers included Higginson, Charles R. Codman, William Endicott, Jr., Moorfield Storey, Edward Atkinson, Charles W. Eliot, Charles Francis Adams, Jr., Winslow Warren, William Lloyd Garrison, Jr., Erving Winslow, Gamaliel Bradford, and Thomas Bailey Aldrich—all known as "mugwumps" in 1884 and later to be among the anti-imperialists of the 1890s.[2] In fact, a large proportion of the most active anti-imperialists were political independents, "mugwumps" in the strictest sense. They had spent a good part of their mature lives bolting from one party to another or systematically proclaiming their independence of any party. They were political mavericks who saw no value in party loyalty as such. Regardless of its origins or onetime virtues, they believed a party was no more than what its current principles, policies, and leaders made it.

The term "mugwump" had originated in the 1884 Presidential election, but the guiding principles and independent political tradition of many mugwumps went back to
the anti-slavery politics of the 1840s and 1850s. A number of
the more venerable anti-imperialists had personally taken
part in the political uprisings that led to the formation of
the Free Soil and Republican parties. Quite early in their
careers, they had lived through the experience of abandoning one party for another in the name of principle. These
men had regarded the Republican Party as the savior of the
Union and as a great moral agent in the destruction of
slavery. But the fruits of victory in the Civil War became
ashes in their mouths as they disapprovingly watched the
rigors of radical reconstruction, with its carpetbagger and
army rule. The corruption of the Grant regime left an even
worse taste, and in 1872 many of their number left the
Grand Old Party when Grant ran for re-election (in many
cases to return in the same year because of their dissatisfaction with the Liberal Republicans' nomination of Horace
Greeley for President). This was but the first of many
changes of party allegiance made by the mugwumps in the
ensuing years. When the English socialist Beatrice Webb
toured the United States in 1898 she was amused to hear a
current riddle that alluded to these numerous switches:
"Why is a Mug Wump like a Ferry: because he spends his
life in going from side to side." [3]

The rationale for this kind of political behavior varied
from man to man and from election to election, but certain
elements were consistently present in all mugwump political
thinking. Of fundamental importance was the mugwump's
view of himself as an "independent" voter. Charles W. Eliot
referred to this cardinal tenet when he wrote in 1886 that, as
an "independent," he was "a citizen who looks upon the political party solely as a means of promoting public principles
and who will therefore act with any party only so long as it
seems to promote those principles in which he believes." Or,

as Edward Atkinson succinctly expressed it in a letter written in 1898, mugwumps were those "who put principle above party." [4]

Mugwumps also looked upon themselves as heralds of reform, at liberty to use their uncommitted votes to force reform upon the existing political parties or, if reforms were resisted, to threaten the parties with destruction. If need be, the mugwumps stood ready to create a new political grouping of high moral commitment, just as they had done when they helped found the Republican Party in the 1850s. As Thomas Wentworth Higginson explained to a Boston audience in 1873, party organizations "are truly prosperous only in advancing that idea which gave them birth," and, just as the Democrats had long outlived their Jeffersonian beginnings, so now the Republicans were losing sight of their founding principles, thus proving once again that "reform must be accomplished first by the free lances ... " [5] The mugwump was seldom deflected from his purpose by the knowledge that as a "free lance" reformer he would often be in the minority or by the certainty that at times he would be derided and persecuted in the pursuit of his vision. Political virtue was its own reward, and, in any case, the truth would ultimately prevail and he would be vindicated. The mugwumps of 1898 knew they were right and likened themselves to reformers of the past:

> Witness the little minority which began the anti corn law agitation. Witness the little squad of abolitionists, their long hair, their vituperation and their folly. Both were right and righteously impatient.[6]

The years 1854–1865 were often in the thoughts of the mugwumps. It was then that moral reformers had founded a new party which won control of the federal government only seven years after the party's creation and then proceeded to save the Union and free the slaves. The dazzling and historic success of this new party was indelibly branded into the mugwump consciousness, and mugwumps were constantly tantalized by the thought that they might be able to do something like it again. William James described his decision to vote for a Democrat in 1884 as an attempt to "get the present Republican party permanently killed, and to be able four years later to drive out the Democrats in the same way in the name of a new national party." [7] Similarly, E. L. Godkin had written a fellow mugwump during the 1872 campaign that what he sought was not "a sham break up of parties, such as the Greeley movement promises, but a real break up, involving something more than the construction of a new party machine, out of the pieces of the old ones." [8] Twenty years later Godkin still hoped that the Democratic Party might nominate "a firstrate man on a first-rate platform" to run against Benjamin Harrison, even if defeat was inevitable. Regardless of the outcome, he explained, such a campaign would leave behind it "the nucleus of something better than either of the existing parties—the party of decent and intelligent people, to belong to, and work for, hereafter." Godkin added that, should the Democrats refuse to name a good man or write a good platform, it was up to the reformers to organize an independent group to let the world know that "however few in numbers, we exist, we are sane, and are fighting." All over the country "there are tens of thousands waiting as the anti-slavery men waited for some organization to deliver them from 'the body of this death.'" [9]

Above all, the mugwump thought that his first duty in politics was to be true to himself. He did not look to successful results for justification of his position. He believed that as long as he pursued the right as he saw it, no other defense of his conduct was necessary. Neither party nor country could hope to receive his loyalty if it afforded him no moral justification for extending it. "A man's first duty," wrote Mark Twain to William Dean Howells in 1884, "is to his own conscience & honor—the party & the country come second to that, & never first . . . the only necessary thing to do, as I understand it, is that a man shall keep *himself* clean, (by withholding his vote for an improper man), even though the party & the country go to destruction in consequence." [10]

Being a mugwump involved more than voting according to certain moral principles. It also involved belonging to what Richard Hofstadter has called a "mugwump culture." [11] In their own eyes mugwumps were the representatives of the "highest intelligence and the best culture of the country," [12] the people who possessed "moral weight" or "solid character." More often than not, the mugwump saw himself as a person with an indisputable right to lead his country. This complacence reflected the fact that most leading mugwumps were men of substantial backgrounds, comfortable circumstances, and long-established Anglo-Saxon stock, in many cases the direct descendants of seventeenth-century New Englanders. They had received excellent educations, often at Harvard. Some of them lived on independent and inherited incomes. A recent study of the mugwumps in the state of New York who led the campaign for Cleveland in 1884 shows that out of a sample list of 396 mugwump names, 100 (or 25 per cent) could be found in the *Social Register*. Included in the sample were 101 lawyers, 97 businessmen, 57 financiers, 27 journalists, 25 physicians, 25 teachers, 22 white-collar workers, and 13 clergymen. It comes as no surprise to find that "only one labor leader and one farmer were found in the sample." [13]

Although many of the New York mugwumps of 1884 were young men in their twenties and thirties, the leading mugwump anti-imperialists of the late 1890s, most of them New Englanders, were a much older group. Among them were Thomas Wentworth Higginson, who turned seventy-five in 1898; William Endicott, seventy-two; Charles Eliot Norton and Edward Atkinson, both seventy-one; James Burrill Angell, Charles Codman, and Carl Schurz, all sixty-nine; E. L. Godkin and Gamaliel Bradford, sixty-seven; Horace White and Charles W. Eliot, sixty-four; Charles Francis Adams, Jr.,

Mark Twain, and William Croffut, sixty-three; Thomas Bailey Aldrich, sixty-two; William Dean Howells, sixty-one; William Lloyd Garrison, Jr., sixty; Wendell Phillips Garrison and William Graham Sumner, fifty-eight; William James, fifty-six; Richard Watson Gilder, fifty-four; and Moorfield Storey, fifty-three.*

These mugwump anti-imperialists—men full of years, long experienced as critics and political independents, and unshakably convinced that they were the authentic spokesmen of old-line America—were not inclined to look kindly on imperialism or to shrink from denouncing its sponsors. They were gentlemen of the old school, representatives of a past era, and imperialism did not appeal to them as an exciting new national adventure. In their view the tone of American life had deteriorated lamentably since the Civil War; it pained them to reflect that New England's most famous figures were no longer Daniel Webster, Theodore Parker, and Ralph Waldo Emerson, but "The Beast" Ben Butler, Dwight L. Moody, and P. T. Barnum.[14] They sensed without fully understanding that the growth of industrialism was at the root of the change, and they bemoaned the spectacle of the new and ostentatious rich—flaunting their ill-gotten wealth, corrupting the taste of the nation, and shoving aside the old leaders of public opinion and guardians of public power. Their contempt for the *nouveaux riches* did not ally them with those others who felt more immediately wronged by the wealthy, namely the European immigrant and the workingman. On the contrary, most mugwumps were alarmed by the sight of hordes of poor and untutored Europeans crowding the Anglo-Saxon cities of America. They

---

* It might be worthwhile to note here the ages of some of the older non-mugwump anti-imperialists, as of 1898: Justin Morrill, eighty-eight; George S. Boutwell, eighty; Edward Everett Hale, seventy-six; John Sherman, seventy-five; George F. Hoar and John B. Henderson, seventy-two; George F. Edmunds, seventy-one; Benjamin Harrison, sixty-five; Andrew Carnegie, sixty-three; Eugene Hale, sixty-two; Thomas B. Reed, fifty-nine; John Lancaster Spalding, fifty-eight; and Hermann von Holst, fifty-seven.

viewed the laborer with fear because he represented a prole-
tarian side of American civilization which they preferred not
to acknowledge and because he was the potential harbinger
of social revolution. Even William James, the genial Harvard psychologist and philosopher, and probably as sanguine
and tolerant as any mugwump, called the 1886 Haymarket
Riot in Chicago "the work of a lot of pathological Germans
and Poles." [15] And Charles Eliot Norton, who advocated using state militia to break industrial strikes, called the Pullman Strike of 1894 the most "wrongheaded since the world
began" and declared that Eugene Debs, its leader, was a
latter-day counterpart of "the mediaeval baron who levied
war on the roads." [16]

Mugwump fears, although partly the exaggerated fantasies
of frightened conservatives, were also based upon realities of
social conflict and change. In Boston, for instance, there
were 555 strikes in the mid-1880s. Arthur Mann has written
that the "Protestant and Yankee character" of Boston had so
changed by 1880 that

> the foreign-born and their children comprised three-fifths of
> the 362,839 populace; in 1900, with Boston's population at
> 560,892, the newcomers outnumbered the descendants of co-
> lonial stock by nearly three to one. Sufficiently numerous
> by 1885 to elect Hugh O'Brien as one of their own for may-
> or, the Catholic Irish contended with the Protestant Yankee
> over the school system, modernism in religion, the control
> of the police department, discrimination in employment.
> The Jewish community, which expanded from 10,000 to
> 30,000 with the coming of coreligionists from the Russian
> and Austro-Hungarian empires, formed a third angle in the
> triangle of ethnic-religious relations.[17]

Many mugwumps questioned the wisdom of an immigration
policy that gave entry to such various peoples at such a
whirlwind rate and suspected the motives of the prevailing
party system that made such quick, and often corrupt, use of

them. The mugwump poet Thomas Bailey Aldrich warned of the consequences of keeping "Unguarded Gates":

> Wide open and unguarded stand our gates,
> And through them presses a wild motley throng—
> Men from the Volga and the Tartar steppes,
> Featureless figures from the Hoang-Ho,
> Malayan, Scythian, Teuton, Kelt, and Slav,
> Flying the Old World's poverty and scorn;
> These bringing with them unknown gods and rites,
> Those, tiger passions, here to stretch their claws.
> In street and alley what strange tongues are loud,
> Accents of menace alien to our air,
> Voices that once the Tower of Babel knew!
>
> O Liberty, white Goddess! is it well
> To leave the gates unguarded? On thy breast
> Fold Sorrow's children, soothe the hurts of fate,
> Lift the down-trodden, but with hand of steel
> Stay those who to thy sacred portals come
> To waste the gifts of freedom. Have a care
> Lest from thy brow the clustered stars be torn
> And trampled in the dust. For so of old
> The thronging Goth and Vandal trampled Rome,
> And where the temples of the Caesars stood
> The lean wolf unmolested made her lair.[18]

The mugwumps felt dislike and contempt not only for swarming immigrants and striking railroaders but also for the methods and manners of the businessmen of the age. As early as 1868, E. L. Godkin had commented upon "the immorality which pervades the commercial world, and taints nearly every branch of business."[19] Charles Francis Adams, Jr., who more than any other member of his family entered into America's new commercial life, recorded in his memoirs what must be some of the most scornful lines ever penned about American businessmen:

> As I approach the end, I am more than a little puzzled to account for the instances I have seen of business success—

money-getting. It comes from a rather low instinct. Certainly, so far as my observation goes, it is rarely met with in combination with the finer or more interesting traits of character. I have known, and known tolerably well, a good many "successful" men—"big" financially—men famous during the last half-century; and a less interesting crowd I do not care to encounter. Not one that I have ever known would I care to meet again, either in this world or the next; nor is one of them associated in my mind with the idea of humor, thought or refinement. A set of mere money-getters and traders, they were essentially unattractive and uninteresting.[20]

Ever since the Civil War, in the opinion of these mugwumps, humorless, grasping, and uncouth businessmen and the growing industrial masses had been corrupting the taste and tone of the nation. Evidence of the cultural decline was visible on all sides. Charles Eliot Norton bewailed the lack of good literature, the absence of good taste everywhere, while Godkin characterized the men of ill-gotten wealth as a "gaudy stream of bespangled, belaced, and beruffled barbarians" who knew well enough how to enrich themselves ("Plenty of people know how to get money") but who had no "culture," no "imagination," and no "character," and thus were incapable of being "properly" rich.[21]

Of all the social evils in America, corruption and machine control in politics attracted the special attention of the mugwumps. This one problem encompassed a number of others which preoccupied these men—the decline in political morality, the influence of businessmen in politics, and the place of the immigrant in America. E. L. Godkin once characterized politicians as "lewd fellows of the baser sort" and charged in 1884 that James G. Blaine had "wallowed in spoils like a rhinoceros in an African pool." That political life had degenerated to such a point that it appealed almost solely to "lewd fellows" was owing, he thought, to the growth of the political machine, an institution which represented the ultimate triumph of the idea "that one's own party is the best party to have power." The principle of party loyalty stifled all open discussion and debate within the party organization. It paved the way for the machine boss who paid no heed to the needs of society or the wishes of the "intelligent" voter when he personally selected candidates for public office to suit his own nefarious purposes. Accustomed as the mugwump had once been to positions of leadership and to having his views respectfully received and implemented, he found it especially painful to discover that educated men like himself retained so little political influence. The party boss had no use for counsel from persons of his caliber. Godkin, unlike most mugwumps, also recognized how much beneficial influence over machine politics was forfeited when intelligent and independent voters voluntarily removed themselves from the existing political parties. He realized that this tactic was one of the most self-defeating in the political behavior of the mugwumps, for the party "in getting rid of its more mutinous or recalcitrant members, solidifies the power of the machine, makes insurrection less frequent, . . . [and] weeds out of the party management . . . the element most sensitive to public opinion, and most anxious to secure the approbation of the more thoughtful class of the community." [22]

The mugwumps saw in the many disquieting new trends of the 1870s and 1880s a departure from the traditions they valued, an unsettling indication that the quality of American life had been irrevocably damaged and altered. The country—with its brash new industrialism, corrupt politics, immigration, and strikes—appeared to have turned its back on the mugwump, who, feeling personally rejected along with the nation's time-honored traditions, concluded that America had lost much of its fineness. He was acutely aware of all the changes that signaled the close of an older, simpler, better era. So it was with Charles Francis Adams who chronicled the deterioration of town-meeting government in Quincy, Massachusetts, where he lived:

In place of the few score rustics following the accustomed lead of the parson and squire, and asserting themselves only when they thought that their traditions of equality were ignored,—in place of this small, easily-managed body, there was met a heterogeneous mass of men numbering hundreds, jealous, unacquainted, and often in part bent on carrying out some secret arrangement in which private interest overrode all sense of public welfare.

In the late 1880s Quincy's town-meeting government—under the pressure of a growing population, the rising influence of labor unions and immigrants, and the increasingly professional nature of politics—gave way to a new city government. Adams regretted both the change and the way it had come about. If inevitable, the change should have been lamented, not "rejoiced at," and the "ancient system" should have been "laid away as a parent that was gone,—silently, tenderly, reverently." [23]

The more America departed from her original character, the more it seemed to the mugwumps that she began to resemble the old nations of Europe. Such a trend, if unchecked, would be fatal to a nation that had been created as an escape from and an improvement upon an imperfect European civilization. A New England Brahmin commented in 1869: "It does not seem to me as if I were living in the country in which I was born, or in which I received whatever I ever got of political education or principles. Webster seems to have been the last of the Romans." [24] And when the Frenchman Guizot asked James Russell Lowell how long the United States would endure, the latter replied with the remark quoted forever after by fellow mugwumps and anti-imperialists: "So long as the ideas of its founders remain dominant." [25]

Such jeremiads and demands for politial purity aroused the wrath of the professional politicians. Theodore Roosevelt called the mugwumps "perverse lunatics," and Blaine, the target of mugwump scorn in 1884, said of them: "They are noisy but not numerous; pharisaical but not practical;

ambitious but not wise; pretentious but not powerful." [26]
Senator John J. Ingalls of Kansas described the mugwumps
as "effeminate without being either masculine or feminine;
unable to beget or to bear; possessing neither fecundity nor
virility; endowed with the contempt of men and the derision
of women, and doomed to sterility, isolation, and extinc-
tion." [27] When the mugwumps walked out of the Republican Party in high dudgeon in 1884, their opponents responded with ridicule:

> Sing ho! the political flirts!
> The moral immaculate few!
> There's Curtis and Godkin and Corporal Schurz
> And the Boston Tiger too!
>
> Sing bah! you political flirts!
> You dubious dudish few!
> Sing bah to you all, especially Schurz
> And calico Curtis too.[28]

Criticism of the mugwumps came from others besides the
professional party men who were the special targets of their
attack. Many thought that the mugwumps were too self-
righteous in their rhetoric, too negative in their program, or
too naïve in their policies. The unrelieved negativeness of
the mugwumps, who were against political machines and
corruption, against the high tariff, against free silver, and
against monopoly, was not lost upon their opponents. One
critic described an important anti-imperialist meeting in
Boston in June, 1898, as an opportunity for mugwumps to
toot on their "pharisaical rams-horns, hoping to control
Congress to do their bidding, to wit: *not* to annex Hawaii,
not to acquire Spanish pos[ses]sions beyond the sea, *not* to
ask territorial or money indemnity from Spain, *et cetera
similia*." [29] Whenever the mugwumps insisted that politics
could be purified by replacing bad men with good men, they
exposed themselves to the kind of retort made years later by
H. L. Mencken, who described gentleman reformers as peo-

ple who simply argued "that the remedy for prostitution is to fill the bawdy houses with virgins," an impractical suggestion since "either the virgins would leap out of the windows, or they would cease to be virgins." [30]

By far the most damaging criticism which could be raised against the mugwumps was that, in their preoccupation with such matters as civil morality and public manners, even with tariff reform and "sound money," they neglected to face the truly crucial problems of their day, problems that sorely needed the attention of men of their position and intelligence. Instead of bringing their superior capabilities and considerable influence to bear on the issues that affected the New Americans, the farmers, and the workers, they shrank in disgust from the teeming immigrant population, ridiculed the simple economics of the agrarians, and urged the state militia and federal army to discipline the striking industrial workers. Rather than directly confront the central social and political issues of post–Civil War America, they "seemed constantly to be engaged, heroically enough, in minor skirmishes while the real battles for the control of the government raged elsewhere." [31] It was William Allen White who observed that the mugwumps wanted reform only "in a certain vague, inarticulate, bullfrog fashion." [32] The tame nature of their reform activities was a reflection of their habitual concentration upon the margin rather than the center of American life.

It took the issue of American imperialism in 1898–1900 to arouse the fears of the mugwumps and bring them back to the center of political controversy. They held that the price of expansion abroad would be the repudiation of America's past and the abandonment of her special place in the world —a coin too valuable to pay. In their campaign against imperialism, the mugwumps made their last great fight and returned to the heart of national affairs for the last time.[33]

CHAPTER TWO

Carl Schurz: The Law and the Prophet

Carl Schurz was the most romantic of all the anti-imperialists. He was born in Prussia in 1829, the son of a schoolmaster. Although the circumstances of his birth were ordinary enough, his initiation into public life took the unusual form of political revolution, an experience unavailable to native American statesmen of his time. Having taken part and been wounded in the Prussian Revolution of 1848, Schurz fled into exile in 1849, only to return to his country the following year to arrange the breathtaking prison escape of a fellow revolutionary. This daring exploit made him "suddenly famous" and thenceforth "a marked man among Germans"; [1] it was to be an important factor working in his favor when he embarked upon a political career in the United States. Having resolved that if he could not "be the citizen of a free Germany" he would "at least be a citizen of free America," Schurz came to the United States in 1852 with his eighteen-year-old wife.[2] He plunged almost immediately into political activities, discovering in the anti-slavery cause a substitute for his dashed hopes of German revolution. By the beginning of the Civil War this Wisconsin immigrant was a minor power in the Republican Party, wielding significant influence among the many German voters of the Midwest. Schurz served the Union during the war as minister to Spain and as brigadier general in the field and was on reasonably close terms with President Lincoln. Success and public renown had become his with fantastic swiftness.

Schurz was a man of parts—a skilled orator, a talented musician, and a famous exile of '48—and he made a marked impression upon those who met him. With his wild appearance and long hair, he struck John Hay as the kind of man who would make "a wonderful land pirate, bold, quick, brilliant, and reckless,—hard to control and difficult to direct." [3] This basically ungovernable and independent character remained with Schurz all his life. He possessed to the fullest degree the mugwump's sense of righteousness and moral superiority. There was in him no humility, no flexibility, no mitigating humor. His speeches were virulent and sarcastic harangues, humorless in their self-appraisal and merciless in their appraisal of others. His entire political life was marked by an unshakable belief in his own rightness and an incredible egoism, characteristics that had taken shape in his youth and are best illustrated by his own words:

> I spoke like a god, and today I cannot get away from the praises of my speech. [Letter to his wife, April 19, 1859.]

> My success in Massachusetts was decidedly brilliant. [Letter to his wife, April 21, 1859.]

> I want him to point out in my record a single principle that I have ever betrayed. I want him to show that in the platforms of policy I have favored a single contradiction. He will not find one. He has never left his party. I have never betrayed my principles. That is the difference between him and me. [Remarks referring to Senator Oliver Morton in the United States Senate, in the early 1870s.]

> As to my personal relations with the President, I undertook the ungrateful rôle of the friend who utters disagreeable truths, because I thought nobody else would do so

while it was most necessary. It was an act of self-sacrifice.
[Letter to Charles R. Codman, February 3, 1887.] [4]

After the Civil War Schurz pursued a varied career. He
was a United States senator from 1869 to 1875 and later
served as Secretary of the Interior in the administration of
Rutherford B. Hayes. He edited newspapers in St. Louis and
Detroit, worked for a few years with E. L. Godkin and
Horace White on the *New York Evening Post,* and served in
the 1890s as editor of *Harper's Weekly.* Both as senator and
editor, Schurz associated himself with the traditional mugwump causes. Although originally a radical reconstructionist
who demanded the impeachment of Andrew Johnson, he
changed his position shortly thereafter and became a consistent advocate of liberal treatment for the South. He stood
for tariff reduction and a hard money policy, declaring in
1874 that he was "absolutely against inflation of any kind."
As Secretary of the Interior he made some modest but pioneering efforts in the conservation of natural resources and
attempted to reform the government's Indian policy. For
many years his consuming interest was the issue of "good
government"; in 1892 he became president of the National
Civil Service Reform League, which he had helped to found
in 1881, the year in which he took up residence in New
York. Throughout the remainder of his life Schurz partici-
pated actively in the struggle for "good government" in
every one of New York's mayoralty elections. [5]

In his defiantly proclaimed independence of party control,
Schurz was a pure mugwump. Even before the Civil War,
when the Republican Party had yet to taste real power,
Schurz warned that if it chose to sacrifice its principles on
the altar of party loyalty it would die a deserved and unre-
gretted death. Campaigning for Lincoln in 1860, the thirty-
one-year-old Schurz prophetically declared: "I do not plead
the cause of party discipline. That is not one of the deities at
whose shrine I worship. It never will be." [6] And he was as
good as his word. By the time he had held a seat in the Sen-

ate chamber for slightly over a year, Schurz was in open revolt against the regular Republican leadership, and in 1872
he took the chair of the Liberal Republican Convention
that named Horace Greeley to challenge the re-election of
President Grant.

The sharpest expression of Carl Schurz's mugwumpery
came in the 1884 campaign against Republican James G.
Blaine. Schurz contended that the country was plagued by a
"moral disease" whose symptoms included corruption, materialism, and excessive corporate power. In order to check the
growth of this malady and prevent the United States from
going the way of past republics—to wit "grow, flourish,
become corrupt, rot and perish"—he advocated the destruction of the political party most guilty of spreading the
deadly germ. This was the Republican Party, which he had
once lauded as "the standard-bearer of National honor," but
which was no longer the party "I have been serving." [7] A
reporter described Schurz at this time as a man who "must
be undermining somebody to be entirely virtuous," [8] and
Blaine, one such "undermined" person whose attempt to get
into the White House Schurz helped to thwart, caustically
described the latter's political career as one "consistent only
in the frequency and ability of its changes." He asked who
would welcome this traveler at the end of one of his independent journeys if he almost certainly carried with him a
round-trip ticket? "The party he upheld yesterday met with
his bitterest denunciations the day before, and to-morrow he
will support the political organization of whose measures he
is the most merciless censor today." [9] Instead of taking the
position "of a man sitting on a fence with clean boots,
watching carefully which way he may leap to keep out of the
mud," Blaine argued that Schurz would better serve the
cause of reform by entering the fray and risking a little "bespattering" in the process.[10]

Over a period of many years Schurz established a reputation not only as a mugwump but also as a major critic of expansionist foreign policies. In fact, nearly all of the arguments he was to bring forward against imperialism in 1898–1900 were originally formulated more than a quarter of a century earlier at the time the Grant administration attempted to annex Santo Domingo. The treaty of annexation, signed by the United States and the island republic late in 1869, was rejected by the Senate in 1870, and Schurz, then a senator from Missouri, was among those who voted against it. When the proposal was reconsidered the following year, Schurz spoke against it in a Senate speech which was significant in that it anticipated nearly all of the most important ideas he was again to advance at the time of the Spanish-American War.

Schurz's overriding fear was that the proposed annexation of Santo Domingo would threaten the constitutional and social integrity of the United States and contradict or even destroy its governing principles and traditions. While he showed some solicitude for the Dominicans and professed concern that they would be exploited and ruined by Anglo-Saxon adventurers, his predominant regard was for America's own welfare and integrity. The question at stake was basic: "whether we shall incorporate the American tropics in our political system." Schurz replied to this fundamental question, both in 1871 and in 1898, with what might be called "Schurz's Law." This was a circular argument—a kind of permanently revolving syllogism—based upon his conception of constitutionalism, national character, race, and geography. The Law went briefly as follows: the United States, in order to remain true to her political principles, could never rule other peoples undemocratically; thus, if Santo Domingo (for which in 1898 read "Hawaii," "the Philippines," or "Puerto Rico") was to be annexed, it should by rights be made a state and be placed on a footing of equality with Massachusetts, Georgia, California, and so forth; *but,* since the incorporation of a tropical people into the Union would destroy the very framework of American government, such a merger must at all costs be prevented; hence the only sane or desirable alternative was to leave the Dominicans "their own masters." [11] Annexation, in short, would either violate the Constitution or corrupt the homogeneity of the nation that was essential to orderly constitutional operation.

Schurz maintained that tropical peoples could not be successfully assimilated into the American Union because they had nothing in common with Americans: "neither language, nor habits, nor institutions, nor traditions, nor opinions nor ways of thinking; nay, not even a code of morals—people who cannot even be reached by our teachings, for they will not understand or appreciate them." The homogeneity he ascribed to American society would be destroyed by the inclusion of alien peoples. No "tropical" people—no matter who they were—could be a republican people. In all of history there was not a single case of a truly self-governing republic maintaining a sustained existence "under a tropical sun." Schurz seemed to assume that this long record of equatorial failure was due partly to the inherent shortcomings of the tropical races but—more importantly—to the intense heat of the sun itself, which made any self-government in the region impossible. Even the Anglo-Saxons had tried it "under the tropical sun" and had "failed in every instance." Schurz, who predicted that the acquisition of Santo Domingo would lead to an expansionist epidemic, warned that if the United States were actually to acquire a whole string of Caribbean territories and admit them into the Union as states, catastrophe would result:

> Have you thought of it, what this means? . . . fancy ten or twelve tropical States added to the Southern States we already possess; fancy the Senators and Representatives of ten or twelve millions of tropical people, people of the Latin race mixed with Indian and African blood; . . . fancy them sitting in the Halls of Congress, throwing the weight of their intelligence, their morality, their political notions

and habits, their prejudices and passions, into the scale of the destinies of this Republic; and, what is more, fancy the Government of this Republic making itself responsible for order and security and republican institutions in such States, inhabited by such people; fancy this, and then tell me, does not your imagination recoil from the picture? [12]

The dread certainty that American imperialism would lead to a ruinous end for either American principles or the American constitutional system remained the cardinal point of Schurz's case against imperialism from the 1870s to the end of the century. He vehemently opposed Harrison's abortive attempt to annex Hawaii in 1892–1893 and Cleveland's policy in the Venezuela crisis of 1895–1896. In 1896 he campaigned vigorously for McKinley's election but soon fell out with the new administration over the issue of American imperialism. Only a few weeks after the new President's inauguration, McKinley and Schurz met in a New York hotel. The latter was already uneasy about rumors that an expansionist minister was about to be sent to Hawaii, but McKinley blandly reassured him that whoever was chosen for the post would be under strict orders to steer clear of annexationist schemes. Schurz, relieved, shook hands with the President, who added for good measure: "Ah, you may be sure there will be no jingo nonsense under my Administration. You need not borrow any trouble on that account." [13]

Thus Schurz was understandably astonished when a new treaty for the annexation of Hawaii was signed on June 16, 1897, and sent to the Senate on the following day for ratification. Some two weeks later, he talked again with McKinley. With mounting apprehension he raised the subject of Hawaii only to have the President, who had apparently forgotten their recent discussion, chat away amiably about his tactical plans for getting the treaty approved. Schurz noted the oversight and reminded McKinley of their New York conversation and of the position he had taken at that time on Hawaii. "Yes, yes, I remember now," McKinley fumbled.

"You are opposed to that annexation, aren't you?" Schurz, always a bit of a scold, replied that he certainly was and recounted the reasons for his opposition. McKinley tried to extricate himself by muttering something to the effect that the treaty could not possibly pass the Senate during the current session and the people would therefore have a full opportunity to discuss the issue and make their own decision.[14] But thenceforth Schurz was on his guard and took nothing for granted.

In the early months of 1898, while the administration still appeared to be resisting the jingoes' demands for war with Spain, Schurz wrote President McKinley encouraging him in his policy of restraint. War would saddle the United States with the almost impossible task of guaranteeing "the future peace and orderly conduct" of the Cuban people, a terrible obligation that both the American people and history would honor the President for avoiding.[15] But when war came, Schurz, despite his misgivings, gave his complete support to its vigorous prosecution. Before the fighting had actually begun he had written in *Harper's Weekly* that if there was to be a war, patriotic Americans should loyally press it to a quick, honorable, and "advantageous" conclusion. Disassociating himself from any attempts to stop the fighting (which he deemed unavailing in any case), Schurz urged the country to make "the shortest possible work of it" and then quickly to make peace. But not just any "peace." In New York on May 14, 1898, Schurz told a banquet of '48ers celebrating the semi-centennial of their uprisings that any "true advocate of peace" would "oppose every attempt to degrade . . . a war for humanity to an ordinary war of conquest." Otherwise the United States would dishonor its flag and bring "new wars and untold disaster" on its people.[16]

Not long after Dewey's dramatic victory at Manila harbor on May 1 it became apparent that President McKinley was determined to wave aside anti-imperialist misgivings and follow some kind of expansionist course. While many Republicans felt obliged to suffer this development in silence out of party loyalty, the mugwump Schurz was free to attack. No obligation to party could stay his tongue, and nothing in his personal makeup—impatient, self-righteous, and independent as it was—stood in the way of his now loosing an unbridled attack against the administration. On May 9, 1898, with the government's eventual designs in the Pacific and Caribbean not yet precisely known, Schurz, although still willing to congratulate McKinley on America's "brilliant victories," struck hard at the renewed proposal to annex Hawaii. By this annexation the United States would forfeit the good will and respect of the world, which had been told that this was "a war of deliverance and not one of greedy ambition, conquest, self-aggrandizement." [17]

As the weeks passed it became increasingly evident that Hawaii was but the first of the administration's demands. Schurz readied himself for a major contest, and when the Civic Federation called a conference to discuss American policy toward Cuba, Puerto Rico, and the Philippines, Schurz saw in it an excellent opportunity to reacquaint the public with his anti-imperialist formula. Addressing the conference at Saratoga, New York, on August 19, 1898—a week after the United States and Spain had agreed to an armistice —Schurz once more stated the case against annexing tropical territories to the United States. The annexation of Puerto Rico would lead in time to the incorporation of the rest of the West Indies and Central America into the United States; in familiar phrases Schurz drew for his listeners the picture of alien peoples crowding the halls of Congress and shouldering their way into the Electoral College. The annexation of the Philippines would prove even more deplorable. All of Schurz's old arguments applied *a fortiori* to these distant tropical islands, inhabited as they were by "a large mass of more or less barbarous Asiatics." The fact that the Filipinos and Puerto Ricans might actually want to be part of the American Union was irrelevant. America's first obligation was to look to her own welfare and interests, and these did not coincide with the annexing of new territories. As first-class citizens with full civil rights, Filipinos and Puerto Ricans would corrupt the whole American system; as second-class subject peoples with no rights, they would give the lie to America's free political traditions and be a standing reproach to the ideals of American history.

Whatever direction it took, imperialism would cause irreparable harm: colonial patronage would fertilize the fields of political corruption; profiteers would fall upon the ignorant and helpless peoples annexed; the addition of "millions of persons belonging partly to races far less good-natured, tractable and orderly than the negro is" would serve to exacerbate national race problems; American policymakers would be caught up in the tangled skeins of European power politics; and the taxpayers would be left to groan under the exactions of an imperial state.[18] A month after the Saratoga conference Schurz pursued his argument in *Century Magazine* and warned that, if the administration did not quickly drop its expansionist plans, Americans would soon lose the luxury of worrying about the arrival of a "few thousand immigrants from Italy, Russia and Hungary" and have to face up to the problem of incorporating "Spanish-Americans, with all the mixture of Indian and negro blood, and Malays and other unspeakable Asiatics, by the tens of millions!" [19]

Schurz's most vehement attacks against the McKinley administration occurred in 1899 and 1900, after American troops had begun their task of putting down the Filipino insurrection, which began in February, 1899. Schurz charged that the peace treaty had "half a dozen bloody wars in its belly" and should more accurately have been called "an open and brutal declaration of war against our allies, the Filipinos, who struggled for freedom and independence from foreign rule." When the administration claimed that rebellious natives were to blame for the outbreak of hostilities, Schurz (accepting the more reliable story that the first actual shot had been fired by an American) called McKinley a liar and added: "When we hear him say to the people such things, in the face of such facts, we fairly hold our breath and bow our heads." He had once declared it the duty of each person to support the government in time of war. Now he preached that no man owed the government any support whatever in its suppression of the Filipino rebellion. He told an audience of Chicago anti-imperialists on October 17, 1899, that they should offer their unreserved loyalty, not to McKinley, but to the institutions threatened by his high-handed policies. If, with impunity, the administration could "ignore the issues upon which it was chosen, deliberately create a coalition of warfare anywhere on the face of the globe, debauch the civil service for spoils to promote the adventure, organize a truth-suppressing censorship, and demand of all citizens a suspension of judgment and their unanimous support while it chooses to continue the fighting, representative government itself is imperilled." [20]

At the heart of Schurz's anti-imperialist Law there had always been the belief that the United States could not rule over others undemocratically without endangering the freedom of its own institutions. A democracy could not for long "play the king over subject populations without creating in itself ways of thinking and habits of action most dangerous to its own vitality." [21] By October, 1899, Schurz believed that this process was already in motion since the McKinley administration had committed the United States to dangerous imperialist policies without consulting either Congress or the people, censored news reports from the Philippines, and sought "purposely and systematically . . . to keep the American people in ignorance of the true state of things at the seat of war, and by all sorts of deceitful tricks to deprive them of the knowledge required for the formation of a correct judgment." [22]

Schurz thought he saw proof that imperialism would ultimately destroy the best of American ideals and principles.

Americans were hearing all sorts of new and ominous teachings. The imperialists chanted that the United States should grab all the territory it wanted; "the strong must not be too squeamish about the rights of the weak." The Declaration of Independence was "a mere glittering generality and antiquated rubbish." The Constitution was old-fashioned and must not be allowed to obstruct the search for national wealth and glory. "We have power and must use that power for our profit, it matters little how." Schurz believed that Americans who accepted these ideas were rejecting the meaning of their own nation's whole existence and denying their time-honored ideals of "right, justice and liberty." Dire social consequences would inevitably follow this cavalier disregard for moral and political principles. They were the essential glue holding together the various classes and groups in American society, and without them democracy was likely to degenerate into a sordid struggle for political and economic power. Schurz declared in Philadelphia on February 22, 1900, that:

> What a democracy, based upon universal suffrage, like ours needs most to insure its stability is an element of conservative poise in itself. This can be furnished only by popular faith in the principles underlying the democratic institutions; by popular reverence for high ideals and traditions; by popular respect for constitutional forms and restraints. Take away these conservative and ennobling influences, and the only motive forces left in such a democracy will be greed and passion. I can hardly imagine any kind of government more repellent than a democracy that has ceased to believe in anything.

Expansionists who scoffed at the Declaration of Independence and dismissed the teachings of Washington and Lincoln as "antiquated nursery rhymes" were in effect hastening the day when orderly, constitutional government would be overthrown by an uncontrollable mobocracy of their own making. The costs of imperialism were high and far-reaching.[23]

In enunciating his Law, Schurz had always made the point that the United States did not have to acquire new territories in order to achieve its various international goals. This was especially true of the desire to expand trade. In 1893, when Schurz was writing for *Harper's,* he declared that the United States could own all the "plantations and business houses" it wanted in Hawaii, or "build and control railroads; . . . purchase mines, and have them worked for our benefit" in Caribbean regions "without assuming any responsibilities for them which would oblige us to forego the inestimable privilege of being secure in our possessions without large and burdensome armaments." [24] Nothing happened in the ensuing five years to change his mind and on June 1, 1898, six weeks after the beginning of the Spanish-American War, he urged President McKinley to refrain from annexing new territories and adopt a free trade policy, which would result in increased sales to foreign nations and territories. The United States would do well to guarantee the independence of Cuba and Puerto Rico and turn the Philippines back to Spain, or, failing that, to "some Power that is not likely to excite especial jealousy," like the Netherlands or Belgium. "Coaling-stations and naval depots" could be acquired by lease or some other arrangement. The United States, freed of embarrassing colonial responsibilities and the hazardous intrigues of imperialist diplomacy, would be able to concentrate on developing and profiting from its commercial interests. While other countries warred among themselves, America would have the enviable role of "the *great neutral Power of the world.*" [25]

Schurz wrote the President again on September 22, 1898, to suggest that the United States grant independence to both Puerto Rico and Cuba and join them, along with Santo Domingo and Haiti, in an American-supervised "Confederation of the Antilles." The future status of the Philippines could be settled by a conference of all the major powers.[26] Four months later, he specifically recommended that such an international conference be convened to guarantee both the independence and neutrality of the Philippines. With the outbreak of the Filipino rebellion in February, 1899, however, Schurz dropped his proposal for neutrality in favor of immediate Philippine independence under American protection. The United States Army's attempt to quell the uprising was "a war of barefaced, cynical conquest," and in October Schurz proposed an immediate armistice to be followed by official assurances to the Filipinos that the American people favored their independence and would actively assist them in establishing their own government. Leadership for self-rule, he pointed out, was available in the insurrectionary regime of Emilio Aguinaldo.

Just as Schurz had not hesitated to suggest a plan for American suzerainty over a "Confederation of the Antilles," so he now recommended that an American statesman supervise the formation of this native Filipino government. Americans should be prepared to accept and approve whatever government best suited the Filipinos and best conformed to their own circumstances and preferences—"whether it be a true republic, like ours, or better, or a dictatorship like that of Porfirio Diaz, in Mexico, or an oligarchy like the one maintained by us in Hawaii, or even something like the boss rule we are tolerating in New York and Pennsylvania." Finally—and crucially—Schurz suggested that the United States should commit itself to protect the fledging nation from the interference or intrusions of any other power.[27]

Secretary of State John Hay ridiculed Schurz's proposals when he got wind of them:

> What can be the matter with poor dear S[churz], who set forth at C[hicago] the other day this preposterous program:—
> 1. Surrender to Aguinaldo.
> 2. Make the other tribes surrender to him.

3. Fight any nation he quarrels with.
I think our good friends are wiser when they abuse us for
what we do, than when they try to say what ought to be
done.[28]

Hay hit upon the flaw in Schurz's program when he observed that if the United States had to answer for the security of the Philippines, it must also have complete authority
over all policy and decisions which might affect that security.
As Henry Cabot Lodge put it a month after Schurz had
made his remarks: "If we are to have the responsibility, we
will have the power that goes with it." [29] Responsibility
without unlimited authority was tantamount to offering
Aguinaldo a blank check he might choose to cash at a most
inconvenient moment. It was imperative for the United
States, not Aguinaldo, to be in a position to select—or elect
to avoid—the Philippines' quarrels.[30]

Schurz's forte, however, was political theory, not diplomatic strategy, and any assessment of his contribution to the
debate of 1898–1900 must ultimately stand or fall on an evaluation of the Law. Its racial bias can hardly be called enlightened, but it was a bias shared by most Americans of
the time—certainly by the imperialists. As a temperate defense of the merits of national homogeneity instead of an
alarmist emphasis on the horrors of racial contamination, it
deserved a serious hearing. The most important provision of
the Law, however, was its warning that the exercise of tyranny abroad would create tyranny at home. Schurz's exact
meaning on this point (and that of other anti-imperialists
who raised the same argument) was not always clear. Their
fears usually centered around the prediction that America's
rulers would begin to chip away at certain freedoms in the
United States just as they had done in the colonies. At other
times the anti-imperialists seemed to be saying that freedom
in the United States would succumb to the tyranny of returning colonial officers thirsting to indulge their new-found
taste for ruling with whip and gun.

The fear of a proconsular invasion that would lay the heavy hand of autocracy on the seat of empire itself was patently extravagant and was never seriously argued by Schurz. As to the more reasonable fear that imperialism would jeopardize the public's access to important political information, there was little basis in fact beyond a few instances of news censorship and the official suppression of some anti-imperialist pamphlets written by Edward Atkinson.[31] The harsh and corrupt colonial regime which the anti-imperialists had envisaged, and upon which the government's motive to suppress information would have hinged, never came into being. Imperial involvement in the Philippines, moreover, did not cause the American people to lose faith in their traditional democratic values. Most of them convinced themselves that there was no conflict between these values and the mild colonial rule which the United States came to exercise over the Philippines. Others simply accepted a double standard: they insisted on democracy at home regardless of what happened in the Philippines. Indeed, at this point in their national history, Americans not only maintained their belief in democratic values, but, in the years following the Spanish-American War, set about to strengthen their own institutions in accordance with these values. The establishment of colonial government in the Philippines coincided interestingly enough with the beginning of the Progressive Era in America.

Schurz had been headed in the right direction when he claimed that imperialism was contrary to America's traditions and inconsistent with her democratic principles, however benevolent her rule over a particular territory. All the sophistry of the expansionists on this point was ultimately unconvincing. But when Schurz came to predicting the actual consequences of America's imperialist outburst, his extravagant and exaggerative bent undid him. The United States annexed Puerto Rico, a few years later acquired the Panama Canal Zone, and for years thereafter wielded great and at times highhanded influence in the Caribbean, but it did not seize all of Central America and the West Indies as Schurz had foretold it would were it to take just one island. One piece of sugar candy did not cause a fatal rash. The undemocratic rule of new insular possessions did not discernibly shake Americans' faith in democratic ideals, and there is no evidence to indicate that domestic political practices were ever significantly affected by America's colonial experience. The United States has never suffered at the hands of restless proconsuls home from the colonies.

Yet none could say that this veteran of '48 had not fought a long and courageous battle against imperialism. His proposals were often unrealistic, his criticisms exaggerated, and his attitude toward the victims of imperialism no more liberal than the imperialists'. Few other men of his time, however, could claim such unflagging attention to reform and to the means of effecting it as could the intrepid mugwump, Carl Schurz. Was it all for nought? Toward the end of his life Schurz had his doubts. By 1902 the seventy-three-year-old reformer, dismayed by America's plunge into imperialism, concluded that the country to whose shores he had come a half century earlier had ceased to exist:

> Can you imagine the feelings of a man who all his life has struggled for human liberty and popular government, who for that reason had to flee from his native country, who believed he had found what he sought in this Republic, and thus came to love this Republic even more than the land of his birth, and who at last, at the close of his life, sees that beloved Republic in the clutches of sinister powers which seduce and betray it into an abandonment of its most sacred principles and traditions and push it into policies and practices even worse than those which once he had to flee from? [32]

CHAPTER THREE

William James: Paradise Lost

The Singular Mugwump

William James brought to anti-imperialism and mug-wumpery a rare appreciation of America's dominant traits and an unusual optimism about her future. This confidence in the possibilities of human nature and relish for things new and untried set James apart from the average New England mugwump, who was inclined by nature to be rather pessimistic and suspicious of change. James had none of Carl Schurz's irritating cockiness or E. L. Godkin's apocalyptic gloom. Although he credited Godkin's *Nation* for his "whole political education," he often objected to the mugwump editor's bilious and contentious polemics. During the Venezuela crisis of 1895–1896, James urged Godkin to be "as non-expletive and patiently explanatory as you can. . . . Father, forgive them for they know not what they do!" [1] Normally inclined to view the world as an arena in which much that happened was good, James found in the Spanish-American War and American imperialism a hard challenge to his optimism.

James was born in 1842, the son of the elder Henry James, an eccentric Swedenborgian philosopher and member of the

Brook Farm circle. Young William grew up among men who were more at home with heresy than with orthodoxy. His father had been attracted to Fourierism, communism, homeopathy, women's rights, abolition, and spiritualism, and in similar fashion James, who was to become one of America's pioneering psychologists and philosophers, evidenced throughout his life an open-minded interest in mediums, clairvoyants, mesmerists, and crystal gazers. Despite his youthful association with the humanitarian tradition of Brook Farm, it was not until James reached his fifties that he gave much attention to social and political questions. Ralph Barton Perry, his biographer, characterizes the years 1892–1902 as James's "period of reform and evangelism." [2] His earlier years were given over to his academic pursuits at Harvard, where he began teaching in 1873. Although he found little time for politics during this period, he was already in the mugwump camp.

In some respects James typified the mugwump outlook. He traced his political heritage to the days of abolitionism. Like most mugwumps he was saddened by a political atmosphere that kept the nation's best men "sulking in their tents" rather than in active public service. In 1884 he joined the mugwump opposition to James G. Blaine, whom he condemned for venality, "waving the bloody shirt," and addiction to old party shibboleths. When he expressed the hope that the elections of 1884 and 1888 would result in the substitution of a new "national" party for the two old ones, James was envisaging a purely mugwump organization—one "with something of an intellectual character" that would reform the civil service and reduce the protective tariff. Like his mugwump friends, James deplored the growth of radicalism, jingoism, and materialism, and although buoyant by nature, he fell at times into the despair that marked so many of his compatriots. On occasion he could even share their perverse wish for chastening misfortune to descend upon their country, as his letter of 1900 to Havelock Ellis illustrates: "America is too prosperous just now for any but optimistic impressions, but I trust we are only fattening to kill." [3]

But James did not always fit the mugwump mold. Unlike most Boston mugwumps, for instance, he took an irreverent view of the local cultural set:

> Last night [he wrote in 1876] I went of all places in the world to Mrs. Sargent's aesthetic tea in Chestnut Street. Certain individuals read poetry, whilst others sat and longed for them to stop so that they might begin to talk. The room was full of a decidedly good-looking set of people, especially women—but New England all over! Give me a human race with some *guts* to them, no matter if they do belch at you now and then. [4]

He had his own views on social and political matters. Far more than his associates, James accepted the clamor and contention of the America of his time. He was not particularly worried about immigrants. Despite his remark about the "pathological Germans and Poles" involved in the Haymarket Riot, he believed that working-class discontent was "a most healthy phase of evolution, a little costly, but normal, and sure to do lots of good to all hands in the end." The Presidential campaign of 1896, which sent droves of panicky mugwumps into the arms of the arch-protectionist McKinley, thrust James in the same direction, but not in panic. He viewed the canvass with good-humored interest. Where E. L. Godkin looked upon the Nebraskan figure of William Jennings Bryan and saw the shadow of Robespierre, James saw only an honest if deluded man leading a people bowed down by real problems and grievances. In the national debate over free silver he discerned an excellent education for the people and a heartening sign of their growing seriousness. [5]

James was prepared to concede that democracy left much to be desired—for one thing, it encouraged mediocrity—but he rejected the facile assumption of many mugwumps that the fine and noble things of life were never to be found on the flat plains of democracy, but only on the heights of aristocracy. Even the mediocrity fostered by democracy was mitigated by the existence of "a vague ideal of public good." The real danger in democratic states was the ever-present possibility that individuality might be smothered. "Let us be content," he wrote in 1878, "to demand of democracy that it shall not stifle the individual. That is everything." [6]

In line with the mugwump tradition, James assigned to America's intellectuals a crucial role in the perpetuation of a viable democratic system. He urged America's thinkers to organize politically and to develop a "class-conscious" awareness of their peculiar responsibilities to society. They should guard its "tone," choose its leaders, blunt the greed of its corrupt politicians, and temper the destructive fury of its masses. These intellectuals would form a party of "pale reflection" dedicated to the use of reason in the pursuit of orderly progress. James apparently nourished no great illusions about such a party's ultimate effectiveness, however, for unlike most mugwumps he fully appreciated with what ease professional politicians could gain the upper hand in any organization set up to oppose them. He also understood that the professionals frequently succeeded where the mugwumps failed because, in addition to their control of political machinery and occasional use of corrupt methods, they enjoyed some real advantages over educated reformers in any contest for popular favor. They struck most voters as being far more practical than "a lot of pure idealists," and they had no qualms about appealing directly to the voters' self-interest and prejudices in order to keep their favor. The mugwumps, on the other hand, were burdened with an almost insuperable handicap, the nature of which James explained in a speech at Harvard on January 9, 1902:

> [The party of "educated intellect"] has to blow cold upon the hot excitement, and hot upon the cold motive; and this judicial and neutral attitude sometimes wears, it must be confessed, a priggish expression and is generally unpopular

and distasteful. The intellectual critic as such knows of so many interests, that to the ardent partisan he seems to have none—to be a sort of bloodless bore and mugwump. . . . Living mugwumps have indeed a harder row to hoe than members of the regular organizations. Often their only audience is posterity. Their names are first honored when the breath has left their bodies, and, like the holders of insurance policies, they must die to win their wager.[7]

James's mugwumpery did not prevent his holding a less than enthusiastic opinion of England and a "crudely patriotic" view of America.[8] On his visits to England he complained of being cramped and hemmed in. He wrote Charles Eliot Norton in 1901 that he was once again finding England "ungracious, unamiable and heavy." He was fond of needling such Anglophiles as his expatriate brother Henry James and E. L. Godkin, who moved to England in the spring of 1901. James told Godkin that England was "too padded and cushioned" for his "rustic taste." "After all," he wrote from his brother's English home, "in spite of you and Henry, and all Americophobes, I'm glad I'm going back to my own country again."[9]

Such disparaging remarks about England did not really reflect a dislike of the country—in fact he once called it the most "wholesome good humoured spot on the map of Humanity"[10]—but rather a backhanded way of emphasizing his high regard for America. Herein he differed from the main body of mugwumps, whose frequent criticism of American life and politics earned them the special enmity of the Grand Army of the Republic and other patriotic societies.[11] James looked upon his country's shortcomings more calmly; he saw its political corruption as "a mere flyspeck of superficiality compared with the rooted and permanent forces of corruption that exist in the European states."[12] He was strongly attracted to the virtues of his own land and believed it his duty to praise and strengthen them. His frequent travels simply increased his need "to steep [himself] in America

again and let the broken rootlets make new adhesions to the
native soil." It was wrong to divide one's national loyalties:
"A man coquetting with too many countries is as bad as a
bigamist, and loses his soul altogether." America was his lawful mate, and no European siren could contest her legal and
moral claim to his devotion. He loved her precisely for those
ways which seemed to distinguish her from Europe—for her
"youth and youth's infinite and touching promise," her
"transparent, passionate, impulsive variety and headlong
fling." Above all, James exulted in his country's "greenness,
her plasticity, innocence, good intentions, friends, everything." [13]

The Savage Instincts

William James believed that anger and pugnacity were
among the most firmly rooted and enduring of human instincts. Indeed, he thought it likely that the instinct of com-
bativeness would never be suppressed by the civilizing and
socializing process that had succeeded in raising man above
the animals. From the psychologist's vantage point war and
imperialism were historical expressions of man's own time-
less drives. James, though in some measure repelled by these
sudden martial outbursts, which reminded him that civilization was but a thin veneer over a savage base, nevertheless
found himself stirred by their power and attracted by their
potential for good.

He had been profoundly impressed during the Venezuelan
crisis of 1895–1896 with how easily man's belligerence
could come to the surface. With one veiled threat of war
against Britain President Cleveland had erased the "peace
habits of a hundred years" and stirred up a "fighting mob-
hysteria." Apparently it had taken only this to arouse "in all
of us the old fighting instinct." [14] Further dramatic proof of
this fact came when Americans went joyously to war in 1898.
James believed that what most Americans wanted was the

sheer excitement of war. Jingoism was not an expression of hostility to some particular rival nation, but a national yearning for excitement. In league with the desire for greatness and mastery, the "passion for *adventure*" had propelled America into this unnecessary war. After the destruction of the Spanish fleet at Manila and the successful invasion of Cuba, James concluded that Americans were "in so little danger from Spain" that their continued interest in the war could only be explained in terms of their craving for "a peculiarly exciting kind of *sport*." [15] War and imperialism grew out of the same irresistible drives. Americans succumbed to the lure of empire because it promised them intoxicating adventures and an outlet for their domineering instincts. The notion that they were interested in "raising and educating inferior races" was "mere hollow pretext and unreality." [16]

However much James feared "the power of the wardemon when once let loose," [17] he was strongly drawn to its elemental vitality and convinced that it could work for good as well as evil. He pointed out that the jingoistic response to President Cleveland's message on Venezuela had demonstrated "that in spite of party frenzies our republic is still a unit when it comes to a question of obedience to the executive"; instead of viewing such mass obedience as a threat to individual freedom or as proof that the public could be manipulated at will, James saw in it the foundation "of all national safety and greatness." So struck was he by the vehemence of the war instincts Cleveland had aroused that he exclaimed: "by those instincts all the sacred deeds of history have been wrought, and with them all the sacred phrases are associated." [18] In the early days of the Spanish-American War James declared that war and imperialism might be crucial factors in shaping a nation's greatness if they did not first ruin it. It was even possible that war might be the only thing that could "hammer us into decency" as he believed it had done in many European nations. Although he regretted that moderate counsels were being disregarded in the on-rushing tide of adventure sweeping the whole country, he too was partially caught up by the same frenzy:

> After all, hasn't the spirit of the life of all great generals and rulers and aristocracies always been the spirit of sport carried to its supreme expression? Civilization, properly so-called, might well be termed the organization of all those functions that resist the mere excitement of sport. But *excitement!* Shall we not worship excitement? And after all, what is life for, except for opportunities of excitement?! It makes all humdrum moralizing seem terribly dead and tame! [19]

In his personal reactions James reflected the universal ambivalence which is felt toward war and the "martial virtues." In the end his distaste for organized bloodspilling was stronger than his attraction to it. In a speech given in 1897 James had already indicated which side he would be on when the fighting started. While he acknowledged that war had historically been the crucible in which anarchy was transformed into community and man's self-love into "social virtue," he nonetheless insisted that civilization itself was the fruit of a sustained attempt to control and check man's war spirit. To be sure, the effort had met with only partial success: "Man is once for all a fighting animal; centuries of peaceful history could not breed the battle-instinct out of us." All the more reason, therefore, for enlightened men to bend themselves unremittingly to the containment—not the encouragement—of their savage instincts.[20]

Theodore Roosevelt, the very incarnation of pugnacity, was the last man to agree with James on this point. Elected governor of New York upon his return from Cuba, the Rough Rider filled the air with speeches in praise of the strenuous life of the soldier and the ennobling influences of imperialism. James responded in a published letter of April 15, 1899. He began by inquiring whether "Governor Roosevelt [should] be allowed to crow all over our national barnyard and hear no equally shrill voice lifted in reply." He was grateful that Roosevelt had not resorted to sanctimonious statements about "elevating" the Filipinos or sending them "ready-made 'pants' to hide their indecent nudity," but he condemned the future President's unabashed appeal to the fighting instincts as a dangerous threat to civilized life. Roosevelt, he wrote,

> although in middle life, as the years age, and in a situation of responsibility concrete enough, . . . is still mentally in the Sturm and Drang period of early adolescence, treats human affairs, when he makes speeches about them, from the sole point of view of the organic excitement and difficulty they may bring, gushes over war as the ideal condition of human society, for the manly strenuousness which it involves, and treats peace as a condition of blubberlike and swollen ignobility, fit only for huckstering weaklings, dwelling in gray twilight and heedless of the higher life. Not a word of the cause—one foe is as good as another, for aught he tells us; not a word of the conditions of success.[21]

Yet James knew how much pull the "party of red blood" could exert. Its appeal to man's love of "fun, excitement, [and] bigness" commanded a wide and emotional following. And this was precisely why the party of "the educated intellect" would have to mount a vigorous opposition. Since the savage instincts had to be contained at all cost, it was imperative that the mugwump party of "pale reflection" keep up its guard.[22]

The Triumph of Orthodoxy, Abstractness, and Bigness

James was stunned by the American decision to force its rule on the unwilling Filipinos. He described the McKinley administration's statement that it had never promised independence to the islands as "the most incredible, unbelievable, piece of sneak-thief turpitude that any nation ever prac-

tised." [23] In sharp contrast to his ambivalent views toward
the Spanish-American War itself, James reacted to the post-
war American role in the Philippines with singleminded
outrage. "God damn the U.S. for its vile conduct in the Philippine Isles," he wrote as late as 1902.[24] He rejected the
imperialist claim that the Philippines would gain rather
than lose from United States rule: America's continued intervention would destroy "the one sacred thing in the world,
the spontaneous budding of a national life," and leave the
Filipinos empty-handed, since "we can destroy their old
ideals, but we can't give them ours." To think that Americans could liberate, educate, and finally elevate the Filipinos to "ultimate" self-government was to indulge in "snivel-
ing," "loathsome" cant.[25]

James's uncompromising opposition to America's involvement in the Philippines grew out of his personal views on
philosophical and social questions. He saw in imperialism
the rise of a new "orthodoxy," and he was an inveterate
opponent of all orthodoxies. They violated his belief in an
open, pluralistic universe; they offended his respect for ex-
perimentally established proof; and they were inconsistent
with his belief in the greatest possible freedom for the
individual. To James all questions were still open, and he
resisted any attempt to close them in the name of orthodoxy.
This opposition to things official and orthodox helps to account for his avid interest in faith-healing, mental therapy,
Christian Science, and the like. It also explains what would
otherwise seem to be a captious opposition to the examina-
tion and licensing of all doctors—he wanted the less orthodox healers left in peace to experiment with their proposed
cures. James "would still have hoped," wrote George Santayana, "that something might turn up on the other side, and
that just as the scientific hangman was about to dispatch the
poor convicted prisoner, an unexpected witness would ride
up in hot haste, and prove him innocent." [26] Thus James
opposed imperialism as another orthodoxy, another official

policy, another damper on diversity and throttle on history which his free-wheeling spirit could not abide.

James also opposed imperialism on the grounds that it was based on abstract thinking. It was the factual and concrete that interested the pragmatist James. The truth of an idea was found in the bright light of its consequences, not in the shadowy labyrinth of deductive logic. Abstractions obscured truth and blocked the emergence of fresh thought. What was worse, they had a way of congealing into fixed orthodoxies unless quickly challenged and tested. In the midst of the Venezuela affair, James remarked that the Monroe Doctrine should have "cold water pumped on it" to prevent its changing from a "nascent dogma" into a "hardened theory" and observed that President Cleveland's inflammatory appeal to patriotism had banished "concrete reason" and left "abstract emotion" in control.[27]

There were additional dangers in the triumph of theory over practice and the general over the particular. People who were treated in abstract terms or as pawns in the service of some abstract cause rather than as flesh-and-blood entities (for example, "Little Brown Brother" or "uncivilized Malay" instead of "Emilio Aguinaldo") were almost inevitably treated with cruelty and inhumanity. A case in point was the Philippines, where Americans were spilling Filipino blood in the name of abstract ideas. The administration had taken "an intensely living and concrete situation" and had dealt with it on the basis of "bald and hollow abstractions" such as America's "responsibility" for the Philippines, her duty to provide "good government," the necessity of upholding "the supremacy of the flag," and the "unfitness" of the natives. Americans, who had never before been able to comprehend the bloodletting of the French Revolution (which had been carried out in the name of "such bald abstractions as Reason and the Rights of Man, spelt with capitals"), were now themselves killing Filipinos in a "stark-naked abstract" operation.[28]

A "concrete" approach to the Philippines situation would have taken into account the "sentiments of the natives and the ideals they might be led by." United States authorities should have made immediate contact with Aguinaldo and his followers and worked out a firm understanding respecting the rights and jurisdiction of Americans and Filipinos in the islands. McKinley, a man "suckled on campaign platforms and moral platitudes," had attempted instead to pacify the islanders with a bald proclamation of American authority and a vague statement of benevolent intentions.* No one in Washington had ever taken the trouble to reflect "that the Filipinos could have any feeling . . . of their own whatever that might possibly need to be considered in our arrangements." The Filipino people were treated like a "painted picture." They were brushed aside like some inanimate obstacles in the path of "good government." A new national life was crushed by the weight of abstractions.[29]

The situation in the islands reminded James of the way the American people were being dealt with by big business—"where the only relations between man and man are legal." The United States had treated the Philippines exactly as a large corporation treated a small competitive firm. Its performance "reeked of the infernal adroitness of the great department store, which has reached perfect expertness in the art of killing silently and with no public squealing or commotion the neighboring small concern."[30] The "great department store" was to James an apt symbol for a civilization that worshiped size and greatness. "The bigger the unit you deal with," he noted, "the hollower, the more brutal, the more mendacious is the life displayed." James told a friend

* James referred to McKinley's declaration of December 21, 1898, which proclaimed America's sovereignty in the islands but referred to its mission there as "one of benevolent assimilation." Its effect upon the Philippines was to arouse resentment against the United States and increase the chances of eventual military conflict. Fighting did in fact begin approximately seven weeks after the proclamation. See Margaret Leech, *In the Days of McKinley*, Harper & Brothers, New York, 1959, pp. 350–52.

that he hated "bigness and greatness in all their forms" and loved "the eternal forces of truth which always work in the individual and immediately unsuccessful way, under-dogs always, till history comes, after they are long dead, and puts them on the top." [31] It was lamentable that imperialism had emerged as the tainted fruit of modern civilization and that the United States, rapidly becoming the most organized, industrialized, and "rationalized" nation in the world, was bogged down in a dirty war against innocent peoples. Conscious of its role as emissary of the new civilization and bearer of the "white man's burden," in pursuit of "a national destiny which must be 'big' at any cost," America was "destroying down to the root every germ of a healthy national life":

> Could there be a more damning indictment of that whole bloated idol termed "modern civilization" than this amounts to? Civilization is, then, the big, hollow, resounding, corrupting, sophisticating, confusing torrent of mere brutal momentum and irrationality that brings forth fruits like this? [32]

An End to Innocence

William James's conception of America as the abode of innocence was decisively challenged by the events of 1898–1900. Although deeply disappointed by the Spanish-American War and its aftermath, he would periodically put on a cheerful face and declare that, in spite of recent events, Americans were still morally superior to Europeans. He sought comfort in the belief that it was the political leaders of America, not the people, who had transformed a just war into a sordid scramble for colonial spoils.[33] James persisted in these hopeful thoughts because of his natural inclination to see some good in every situation, but like Carl Schurz, he believed in his heart that, in turning to imperialism, the United States had struck a fatal blow against its own na-

tional ideals. "What a rôle our country was born with," he
wrote Schurz, "what a silver spoon in its mouth, and how it
has chucked it away!" [34] Despite some early twinges of
alarm at the time of the Venezuela crisis, James had not
been prepared for the events of 1898; then he learned to his
sorrow that "a nation's ideals [could] be changed in the
twinkling of an eye" and America, with so much at stake,
could "puke up its ancient soul . . . in five minutes without a wink of squeamishness." [35] As late as 1907 he was still
fuming about the question, writing that "the manner in
which the McKinley administration railroaded the country
into its policy of conquest was abominable, and the way the
country puked up its ancient soul at the first touch of temptation, and followed, was sickening." [36] By allowing her
time-honored convictions to give way to brutal passions,
America had turned the "stars and stripes" into a "lying
rag." She had wantonly relinquished her refuge of isolation
to enter the enmeshing trap of European rivalry and conflict. The United States could no longer shine as the world's
favored nation, detached and unstained in her special place
above the fray.[37]

And what were the ramifications of this abandonment of
national ideals? Among the most serious was the harm dealt
to the image of representative government and the "old belief in the *vox populi*." How else was one to interpret a war
which had begun with widespread popular support and had
ended in naked aggression? [38] Even more serious was the dis-
crediting of America's claim to be a uniquely innocent and
virtuous nation. Now she was in no important way different
from other countries:

> We had supposed ourselves (with all our crudity and bar-
> barity in certain ways) a better nation morally than the
> rest, safe at home, and without the old savage ambition,
> destined to exert great international influence by throwing
> in our "moral weight," etc. Dreams! Human Nature is

everywhere the same; and at the least temptation all the old military passions rise, and sweep everything before them.[39]

With the passing of time James came to accept this realization with greater equanimity: Americans were "no worse than the best of men have ever been," he wrote in 1901. "We are simply not superhuman." [40] But for James there was always the lingering regret that his countrymen—even if they were not really superior to other peoples—had been unable to seize the opportunity presented by the fortunes of history and geography to act as if they were. It was terrible to have to acknowledge that "angelic impulses and predatory lusts divide our heart exactly as they divide the hearts of other countries." [41]

The effect of this disillusionment was apparent one sunny autumn day in 1898 when James and his fellow Harvard philosophers George Santayana and George Herbert Palmer were discussing the peace terms forced upon Spain in negotiations at Paris. James seemed "terribly depressed" and told his colleagues that he felt as if he had "lost his country." [42] He agreed that Spain deserved to be expelled from Cuba because her rule had been so unjust, but he was tormented by other questions:

> The annexation of the Philippines, what could excuse that? What could be a more shameless betrayal of American principles? What could be a plainer symptom of greed, ambition, corruption and imperialism?

Palmer smiled blandly and tried to reassure James with a few philosophical commonplaces about the "synthesis" being for the ultimate good of all and the "course of history" reflecting "the true Judgment of God." Santayana felt differently. As a native of Spain, he resented "the schoolmaster's manner of the American government, walking switch in hand into a neighbour's garden to settle the children's quarrels there, and [making] himself master of the place." But he acknowledged that this had always been the way of the world—the United States, like other powerful nations before her in history, had simply pounced upon a neighbor weaker than herself. Why, then, was James so disconsolate? Santayana thought that it was because

> he held a false moralistic view of history, attributing events to the conscious ideals and free will of individuals: whereas individuals, especially in governments, are creatures of circumstance and slaves to vested interests. These interests may be more or less noble, romantic, or sordid, but they inevitably entangle and subjugate men of action. . . . Catastrophes come when some dominant institution, swollen like a soap-bubble and still standing without foundations, suddenly crumbles at the touch of what may seem a word or an idea, but is really some stronger material force. . . . James, who was a physician and a pragmatist, might have been expected to perceive this.

To James, however, Santayana's opinions represented a philosophy of moral irresponsibility and despair. He could never accept the idea that men were only the unwitting instruments of impersonal "forces." If a man's actions were simply the final and remote results of some far-removed Original Cause, there could be no moral content to those actions, nothing to merit either praise or blame. The absence of a moral dimension to life made meaningless the pursuit of such human ideals as freedom and justice. It robbed aspiration itself of all meaning. James could never subscribe to this view; he was always a person who could say of life that at least it *"feels* like a real fight." [43]

Santayana was critical of James for thinking that he had "lost his country." He thought that America was just coming into its own as a world power. James had failed to comprehend and appreciate this important development, blinded by his grief over the abandonment of America's democratic ideal which "he had innocently expected would always guide it, because this ideal had been eloquently expressed in the Declaration of Independence." To Santayana the Declaration was "a piece of literature, a salad of illusions"—certainly nothing that should prevent James from enjoying America's first move toward its destined domination of the Western Hemisphere. James had not lost his country, which had never been more vigorous and youthful; he had, Santayana asserted, merely "lost his way in its physiological history."

It was true that James could not shrug off the principles of the Declaration of Independence, despite his habitual impatience with abstractions. He was too much of a democrat to dismiss as illusory the statement "that all men are created equal." Even if Thomas Jefferson's ideals were only aspirations, without hope of complete realization, James thought them worth defending. Even if America's "eloquently expressed" ideals were nothing but the fabric of a national myth, James understood better than Santayana how precious to a nation were its most noble myths.

Had James lost his country? Santayana, who half-grudgingly admired the "honest enthusiasm and vitality" of "young, ambitious, enterprising America," believed that it was wrongheaded of him to think so, especially since James himself admired these American traits and was in some measure their spokesman. What Santayana failed to appreciate was that, in the aftermath of war, James believed that his country's distinctive traits had been corrupted by imperialism. American enthusiasm had been channeled into an evil course, and American vitality had been put to the service of piracy. James agreed that America was "healthy," but he saw this imperialist "health" as something calloused—athletic, but hardened and unfeeling.

James's error lay in supposing that it had taken imperialism to reveal that Americans had their quota of human frailty and were neither better nor worse than other men. The mistake was not his alone, but was shared by many mugwumps and other idealists. To think that war and the suppression of insurrection in the Philippines had revealed for the first time that the American people shared the universal human condition was to overlook a history which included religious conflict and witch-hangings, slavery and lynchings, corruption and industrial warfare, and the near-extermination of the American Indian. More to the point, it was to ignore a long history of battles for expansion and control.

The anti-imperialists needed William James just as the world has always needed a man who dares to deny that life is "nasty, poor, brutish and short" and has the faith to affirm that man can and does act as he thinks right. If there had been no one to proclaim that America had always been an innocent nation or to carry on the fight for the perfect ideals of the Declaration of Independence, the stage would have been left entirely to those who claimed they saw no discrepancy between the play as it was written in 1776 and as it was being performed in the Philippines. James may have failed to note that there had already been significant departures from the original text, but once he understood that undesirable alterations were being proposed, he stoutly stood his ground against them.

CHAPTER FOUR

E.L. Godkin and Charles Eliot Norton: The Last Straw

It used to be said in Cambridge that all the dogs in town wailed mournfully whenever E. L. Godkin and Charles Eliot Norton got together to exchange their gloomy views on the state of the nation. In the summer of 1897 Norton wrote Godkin that he had recently been forced to put his paper aside one evening "because with each note or article the gloom deepened till it grew darker than it used to be even in my study when after an evening of talk you declared that it was enough to make Rome howl." [1] For more than thirty years Godkin and Norton sustained and fed each other's pessimism, sorely disappointed as they both were with the tone of post–Civil War America. They believed that American morality had declined precipitately since the early days of the republic. They lamented the lack of good men in politics and the domination of the public service by coarse and corrupt men. They watched with jaundiced eyes as millions of immigrants poured into their country. They took in the "General Grant" architecture, read the new literature, deplored the new wealth, saw successful businessmen gain entrance to their private clubs, faced the glaring headlines of the yellow press—and declared it an age of vulgarity and a nation of "chromo-civilization."

There have always been such men, convinced in the core of their being that what had been in their youth a world of gold had lately turned to dross. In the era of industrialism and mass democracy these Jeremiahs have more often than not come from the ranks of the old landed, learned, or professional élites most in danger of being superseded or ignored by a democratic and acquisitive society. The quicker the rate of change and the fresher the memory of better times, the greater the likelihood that these gentle Brahmins would deplore the life around them. The rapidly changing America that emerged from the Civil War provoked such an outcry of genteel despair—a dismay eloquently expressed by E. L. Godkin and Charles Eliot Norton.

Godkin and Norton placed the blame for their unhappiness on precisely those features of American society most highly valued by the majority of their countrymen: material prosperity and democratic government. Here they found the source of America's immorality, vulgarity, and corruption. For years Godkin and Norton brooded over the detrimental effects of wealth and democracy. At the end of the century, on top of all the other evils that had befallen their country, came the plunge into imperialism—final proof that their worst fears had been justified. In their darkest moods they believed that the American Experiment had failed. Imperialism was the last straw.

The Decline of the Republic

Edwin Lawrence Godkin was born in Moyne, County Wicklow, Ireland, on October 21, 1831. His father was a Presbyterian clergyman who became a political journalist after being ejected from the pulpit for advocating home rule for Ireland. Young Edwin, too, went into journalism after making an indifferent record at Queens' College in Belfast. Already the youthful author of a history of Hungary, Godkin left for the Crimea in 1853 as a war correspondent for the *London Daily News*. Upon his return two years later he decided to emigrate to the United States. In November of 1856 he reached America where, for nearly a decade (except for a short period spent in Ireland and Europe), he occupied himself with law studies he had begun in London and writing letters on American affairs for the *London Daily News*. His early friends included a number of important eastern Republicans, and in 1865, when they decided to establish a journal that would reflect their political and economic views, they founded *The Nation* and selected the thirty-four-year-old Godkin to edit it. One of the prime backers of the new weekly and a close friend of its editor was Charles Eliot Norton.

Godkin's sharp and authoritative editorials quickly made *The Nation* a habit for thousands of readers; later on his work performed the same service for the daily *New York Evening Post*, whose editor he became in 1881 while retaining his post on *The Nation*. The critical tone of *The Nation* made it seem to some a "weekly judgment day," [2] and neither it nor the *Evening Post* ever attracted a large circulation. Both, however, exercised wide influence. College students adopted Godkin's opinions as their own the way later generations of students would parrot H. L. Mencken and Walter Lippmann. Other newspapermen paid close attention to Godkin's editorials, one explaining to a person who had complained about the *Evening Post's* small circulation: "You idiot, don't you know that there isn't a decent editor in the United States who does not want to find out what it has to say on any subject worth writing about, before getting himself on record in cold type?" [3] Governor David B. Hill of New York, a frequent target of attack by the *Evening Post*, once remarked: "I don't care anything about the handful of Mugwumps who read it in New York [City]. The trou-

ble with the damned sheet is that every editor in New York
State reads it." [4] According to his admirers Godkin exerted
the era's most potent and beneficial influence upon public
opinion. Norton observed in 1902 that he "did more than
any other writer of his generation to clarify the intelligence
and to quicken the conscience of the thoughtful of the community in regard to every important political question of
the time." [5]

Yet Godkin's critics were legion. The most vehement
among them was Theodore Roosevelt, who called Godkin
almost every disagreeable name that came to his fertile
mind. To him Godkin was an unpatriotic man, "a malig-
nant and dishonest liar" who suffered from "a species of
moral myopia, complicated with intellectual strabismus." [6]
Roosevelt's outbursts may be regarded as the venom of a
party regular and jingo who had often felt the sting of Godkin's sarcasm, but the testimony of those with no scores to
settle is not so easily dismissed. Lincoln Steffens, who worked
for a short time with Godkin, thought that his editorials
were "clever, forceful, [and] ripping," but also "personal
and not very thoughtful." Boston banker and philanthropist
Henry L. Higginson believed that as Godkin's career un-
folded his words became "so twisted and stained by great
conceit, arrogance, evil temper, that they lost their fairness,
their perspicacity, their virtue and therefore their value." [7]
It was Godkin's skill as an editorialist—a lucid and self-
assured style which lent itself readily to either hilarious
burlesque or snarling sarcasm—that engendered much of the
criticism he encountered.

Charles Eliot Norton had the gentle qualities his friend
Godkin lacked. He too was the son of a clergyman, Andrews
Norton, a prominent Unitarian divine. Born in Cambridge,
Massachusetts, in 1827, Norton spent his youth in the schol-
arly surroundings of a home frequented by such distin-
guished visitors as Francis Parkman, George Bancroft,
George Ticknor, and Henry Wadsworth Longfellow. While

still a child he developed a great passion for rare books and art objects, an enduring interest to which he was unable to devote his full attention until he was nearly fifty. He made Phi Beta Kappa at Harvard, and after his graduation in 1846 he spent a number of years with a firm of Boston merchants engaged in the East India trade. After his stint in business he spent some twenty years studying, living and traveling in Europe, writing and editing books, supervising Union propaganda activities during the Civil War, and working as either editor or contributor for the cream of American journals—the *Atlantic Monthly, North American Review,* and *The Nation.* Finally, after the death of his wife, Norton ceased his travels and returned to the United States for good in 1875 to settle down at "Shady Hill" in Cambridge and serve as Harvard's first professor of the fine arts, a post that he retained until his retirement as professor emeritus in 1897.[8]

As a scholar Norton was an acknowledged master of medieval studies and a respected translator of Dante. He wrote an important volume of *Historical Studies of Church Building in the Middle Ages* as well as studies of many writers and artists, among them Dante, Donne, Ruskin, Gray, Michelangelo, Holbein, and Turner. In addition, he edited the letters of James Russell Lowell, the Thomas Carlyle–Ralph Waldo Emerson correspondence, the Carlyle-Goethe correspondence, and the letters he had received from John Ruskin.

As a teacher Norton's aim was to advance aesthetic values and inculcate high standards of taste. Art was not to be studied merely for its own sake. Norton believed that man had reached his greatest moral and intellectual heights in ancient Greece and medieval Italy, and he thought that this superiority could be seen in the artistic achievements of these epochs. It was his habit in class to illustrate this relationship between art and morality with frequent deprecating references to the sterility of American art and the moral and intellectual inferiority of American life. When Norton's son referred to his father's fine arts course as "Lectures on Modern Morals as Illustrated by the Art of the Ancients," the professor was amused and raised no objection.[9]

The story is told that Norton once began a lecture on the idea of "the gentleman" with the airy remark: "None of you, probably, has ever seen a gentleman." It was inevitable that a teacher with such a rarefied taste for the antique would become the subject of parodies and the source of much campus amusement. The Dante scholar no doubt went to his grave unaware that students identified his daughters as Paradiso, Purgatorio, and Inferno, or that (according to a supposedly authentic story) an undergraduate emerged after three meetings of Norton's Fine Arts 3 course with his total notes reading:

(1) Greece.
(2) Bully for Greece.
(3) There are no flies on Greece.

Both Norton's general aesthetic sensibilities and his displeasure with the design of many new buildings going up at Harvard were parodied in a tall story to the effect that he had died and was about to enter heaven when he suddenly drew back, shaded his eyes, and exclaimed: "Oh! Oh! Oh! So Overdone! So garish! So Renaissance!" [10]* Despite the numerous campus jokes at his expense, Norton's encouragement of the fine arts and his efforts to direct public attention to the deterioration of America's landscape and cities made him an important figure in post–Civil War America—a friend of art museums, conservation projects, parks, and schools. In the opinion of Van Wyck Brooks, "no one aroused the country more to a sense of its general ugliness and a will to create a beautiful civilization." [11]

---

* "Old Harvard men," wrote George Santayana, "will remember the sweet sadness of Professor Norton. He would tell his classes, shaking his head with a slight sigh, that the Greeks did not play football." *The Genteel Tradition at Bay*, Charles Scribner's Sons, New York, 1931, pp. 3–4.

Godkin and Norton were both mugwumps. Godkin was aware that the independent was often politically isolated and powerless, but he saw no other acceptable course of action. Accordingly he voted for Grant in 1872 only to avoid supporting Horace Greeley, whom he called a "conceited, ignorant, half-cracked, obstinate old creature." [12] He halfheartedly backed Rutherford B. Hayes in 1876, but when Hayes's victory was disputed, he switched his support to Democrat Samuel J. Tilden. In 1880 Godkin supported the Republican Garfield but shifted his allegiance to the Democrats and Cleveland in 1884, 1888, and 1892. In 1896 he withheld his support from both McKinley and Bryan to vote for the Gold Democrat, John McCauley Palmer. As for Charles Eliot Norton, who was frequently out of the country during election campaigns, his position is best summed up in a letter he wrote Lowell in 1880: "The 'Nation' will give you my politics." [13]

Both men complained about political corruption, inflationary schemes, and high tariffs. Both feared that American politics had rejected the country's "good men" and both hoped for a breakup of the old party organizations. As early as 1859 Godkin had complained that the "nominating conventions toss men like Clay and Webster aside, and fish out from amongst the obscurities Pierces and Buchanans as likely to prove more pliable instruments in factious hands." [14] The political machines put up such bad men for office that "good men," who had no desire to join a "ridiculous and . . . contemptible" office-seeking class, could not be persuaded to enter public affairs. Thus America was left to a mob of dull-witted boodlers. [15]

For Godkin and Norton the evident decline in political morality was but one aspect of a more general and serious decline in the quality of American life. In former times the United States had enjoyed a Golden Age of reason, simplicity, and high morality, but the push toward an industrial way of life was transforming the social and physical landscape of the once-Arcadian America they loved, and wherever they looked they now saw deterioration and decadence. Godkin deplored the "moral anarchy" of modern business methods and despised those who employed them. He fought against the admission of businessmen to the Century Club of New York, complaining that most of them "rarely open a book" and "know no more, read no more, and have no more to say than the bricklayer and the plumber." [16] For his part, Norton was particularly concerned with the aesthetic changes in America and the lamentable tone of society. The country he had known had vanished under a wave of vulgarity. The "barren" art and literature of the late nineteenth century depressed him:

> Nowhere in the civilized world are the practical concerns of life more engrossing; nowhere are the conditions of life more prosaic; nowhere is the poetic spirit less evident, and the love of beauty less diffused. The concern for beauty, as the highest end of work, and as the noblest expression of life, hardly exists among us, and forms no part of our character as a nation. [17]

Norton felt increasingly pessimistic and isolated. He told Lowell in 1873 that America had lost its original bright promise and was no longer "a pleasing child." Only Harvard, Yale, *The Nation,* and the *North American Review* stood firm as "solid barriers against the invasion of modern barbarism & vulgarity." The other landmarks and manners of an earlier and better day were disappearing before his very eyes. Once, while staying a night in Northampton, Massachusetts, which was rebuilding after a bad fire, Norton reported that the town "has lost much of its old, tranquil charm, and has put on the showy looks and pert airs of a chromo-civilized country town. There is nothing pretty, refined, or other than inelegant in all its newness." Cambridge, too, was slipping away, and Norton felt himself a stranger in his birthplace. "New people" occupied the few houses remaining from his childhood. He could find only "half a dozen men or women" who could converse on those general subjects once familiar to all people of education— "My fair neighbor asks, 'What are Pericles?'" [18] Condemned to live in an age of industrialization and specialization, he sighed under his burden of nostalgia, a sigh audible in his classrooms where it was once recorded by young Josephine Peabody who heard him lecture at Radcliffe College in the autumn of 1895: "The dear old man looks so mildly happy and benignant while he regrets everything in the age and the country—so contented, while he gently tells us it were better for us had we never been born in this degenerate and unlovely age." [19]

What had brought America to this pass? Godkin had initially attributed the brashness and materialism of American society to its continued preoccupation with pushing a frontier through the wilderness, not to its democratic organization. In an essay published in 1865 he had maintained that, because Americans were so busy building a new country, it was understandable that they were heedless of history and deficient in taste. As soon as the West was fully settled and the frontier lost its dominant influence on American society, the United States would begin to display the more decent and "civilized" qualities of an older and fully established nation.[20] But as the years passed, the promise which Godkin had once seen in the West seemed never to materialize. Instead, the West was a continuing cause of America's shortcomings. After Populist victories in the 1890 elections, he remarked: "We do not want any more States until we can civilize Kansas." [21]

There were other causes of the nation's troubles, and the new science was one. It had "killed the imagination," suffocated literature, art, and religion, and snuffed out interest in human life and experience, "except as a field for mechanical discovery, with its resulting worship of material things." [22] American prosperity was another villain. The pursuit of easy money had produced a population of vulgarians and thieves.

"Material prosperity," Godkin wrote in the 1880s, "is now associated in people's minds with so much moral corruption that the mention of it produces in some of the best of us a feeling not far removed from nausea." [23]

Godkin found in the very heart of the American Experiment—in its commitment to democracy and equality—the greatest cause of its failure. These noble ideals simply did not work in practice. The triumph of popular rule had come to mean only that politicians catered to the lowest level of popular understanding. The ideal of equality, which in theory referred to an "equality of burdens," had degenerated into a contempt for the excellent and superior, a "disregard for special fitness." [24] Could anything but disaster be expected from the masses whom this egalitarian democracy had thrown to the top? Godkin wrote in 1870:

> Their rush into the forum and into the temples and palaces and libraries is not an agreeable sight to witness, and it would be foolish to expect that under their ruthless touch many gifts and graces will not be obscured, many arts will not be lost, many a great ideal, at whose shrine the best men and women of three generations have found courage and inspiration, will not vanish from the earth to be seen no more.[25]

At the close of the Civil War Norton, like Godkin, had been full of optimism about America's prospects. The war itself had temporarily convinced him that many of the defects he had once thought inherent in America's popular society were mere "excrescences" that could be quickly shed to clear the way for an advance to "the image of the ideal." [26] But disillusionment was quick to follow: as early as 1867 he had come to believe that the downfall of American civilization was at hand, with prosperity and democracy operating as agents of destruction. Norton's studies had persuaded him that there was a direct causal connection between great wealth and the dissolution of national character. The decline of Greece had been set off by the "increase of private luxury [and] selfishness" and the rise of "unrestrained individuality." Fourteenth-century Siena was another example of a strong and rich society succumbing to "luxury and wantonness":

> The sources of civic virtue and of public spirit were beginning to run low. Men were less honest, women less modest, than of old. . . . The new generation was growing up less hardy, more passionate and lustful, than the old had been. The laws became ineffectual to restrain men who no longer reverenced justice.[27]

Surely it was vanity to believe that America could be spared the disastrous effects of excessive material wealth. As early as 1853 Norton had warned that the long and uninterrupted history of prosperity enjoyed by the United States was beginning to take its toll in a blighted national character.[28] After the Civil War the blight grew worse and spread beyond the frontiers and across the ocean. In America—and, as a result of her influence, in Europe too—"society" was being suffocated by materialism. Money-getting was proving the ruin of literature and was blunting the intelligence of the people. A foolish optimism was in the air. From Florence in 1869 Norton wrote that:

> Italy in losing tyrants, in becoming constitutional, in taking to trade, is doing what she can to spoil her charm. The railroad whistle just behind the church of Santa Maria Novella, or just beyond the Campo Santo at Pisa, sounds precisely as it sounds on the Back Bay or at the Fitchburg Station, —and it and the common school are Americanizing the land to a surprising degree. Happy country! Fortunate people! Before long they may hope for their Greeleys, their Beechers, and their Fisks.[29]

If trade and prosperity produced vulgarity, democracy threatened to destroy the very foundations of civilization. Speaking at the Tercentenary Celebration of Emmanuel College, Cambridge University, in 1884, Norton posed the question that had tormented him for so many years. What would be the price of America's egalitarianism?

> We are raising in the level of civilization in America the classes which have heretofore been depressed. The natural result of that work is that the higher levels—that the peaks of civilization—sink, and the mass—the average level—is raised to unexampled elevations. Now the point we have to consider is whether this process can go on without risking the very existence of the most precious fruits of civilization and culture.[30]

Norton's answer to the question was essentially negative: democracy and prosperity were doing serious harm to American society. Men no longer had the courage to be different, the capacity to be original, the inclination to be independent. Instead they shared a "uniform level of thought and effort." The "true gentleman" had become as exceptional as the "true genius" because democracy was "not favourable to the existence of either." [31]

Norton did not deny that democracy could "work," but, as he told Lowell after the election of 1884, it appeared to work "ignobly, ignorantly, brutally." Or it could work as it had begun to in Europe where it was bringing about "the destruction of old shrines, the disregard of beauty, the decline in personal distinction, the falling off in manners." Democracy clearly did not work as Norton and his friends had hoped it would. In his view democracy was supposed to ensure that everyone in society would be public-spirited. But it had worked out in practice to mean that everyone was involved in the selfish pursuit of his own interests. Rather than heightening the individual's awareness of his civic responsibilities, universal suffrage had furnished "a distinct source of moral corruption." Rather than increasing the wisdom of all citizens, democracy had diminished the respect for intelligent counsel and produced a general "rejection of authority." The sense of license and the smug complacency created by democracy and prosperity had made "extravagant self-confidence" and willful conduct the hallmarks of the American people. Writing in 1896 Norton declared that for the indefinite future he anticipated "an increase of lawlessness and of public folly." [32]

It need hardly be noted that misgivings of this sort came in part from a deep mistrust of the masses who formed the base of democracy. Godkin was savage in his dislike for the immigrants who were daily being incorporated into the American political system. Their votes gave power to the corrupt urban bosses who exploited them in turn. On every hand, Godkin exclaimed, there was the "ignorant" foreign voter "eating away the political structure, like a white ant, with a group of natives standing over him and encouraging him." As early as 1866 Godkin had hoped that the unrest caused by Chinese immigration would lead to a restriction of universal suffrage. A quarter of a century later in 1891 (two years after "200,000 ignorant and obscure Italians" entered the United States), he proposed that all immigrants be shut out unless they could read and write the English language. He admitted that this would mean that all but a few immigrants would perforce come from the British Isles, "but why not, if the restriction be really undertaken in the interest of American civilization? We are under no obligation to see that all races and nations enjoy an equal chance of getting here." [33] Norton was similarly troubled by the demographic change being wrought by unrestricted immigration. In the 1850s he had sympathized with the anti-Catholic and anti-immigrant goals of the Know-Nothing Party, and toward the end of the century he became concerned about the Irish and Jewish invasion of New England.[34]

Both men believed that much of the radicalism of the period could be blamed on the ostentatious display of wealth by the *nouveaux riches.* Little wonder that humble people craved for more than they possessed! But Norton and Godkin held that the poor would simply have to accept their condition, and both adamantly opposed any public welfare measures which might have improved it. Godkin, called a "fanatic for laissez faire" by Edward C. Kirkland, declared it a natural law "that the more intelligent and thoughtful of the race shall inherit the earth and have the best time, and that all others shall find life on the whole dull and unprofitable." He shrugged off socialism as a vain effort to contravene this law and provide "a good time to everybody independently of character and talents." In a socialist system:

> The rich man is called on to strip himself of his riches; the frugal man of his savings; the able man to treat his ability as an incumbrance; and the whole community, as a community, to give up all it loves and glories in. Smoking is to be allowed at funerals, and the men and women are to mate in the streets. Children are to go to the foundling hospital. Whatever power there is anywhere is to be lodged in the hands of the most stupid and incapable. The lazy are to lie on their backs and the industrious to get nothing for their industry.[35]

Norton ordinarily was not as rigid on these matters as Godkin, but after a rash of strikes in 1877 he wrote Lowell that society would have to learn to defend itself more vigorously against worker agitation. Threats to property rights would have to be met with a force far more powerful than that provided by the state militias, regardless of the political principles which might be disregarded in the process. Godkin was more direct. When the Pullman workers went out on strike in 1894, *The Nation* stated that they would have to be dealt with "in the old-fashioned way"—the government would have to "shoot them down." [36]

E. L. Godkin had no answer to the problems of his age. The structure of American life seemed too corrupt to save, too rotten to shore up with marginal improvements. He knew that he did not want America converted "into a republic of kindly patricians charged with the board, lodging, washing, and amusement of a vast and discontented proletariat," [37] but apart from ridicule, preachments on manners, and Manchester economics, he had little to offer. Charles Eliot Norton had no answers either, but his pessimism was relieved by a limited belief in ameliorative action, and his distrust of acquisitiveness and democracy was mitigated by a genuine interest in the unprecedented material and educational achievements of America's lower classes. He was better equipped than Godkin to react constructively to the social problems that disturbed him, and in even the most unpromising situation he was more disposed to find some ray of hope.

As an active participant in the social and political process, Norton established a night school for the poor in 1846; he promoted better housing for the underprivileged; he was in the forefront of the campaign for female suffrage and education (with the hope that women would raise the ideals and tone of American society). In the interest of preserving at least the landscape of America, he fought hard and effectively to save both the Adirondacks and Niagara Falls from exploitation and desecration. In an effort to exert direct influence upon public opinion, he founded the Ashfield "Academy Dinners," held each summer from 1879 to 1903 in Ashfield, Massachusetts. On these occasions civil service reform, tariff reduction, Negro education, and anti-imperialism, as well as many other "mugwump" interests and causes, were discussed by William Dean Howells, George Washington Cable, Edward Atkinson, William James, Moorfield Storey, James Russell Lowell, Booker T. Washington, George W. Curtis, and many others, including Norton himself.[38]

Norton found it reassuring to know that the economic and educational level of the lower classes in his country had been elevated to the highest point in history. When Howells inquired of him: "Well, after all, if you could change, would you rather have been an Englishman than an American?" he unhesitatingly replied: "No, if I could choose I would rather have been American." [39] He urged others not to give up on the American people. Their shortcomings, he wrote in 1894, could have been far more pronounced than they were:

> Here are sixty or seventy millions of people of whom all but a comparatively small fraction have come up, within two or three generations, from the lower orders of society. They belong by descent to the oppressed from the beginning of history, to the ignorant, to the servile class or to the peasantry. They have no traditions of intellectual life, no power of sustained thought, no developed reasoning faculty. But they constitute on the whole as good a community on a large scale as the world has ever seen. Low as their standards may be, yet taken in the mass they are higher than so many millions of men ever previously attained. They are seeking material comfort in a brutal way, and securing in large measure what they seek, but they are not inclined to open robbery or cruel extortion. On the whole they mean "to do about right." I marvel at their self-restraint. That they are getting themselves and us all into dangerous difficulties is clear, but I believe they will somehow, with a good deal of needless suffering, continue to stumble along without great catastrophe.[40]

But at best progress came at a maddeningly slow pace, and Norton succeeded only intermittently in maintaining any semblance of optimism. In 1871 he predicted that the creation of a really sound republic would take as long as the evolution from monkey to man. In 1884 he described himself as an "absolute" pessimist—a man who had learned not to hope for any good in the world and who thus lived a life free of expectations and complaints:

> Your out-and-out pessimist is cheerful, even though nature herself plays false, and uses loaded dice against him in the game. Darwinism has helped us a good deal. You expect less of men when you look at them not as a little lower than the angels, but as a little higher than the anthropoid apes.

America might improve, but as John Adams had once remarked, it would first have to be "purified in the furnace of affliction." Norton was in the habit of proclaiming that only a "calamity" could redeem the United States, that "nothing short of seven lean years, or the plagues of Egypt will make this nation serious, honest, full-grown, and civilized." [41]

By the mid-nineties Godkin and Norton had lived for a third of a century believing that their country was sinking, that its onetime promise had been largely submerged by the rising tide of corruption, immorality, tastelessness, and stupidity. It was more than coincidental that the thoughts of each man turned to the fall of Rome as the nineteenth century came to a close. In 1895 Godkin wrote Norton:

> You see I am not sanguine about the future of democracy. I think we shall have a long period of decline like that which followed the fall of the Roman Empire, and then a recrudescence under some other form of society.

A year later Norton wrote an English friend:

> It is hard to have the whole background of life grow darker as one grows old. I can understand the feeling of a Roman as he saw the Empire breaking down, and civilization dying out. It will take much longer than we once hoped for, for the world to reorganize itself upon a democratic basis, and for a new and desirable social order to come into existence.

With the faith that never completely left him he added: "But if we set our hope far enough forward we need not lose it." [42]

The Last Straw

By 1895 Godkin and Norton had come to sound like men who were close to abandoning all hope for their country. From *The Nation* and from Harvard they watched the ailing American Experiment falter and fail, little hoping that recovery was possible. They had been watching for many years, waiting for the death that always seemed imminent, when imperialism appeared on the scene to administer the *coup de grâce*. What had seemed to William James a horrible, sudden, unlooked-for shattering of the Experiment seemed almost an anti-climax to Godkin and Norton. They were angry and saddened but not surprised, for they had expected all along that something of the sort would happen. The times had long been out of joint, and imperialism was but another blow—albeit the heaviest—against the America they had known. The only question that remained for them was whether the blow was fatal—whether a resurrection of the American Experiment was possible.

Both men for years had been sharply critical of American foreign policy. Almost half a century before the Spanish-American War—in 1857—Norton had welcomed the prospect of a depression because he felt that it would hamper filibustering expeditions in Nicaragua and eliminate any hope of raising money for purchasing Cuba.[43] Four years earlier, in an anonymously published book, he had criticized popular talk about "manifest destiny" expansionism as a sure sign that prosperity had weakened the character of the American people. He warned that American political principles would be put to a severe test by further expansion, which would result in intermingling with the "half savage descendants of the Spanish conquerors and the conquered natives of America" or the "semi-civilized" people of the Sandwich Islands. These people were unworthy of self-government, which was a right "not to be intrusted to the whole human race."[44] After the Civil War Norton opposed the proposed annexation of Santo Domingo and criticized the government for negotiating a treaty for the purchase of the Danish West Indies, especially since it was obvious that the Senate would never agree to the transaction. In the latter case he was as displeased with the manners as with the goals of American diplomacy, just as he was when he complained of the unbecoming behavior toward Great Britain in the arbitration of the *Alabama* claims. The United States had demanded payment for contingent or indirect damages * as well as for the direct damages caused by the English-built Confederate cruisers of the Civil War. The United States was bound to get its comeuppance before long, he wrote Godkin from Germany: "A bully gets thrashed some time or other, & a trickster in the long run loses more than he gains." [45]

As an editor Godkin was continually obliged to take a public stand on issues of foreign policy and was thus a more prominent opponent of American policy than Norton. For a quarter-century he hammered away at every annexation scheme that came along, and at every other project that might lead in the same undesirable direction. In the process he formulated a large and useful set of anti-imperialist ideas. Shortly after Appomattox and the founding of *The Nation* he joined the thin ranks of those who criticized America's efforts to bring down the French puppet empire of Maximilian in Mexico. He feared that intervention might create a Mexican political vacuum that the United States would have to fill, a prospect appalling in itself and liable to produce the evils which Godkin habitually associated with imperialism: extravagant spending, increased patronage for brigand politicians, and the descent of sharpers and carpetbaggers like famished locusts upon the miserable Mexican nation. Godkin was always repelled by the idea of getting mixed up with the "alien" peoples of Latin America, and on July 18, 1867, after the departure of the French soldiers from Mexico and the inglorious death of Maximilian, he wearily confessed that he could see "nothing especially impressive or valuable" in the episode. "It will, we fear, teach princes and invaders nothing, except that Mexico is a disgusting country peopled by ruffians, into which a Christian and a gentleman is a fool for venturing." [46]

Godkin was mildly and only temporarily unsettled by the annexation of Alaska, which he originally termed "a frozen

---

* For example, increased insurance rates, loss of commerce owing to fear of shipping in the area of the Confederate cruisers, the costly prolongation of the war, etc.

desert of a colony," [47] but he joined Norton in criticizing American policy during the arbitration of the *Alabama* claims and the negotiations to purchase the Danish West Indies. Grant's attempt to acquire Santo Domingo stirred his anger more deeply. He wanted nothing to do with a "policy of absorbing semi-civilized Catholic states." To annex Santo Domingo would be to admit 200,000 "ignorant Catholic Spanish negroes" into the United States as citizens. It would also make inevitable the incorporation of the neighboring black republic of Haiti. When it became apparent that the defeat of the treaty in 1870 had failed to discourage its proponents, Godkin continued his protests and ridicule:

> New reasons for annexation will every day make their appearance. "Commerce," we shall be told, "demands it; manufactures demand it; the army and navy demand it; posterity looks for it . . . ; art, science, and literature will be the better for it; the prairie breezes sigh for it; the lonely loon of the Northern lakes cries for it. In the name of our common humanity, then open the door to this dusky daughter of the sun-kissed seas, and let her take her seat in her golden robes among her frost-crowned sisters of the continent." [48]

Through most of the 1870s and 1880s the United States kept clear of new territorial moves. Nonetheless, Godkin, "a sort of Gloomy Dean of the period," [49] was as acidulous and irritable as ever, perpetually harping on the "spirited foreign policy" of the time, a phrase that he took to mean "that we should constantly carry a chip on our shoulder, daring anybody to knock it off; that we should . . . act the universal bully, shaking our fists in everybody's face to inform the world that we can 'whip all creation.'" He attacked every manifestation of this spirit, whether it took the form of proposals to intervene in the Cuban civil war of the 1870s, "meddling" in the War of the Pacific between Chile and Peru, or participation in the 1884 Berlin Conference on the

Congo.[50] When the Arthur administration tried to acquire rights for an American-owned canal in Nicaragua, Godkin saw in the proposal the threat of bringing three or four new territories into the Union and extending American citizenship to 15 million "slightly Catholicized savages." Anyone given to calling Mexicans "greasers" and describing Cubans as a "motley" crowd no more capable of understanding "our religion, manners, political traditions and habits, and modes of thought" than "the King of Dahomey" was unlikely to look with charity on the inhabitants of Nicaragua, Guatemala, or Honduras, a region containing "more 'rum, Romanism, and rebellion' to the square mile than probably any other part of the world." [51] As to efforts to press other countries into buying American products, he condemned them as mischievous and economically unnecessary. When James G. Blaine complained that the United States was missing a golden opportunity to develop trade with Chile and Peru, Godkin observed that the loss would have about as much impact on the American economy as "the failure of a dry goods store in Bangor, Maine." [52]

In the late eighties and early nineties the irascible editor continued to lash out against American policy—in Samoa where it seemed "a wild goose chase," in Chile where it was "childish," in Hawaii where it took advantage of a local revolution "of sugar by sugar and for sugar." [53] As all of these schemes passed before his review Godkin did his sardonic best to deflate them, but he also tried to figure out what trend they were setting for his country. He foresaw worse calamities ahead. He had long believed that expansionism and jingoism were growing in tandem with the growth of democracy. War itself was being democratized, with the masses laying their rude hands upon what had once been the affair of a small circle of gentleman statesmen. In an essay written during the Franco-Prussian War, Godkin observed that the rank and file now determined when war should be waged—it was "the people's work." Since war was more democratic it was more impetuous and unreasoning and hence more dangerous. Godkin therefore thought it imperative to counteract the various ideas and trends that were making the common people so "ready to fight," including the popular belief that one nation could gain only at the expense of another, the outmoded dogma that "the less commercial intercourse nations carry on with each other the better for both, and that markets won or kept by force are means of gain," the tendency of newspapers to take a "pugilist's view" of foreign affairs, taunting and goading governments into unnecessary conflicts, and the romantic proclivity to think of national honor in the outdated terms of individual honor—to believe that it was "always more becoming to fight than apologize." Since all of these influences on the popular mind could be fanned by the emotions, it was necessary above all to teach the people that law instead of sentiment should be the basis for all foreign policy. It was the citizen's duty to see his nation—as he ideally saw himself—as subject to laws and rules rather than whims and passions.[54]

In the middle 1890s Godkin directed his attention to the jingoistic newspapers which filled "the heads of boys and silly men with the idea that war is the normal state of a civilized country."[55] In May of 1895 in the pages of the sober and influential *North American Review* he analyzed the prevailing public temper created in part by the yellow press. The American people, he wrote, were confident, yet oversensitive to foreign criticism—shortsighted, yet full of an expansive sense of national destiny. At the root of their buoyant temper lay the "abounding, unparalleled prosperity" that had made them a reckless people, ripe for agitation by the yellow press. This admixture of giddy people and irresponsible newspapers had already so corrupted the meaning of "Americanism" that the term could now be defined as the "simple readiness to take offense." The "true-blue American" was contemptuous of any man who possessed doubts of the ability of the United States to thrash other nations; or who fails to acknowledge the right of the United States to occupy such territories, canals, isthmuses or peninsulas, as they may think it desirable to have, or who speaks disrespectfully of the Monroe doctrine, or who doubts the need of a large navy, or who admires European society, or who likes to go to Europe, or who fails, in case he has to go, to make comparisons unfavorable to Europe.

As the influence of the common people increased throughout the world, so did the power of the newspapers to force countries into unnecessary collisions with one another. Normally circumspect diplomats, pushed on by press and public breathing hotly down their necks, shook the world with their intemperate words and bellicose actions. Godkin found the whole thing extremely dismaying.[56]

The Anglo-American diplomatic crisis of 1895–1896 arising from the border dispute between British Guiana and Venezuela convinced Godkin and Norton that they were in for an extended period of expansionist violence. In a message to Congress President Cleveland indicated that America was willing to go to war with Great Britain if it were deemed necessary. Godkin was "thunderstruck" by the thought. In *The Nation* he castigated Cleveland's act as a "dishonorable and traitorous attempt to imperil peace," a "betrayal of the nation," a "mad appeal to the basest passions of the mob," a case "of a civilized man throwing away his clothes and joining the howling savages." He feared that America—now controlled by a huge, ignorant, and provincial mob—would henceforth be "constantly on the brink of some frightful catastrophe." [57] Norton was, if anything, more pessimistic than Godkin and wrote him that the crisis made "a miserable end for this century." It had encouraged the worst tendencies in American democracy—its growing Anglophobia, arrogance, and barbarism—and had demonstrated that "the rise of democracy to power in America and in Europe is not, as has been hoped, to be a safeguard of peace and civilization." The triumph of democracy was instead the triumph of the "uncivilized," and America, under the rule of a petty-minded and amoral people, faced a terrible future "of error and of wrong" that would make her "more and more a power for disturbance and for barbarism." [58]

Godkin, with his thirty-year record of anti-imperialism, was profoundly disturbed by the outbreak of the Spanish-American War. In line with his long-standing aversion to things Latin American, he was unable to respond to the cry for "Cuba Libre." In fact, he actually applauded Spain's efforts to suppress the island's rebels.[59] The jingoism which accompanied American entrance into the war also raised his temper. "The blowing, the blatherskite, the mendacity" of the press prompted him to the rhetorical question: "Are there no gentlemen left in American public life?" He was convinced that Americans would never be proud of this war.[60] Three months before it began, when the Senate was considering the annexation of Hawaii, he repeated some of his familiar objections to expansion in a *Nation* editorial:

> The sudden departure from our traditions; the absence from our system of any machinery for governing dependencies; the admission of alien, inferior, and mongrel races to our nationality; the opening of fresh fields to carpetbaggers, speculators, and corruptionists; the un-Americanism of governing a large body of people against their will, and by persons not responsible to them; the entrance on a policy of conquest and annexation while our own continent was still unreclaimed, our population unassimilated, and many of our most serious political problems still unsolved; and finally the danger of the endorsement of a gross fraud for the first time by a Christian nation.[61]

At the close of the war in August, 1898, he maintained his opposition to all annexation projects although, in the case of

Cuba, he was not sure that the United States could free itself entirely of future involvement. Puerto Rico could certainly be left alone, and Spain could either be obliged to improve her administration of the Philippines or grant the islands their independence. The future of the Philippines was, in any case, no concern of the United States.[62]

To those who took issue with him Godkin pointed out the difficulties the United States would face as an imperialist power. Twice before within its territorial limits, with the Indians and with rebellious Southerners after the Civil War, the United States had attempted to govern others as subject peoples. Neither experience was in any way worthy of repetition. America had made "a fist" of its dealings with the red man, and during Reconstruction it had loosed against the South "large bands of characterless adventurers called 'carpet-baggers' to humiliate the vanquished and plunder them, until the abuse grew too strong to be defended or even apologized for."[63] No, if the United States were ever to establish a successful colonial administration, it would have to effect a drastic change in its entire political system. In order to defend the Philippines from the covetousness of other powers, it would have to arm to the teeth, pour all its energy into the creation of a military force more mobile and efficient than any yet required in the nation's history, and set up a professional colonial service on a permanent basis. Godkin was convinced that the United States could not meet these requirements of colonialism without a fatal weakening of its republican principles. It was not possible for a government to execute a consistent colonial policy when it was accountable to the "rapid and uncontrollable vagaries of public opinion" and "the furious influence of irresponsible editors." It was not possible for a President to direct an efficient colonial administration if he had to fight for his political existence every four years. "Unquestionably," Godkin asserted, "our present Constitution was not intended for a conquering nation with several different classes of citizens."

Empire and democratic government simply could not co-exist.[64]

When the McKinley administration decided to acquire direct control over the Philippines, native forces under the leadership of Emilio Aguinaldo resisted and launched a guerrilla war that ended only with the complete suppression of the insurgents some three years later. To Godkin this war was "the most savage which was ever known in the history of our republic." For over a hundred years the United States had adhered to a political creed which taught that "all just power is derived from the consent of the people who live under it" and which further taught that power exercised without popular consent should be resisted with force. In accord with this philosophy Americans had repeatedly demonstrated their sympathy for the great popular and nationalist revolutions of the nineteenth century—whether in Greece, Italy, Poland, Ireland, Hungary, Latin America, or, most recently and significantly, in Cuba.* Now this long and honorable history was being rejected. The American government, in the name of its citizens, was denying another people the right of self-determination, a "shameless abandonment of the noble faith under which we have lived for a century, and have achieved everything that has won for us the respect and confidence of mankind." [65]

In his anger Godkin railed at the expansionists for their betrayal of American principles. In the Philippines McKinley, now "drunk with glory and flattery," had substituted "keen effective slaughter for Spanish old-fashioned, clumsy slaughter." When eager missionaries began planning new translations of the Bible in the various tongues of the Filipinos, *The Nation* derisively suggested that they read: "Mow down the natives like grass and say unto them, the Syndicate has arrived." [66] But Godkin could no longer put

---

* Godkin at this point was conveniently overlooking the contempt for the Cuban rebels that he had expressed before the beginning of the Spanish-American War.

much heart in his protest, for it seemed to him that the fight was virtually lost. Even before the beginning of the Filipino insurrection, he had written: "I can not help thinking this triumph over Spain seals the fate of the American republic." [67] In late 1898 and early 1899 he gave way to utter despair, publicly declaring that "the old American republic is in a bad way." [68] In private letters he poured out his full sorrow:

> Morals in this community, except sexual morals, are entirely gone. I fancy that the press has had a good deal to do with this awful decline—the greatest in human history.

> I have never . . . felt more confident of anything in my life, than that you [in England] will have a rude awakening, & that if the American anti-imperialists fail to stem the present tide of barbarism & rascality, you will, before many years, have to deal with a new & more formidable America, without either religion or morality, under a government better fitted for predator purposes.

> I am, heart and soul, an American of the *vieille roche*. American ideals were the intellectual food of my youth, and to see America converted into a senseless, Old World conqueror, embitters my age.

> I came here fifty years ago with high and fond ideals about America. . . . They are now all shattered, and I have apparently to look elsewhere to keep even moderate hopes about the human race alive.

> I have suffered from seeing the America of my youthful dreams vanish from my sight, and the commencement on this continent of the old story; and I must confess I think I have seen great decline in both morals and politics, within my forty years.[69]

Godkin suffered a stroke in February, 1900. Fifteen months later he turned his back on his adopted country and returned to England. Occasionally the bitter humor of former days would return to him, as when he wrote James

Bryce: "Do come over soon, and we'll lie under a tree at Dublin while you abuse Great Britain and I abuse the United States." [70] He died in Devon on May 21, 1902, and was buried in the Hazelbeach churchyard, Northampton, to rest forever in England. In America, the country he had left behind, *The Nation* published a fitting epitaph:

> He grew old in an age he condemned,
> Felt the dissolving throes
> Of a Social order he loved,
> And, like Theban seer,
> > Died in his enemies' day.[71]

Charles Eliot Norton, like Godkin, interpreted the Spanish-American War and its aftermath as final proof that his early hopes for a special American destiny had been in vain. Amid the popular enthusiasm aroused by early victories in Cuba and at Manila Bay, he advised students not to enlist and declared before an audience in Cambridge that America's rash eagerness for a totally unnecessary war was "a bitter disappointment to the lover of his country; it is a turning-back from the path of civilization to that of barbarism." To wage such a war was "a national crime." It was immoral to try to relieve Cuban suffering "by inflicting worse suffering still." It was futile to enter this fight because Spain's expulsion from Cuba would mean either "anarchy" or the substitution of America's authority for that of Spain, and either alternative seemed bleak to Norton.[72] *

Norton feared that the responsibilities of empire would bring upon the United States "the misery and the burdens that war and standing armies have brought upon the nations of the Old World." The result would be the destruction of those very virtues that had made America unique in the world. He wrote an English friend that "all the evil spirits of the Old World which we trusted were exorcised in the New,

* Norton's speech evoked an outraged public reaction and a public denunciation by Republican Senator George F. Hoar of Massachusetts. See below, Chapter 7.

have taken possession of her, and under their influence she has gone mad." It was appalling that Americans were "so ready to fling away their distinctive blessings," so willing to take the European road to corruption and guilt. Norton spoke for other anti-imperialists besides himself when he replied to the charge that his views would deprive America of its deserved place in world affairs:

> It is not that we would hold America back from playing her full part in the world's affairs, but that we believe that her part could be better accomplished by close adherence to those high principles which are ideally embodied in her institutions,—by the establishment of her own democracy in such wise as to make it a symbol of noble self-government, and by exercising the influence of a great, unarmed and peaceful power on the affairs and the moral temper of the world.
>
> We believe that America had something better to offer to mankind than those aims she is now pursuing, and we mourn her desertion of ideals which were not selfish nor limited in their application, but which are of universal worth and validity. She has lost her unique position as a potential leader in the progress of civilization, and has taken up her place simply as one of the grasping and selfish nations of the present day.[73]

For Norton the Spanish-American War "sounded the close of the America exceptionally blessed among the nations," [74] a profoundly disturbing development for one who had believed that the "hopes for the advance of civilized man" depended on the successful outcome of the unique American experiment. Like William James, he reacted by blaming himself for having been too hopeful in the past, for having lived in the "Fool's Paradise" of expecting America to point the way to a new social order:

> I have been too much of an idealist about America, had set my hopes too high, had formed too fair an image of what she might become. Never had nation such an opportunity,

she was the hope of the world. Never again will any nation have her chance to raise the standard of civilization.[75]

Godkin and Norton were among those nineteenth-century idealists who had hoped, like the Puritans of two centuries before, that America would be a City upon a Hill—a state and civilization that would attract the admiration of the whole world. They had believed that America had a unique opportunity to demonstrate the true design of a proper and just society for mankind. Schooled in the Anglo-Saxon genteel tradition, they were confounded by the vulgarity that had emerged in place of the New World perfection for which they had hoped. The strength and vitality of America completely eluded them, for they noted only its slums, aliens, warring classes, philistines, and corruption, its wanton destruction of virgin forests, its shameless surrender to marketplace ethics. Imperialism was the last straw, the final defeat of their original hopes.

Yet even Godkin and Norton were never able to relegate their hopes to total oblivion. Neither was fully able to resist the lingering hope that America might yet be saved, and they flattered themselves that men such as they might yet create in the distant future a superior civilization in America. Godkin wrote in December of 1898:

> The cause of civilization and liberty is eternal, and its claims on our best services are also eternal. They will never die out. Those of us who think this Philippine scheme is born in iniquity and must bear iniquitous fruit, are bound to keep saying so, no matter what the Senate or the President may do, or how much money it may make for the warriors. Nay, if it destroys this government, it will be none the less our duty to labor for its restoration, and it is our firm conviction that those who may now succeed in saving it, or who may have hereafter to work for its revival, will hold as high a place in American history as those who became immortal by founding it.[76]

In 1902—with Americans in control of Cuba, Puerto Rico, and the Philippines, with Emilio Aguinaldo in captivity and his rebellion broken—Norton counseled his friends not to give up:

> While all the congregation of the children of Israel are wandering in the wilderness of Sin, . . . we, the little remnant of the house of Judah that has escaped, must comfort one another as best we may. Happily our feet are planted upon a rock whence not even the Lord in his present mood can dislodge us.
>
> Prosperity has materialized the souls, hardened the hearts & dulled the consciences of our people,—and "Humpty Dumpty had a great fall."
>
> Well, we are defeated for the time; but the war is not ended, and we are enlisted for the war.[77]

CHAPTER FIVE

Edward Atkinson: The Informal Empire

Trade and Empire

Most leading anti-imperialists who had given the subject much thought subscribed to the principles of laissez-faire economics laid down by Adam Smith in the eighteenth century. Many had doubtless read *The Wealth of Nations* and were familiar with Smith's own condemnation of imperialism on the grounds of national self-interest:

> After all the unjust attempts . . . of every country in Europe to engross to itself the whole advantage of the trade of its own colonies, no country has yet been able to engross to itself any thing but the expence of supporting in time of peace and of defending in time of war the oppressive authority which it assumes over them. The inconveniences resulting from the possession of its colonies, every country has engrossed to itself completely. The advantages resulting from their trade it has been obliged to share with many other countries.[1]

Colonies afforded their owners only trouble, expense, and unfulfilled expectations. British opponents of colonialism had long contended that trade did not follow the flag, and in the last third of the nineteenth century many Americans who opposed the annexation of foreign territories but favored an expansion of American trade adopted this classic argument for their own purposes. Both businessmen and statesmen were searching for new foreign markets, which seemed essential to continued profits, economic growth, and employment. Most of them believed with Adam Smith, at least until the late nineties, that a large increase in exports could be effected without seizing the nettle of empire. Fashioning a "trade empire" happily would not require the creation of a political empire. As John Kasson, a former minister to Austria, wrote in 1881, the United States, by expanding its economic power in Latin America, could acquire not only profits but also "irresistible arguments to sustain our non-colonization policy." [2]

Some historians have fastened upon this trade-without-territory policy and contended that it was merely the anti-imperialists' own, shrewd version of "imperialism"—that, when all is said and done, the anti-imperialists were not "real" anti-imperialists. They may have made a great fuss about the moral and constitutional implications of colonialism, but they actually had their sights set on an American economic empire. William A. Williams has written that "some leading politicians and intellectuals like Carl Schurz advocated a more sophisticated kind of empire based on economic power" and divorced from the "unnecessary (and even harmful)" burdens of formal colonialism.[3] Another writer has described the anti-imperialists as "confident of America's ability to conquer the world without paying the traditional costs of colonial expansion." They "offered the anti-colonial expansion of the marketplace as the solution for the problems facing American policy makers in the 1890's."[4] Instead of capitulating to the jingoistic clamor for empire, the anti-imperialists cleverly pointed the way to an imperial system unsullied by the brutalities and unburdened by the costs of formal empire. They were "anti-colonial imperialists."

There *were* men who called themselves anti-imperialists but stood for policies that might well be called "imperialistic" by mid-twentieth-century standards. There was the anonymous writer in the *Yale Review* of August, 1898, who declared that the rapid increase in American production made an expansion of foreign trade imperative and insisted that this could best be achieved "by repudiating the doctrine of expansion by acquisition after the Roman type, and insisting simply upon freedom of intercourse . . ." He wrote that true American imperialism consisted "in the empire of trade, coupled with fair dealing, justice, and freedom, not in the empire of conquest." [5] This writer certainly professed to see nothing exploitative in the "empire" he described. The same was true of most economic expansionists, who believed that everyone would gain from an increased sale of American goods. It is reasonable to question the credentials of those anti-imperialists who were disposed to press or force other peoples to open their doors to American products, who insisted upon retaining harbors and coaling stations in distant territories, or who believed that the United States should have the last word over the decisions of ostensibly independent governments. It makes little sense, on the other hand, to force the label of "imperialistic" on the widely held belief that a policy of free trade could enlarge the sale of American goods to countries willing to purchase them. As one writer has observed, "the doctrine of comparative advantage in international trade theory can hardly be classed as expansionism." [6]*

* The doctrine of comparative advantage is the classic theoretical argument for free trade.

A large volume of free trade between two nations can result in the development of a dominant-subordinate relationship between them, especially when a poor country with an undiversified economy depends heavily on the continued willingness of a stronger country to purchase the bulk of its one or two cash products. The villains here are dependence, which can result from a variety of political, economic, or geographic circumstances, and the absence of diversification—not free trade itself. It is certainly a vast oversimplification to *equate* close economic relations with "imperialism."

The question remains: was the anti-imperialist movement at bottom a camouflaged campaign for an informal empire? Was the primary aim of its leaders to expand American economic strength around the globe by means more sophisticated than those of the spread-eagle imperialists? The answer is No. A large number of leading anti-imperialists gave no thought at all to the economic implications of imperialism, and those who did almost invariably subordinated them to moral, racial, historical, and constitutional considerations. Charles Eliot Norton had not been reading American commercial reports when he formulated his protest against imperialism. E. L. Godkin, though a prominent exponent of free trade, did not belabor the McKinley administration for carelessly choosing the wrong way to increase the profits of American business. When William James lamented that America had lost its unique place in the world, he was in no way referring to its economic position. And neither the mugwump Charles Francis Adams nor the Republican George F. Hoar placed any emphasis on markets and trading profits in their contributions to the anti-imperialist protest.[7]

To be sure, a number of anti-imperialist spokesmen—among them Edward Atkinson, Carl Schurz, David Starr Jordan, William Graham Sumner, Andrew Carnegie[8] —sometimes sounded like men searching for a cheap and clean route to American economic expansion. But none of them considered this particular aspect of the issue to be as important as those of a moral and political nature. Atkinson entertained dreams of American economic predominance throughout the world, but he also edited *The Anti-Imperialist*, a polemical sheet described by Thomas Wentworth Higginson as "the most elaborate single battery which the war-party had to encounter" and the repository of every conceivable anti-imperialist argument.[9] Although Schurz hoped that the United States would avail itself of every possible commercial advantage in the various pieces of Spain's broken empire and did recommend the establishment of a

protectorate over the Philippines, it would be grossly misleading to characterize a critic so preoccupied with racial, social, and constitutional questions as the advocate of "a more
sophisticated kind of empire based on economic power." [10]
David Starr Jordan, president of Stanford University, did in
fact formulate what seemed to him an innocuous program
for "permeating" rather than taking over Oriental territories, but his overriding concern was his fear that American
policy might have a disastrous effect on the nation's political
traditions and institutions. William Graham Sumner stated
the case for informal imperialism in unmistakable terms, but
at the same time he upbraided the McKinley administration
for "stretching" the Constitution, trampling on American
traditions, and arousing the hatred of the Filipinos. In short,
to describe the anti-imperialist movement as a campaign to
create a less bothersome and more sophisticated empire than
the one being forged by William McKinley and his cohorts
is to miss the essential point of the protest.

As a strain of the complex anti-imperialist impulse, however, the informal empire approach must be taken into account. Edward Atkinson, who was its most energetic exponent, never visualized it as a policy of exploitation. More
important, he finally rejected it as economically unnecessary.

The Open Door and the Hell of War

Edward Atkinson was a person with a decided opinion on
every subject. His views were usually buttressed by a mass of
statistics that did not always prove what he thought they did
but were impressive by virtue of their sheer bulk. Atkinson
was born near Boston in 1827 and never attended college;
his extensive use of statistics was no doubt an effort to show
the world and convince himself that he was as good as any
Harvard scholar. His father, an old-line merchant, had come
on hard times and was unable to finance an advanced educa-

tion for his son, who left school at fifteen to seek his fortune. Starting out with a dry-goods firm, he quickly became an expert accountant and was soon launched on a successful career as treasurer and financial agent for several large manufacturers.

A tall, massively built man, Atkinson possessed an extraordinarily optimistic view of the world and an ample quota of self-esteem. All his life he moved with evident satisfaction and gusto from one career and enthusiasm to another. In 1878 he branched out from his main work in cotton manufacturing to become president of the Boston Manufacturers' Mutual Fire Insurance Company, and this remained his chief business interest until his death in 1905. Apart from his business activities, he attracted public notice as tariff reformer, sound money agitator, popular statistician, public speaker, dietician, and sometimes inventor. He thrived on controversy and jumped into the midst of any fray, as evidenced by his authorship of more than 250 polemical pamphlets and countless "Letters to the Editor." Everything from cotton mills to automatic fire sprinklers caught his interest and the attention of his ready pen. His interests were, in fact, too diverse for the intellectual equipment he could bring to bear on them. His "quick apprehension and fluency of speech," the *Boston Journal* declared in 1899, "have tempted him to spread himself over fields too broad for a score of good men to cover effectively. His weakness has been to discuss dogmatically and with affected precision multitudes of subjects upon which his real touch has been purely superficial." [11] As Charles Francis Adams put it, he was "always in evidence." [12]

Atkinson was inventor of the Aladdin Oven, a sort of prototype pressure-cooker which operated on small amounts of cheap kerosene. He recommended his oven, along with suggestions for making the most of a small grocery budget, as a weapon in the battle to rid the world of poverty. He hoped to instruct "the fourteen hour wives of the eight hour men

. . . how to get more appetizing food from the shinbone of beef and the scrag of mutton than workmen commonly get from the finer and better cuts when they can afford to buy them." A family of five that saved a quarter a day on food and fuel by using his machine and advice could lead a life of ease. Jeered at by workers as "Shinbone Atkinson," the inventor himself once suggested that his epitaph should read, "He taught the American people how to stew." He was deadly serious, however, in his belief that culinary economy and a nutrition chart could go a long way toward eradicating poverty.[13]

Atkinson was never one to make an economic or social proposal that threatened the status quo. He supported hard currency, advocated the reduction of tariffs, wrote pamphlets against passage of the Interstate Commerce Act of 1887, fought against working-hours legislation, opposed the statutory abolition of child labor, and ceaselessly criticized labor union activities (once telling a Knights of Labor audience: "you call a man a scab who won't submit. . . . I tell you right here that the 'scab' is the man who will come out ahead, and you will get left").[14] A onetime abolitionist and fund-raiser for John Brown, Atkinson consistently pursued a mugwump line, seeing in it "the only comfortable political position that a man can hold."[15]

In the 1890s when foreign questions became increasingly important in public discussions, Atkinson emerged as a prominent anti-jingo spokesman. In arguments against the annexation of Hawaii and criticisms of American policy in the Venezuela crisis of 1895–1896 he took the position that the United States should do everything in its power to gain world economic supremacy with a minimum of international disturbance and without acquiring a burdensome political empire in the process. He was no "Little American," but he believed that an action like the annexation of Hawaii was simply unnecessary and therefore inadvisable. When expansionists suggested that Great Britain, Japan, or even Russia would snatch the islands unless the United States acted first, Atkinson pooh-poohed their worries and argued that all any nation with maritime interests wanted from Hawaii was the freedom to trade with her and to use her islands as a way station for traffic across the Pacific Ocean. In 1895 he presented these ideas to President Cleveland, urging him to call for an international treaty that would guarantee Hawaii's neutrality and keep her open to the trade of the whole world. The powers interested in Hawaii wanted no territory but only "unrestricted intercourse," coaling station sites, and electric cable landing spots. The Hawaiians themselves could maintain their own government under the protection of the powers, who in council would also decide upon all questions connected with the islands' foreign affairs.[16] Although such an arrangement would surely have been a web of diplomatic intrigue, Atkinson considered his proposal quite sound and was later to advance a similar one for the neutralization of the Philippines.

Despite his belief that the United States could gain what it wanted without creating an empire of its own, Atkinson was not averse to taking advantage of the empires of others to increase American commerical profits. He particularly admired British colonial policy because it opened the door of trade to all comers and increased the ability of colonial peoples to pay for Western goods. He deplored the kind of imperialism that was practiced by France, Spain, the Netherlands, and Germany in an effort to retain the "sole control" of their subjects' commerce. The British, by contrast, were not only merciful to subject peoples but provided an opening for American merchants. "What a boon it would be to the world," Atkinson wrote in the *North American Review*, "if systems corresponding to English law, English administration and the English regard for personal rights, could be extended over the continent of South America."[17]

The United States, untroubled by the burden of imperialist acquisitions, could then exploit the free trade opportunities presented by the British to build up the strongest trade position in the world. Of all the "machine using" nations, he explained in a letter to Cleveland on November 12, 1895, only the United States produced more than it required for its essential needs in all important categories—timber, food, fibers, and metals. All other nations were deficient in at least one and usually several areas, a circumstance which he considered of great significance, for while the United States was increasingly called upon to fill the deficiencies of other countries, it was at the same time "more and more independent of them for everything but articles of voluntary use." If America acted wisely and adopted a policy of free trade she could steadily increase other nations' dependence on her and ultimately control the "commerce of the world." This, and not jingoism, was the road to the "true defense" of the United States, a path Atkinson urged the President to take without delay.[18]

Just a month later, however, the Venezuela crisis erupted, and there was no measuring Atkinson's shock when he realized that, instead of heeding his advice and combating jingoism, Cleveland was himself fanning its flames into wildfire. As soon as he heard reports of the President's threatening message of December 17, he shrieked to a reporter, "This is ridiculous, ridiculous, ridiculous!"[19] He then wrote Cleveland such a sharp letter of complaint that the beleaguered Chief Executive thought that he had perhaps gone mad.[20] In a letter to a member of Cleveland's cabinet Atkinson stated that things could be set right "if the whole of South America could be taken under a British protectorate, supplemented by a commercial treaty with the United States giving equal rights to all English speaking people in commerce therewith."[21]

In the wake of the Venezuela imbroglio, Atkinson came up with a new proposal. The United States and Great Britain, after settling all outstanding issues which divided them, should jointly support a program to establish a system of international adjudication of territorial disputes, set up a method of arbitrating "all other international questions," abolish privateering, and guarantee "the freedom of cities from bombardment which are not part of the defences of harbors." The Anglo-American powers so united would be irresistible, not in conquering, but in "stopping the enormous waste of money for preparation for war and working beneficently in every direction," including the benevolent supervision of economic development in Latin America.[22]

Two years later, as the United States drifted toward war with Spain, Atkinson, who was a vice-president of the American Peace Society, urged churches to petition Congress for peace and implored President McKinley "to avoid the hell of war." [23] Meanwhile he continued to advance his packet of schemes for peace and economic expansion. He suggested that the United States call a conference at which it could join with Great Britain, Russia, and Japan in guaranteeing neutrality and the open door in Hawaii. If Spain could be induced to attend, the seething Cuban question could be submitted to arbitration.[24] Taking a far too optimistic view of developments in the Far East (especially with regard to Russian intentions), Atkinson declared in a speech to the Atlanta Chamber of Commerce on April 14, 1898, that the American cotton-goods industry would soon find a great untapped market for exports in China; he went on to predict that peace on the high seas and Anglo-American-Russian friendship would extend the market even further. In a plea for free trade, he exhorted his audience: "Commerce is today the prime factor in the world's work. Its development is the chief object of nations." If America played her cards well, limitless commercial growth was within her reach.[25]

A week later the United States was at war, despite all of Atkinson's schemes. Atkinson was not happy with this turn of events, but for a brief time he tried hard to reconcile himself to it, hoping that the problems presented by war would not be as formidable as he had feared and that, in

fact, the United States might gain some economic and diplomatic advantage from the conflict. For the moment he
viewed the domestic side of the crisis with composure and
even hope: any increase in taxes and the national debt could
probably be sustained without damage, free silver might be
eliminated from the scene as a political issue, and the lingering bitterness between Northerners and Southerners might
be ended by their unified response to the national call to
arms. Impressed by the difficulties of turning back the clock,
Atkinson temporarily accepted American protection or annexation of Cuba and Puerto Rico as unavoidable and even
remarked that such a development would give the United
States "the command of the Gulf of Mexico and the coast of
South America." [26] Hawaii still seemed unsuited for American control, and Atkinson continued to hope that circumstances would not require the annexation of the Philippines.
But if the United States did find it necessary to annex the
Philippines, this involvement in the Far East would enhance
the chances of creating an alliance with Britain to halt the
partitioning of China and keep the doors of the ancient
kingdom open to the products of the English-speaking
world. Through the spring and early summer of 1898 he put
the best face he could on these prospects, since it appeared
that the United States had become "one of the great powers
of the world" in spite of itself and had entered an era in
which its traditions of "non-extension and non-interference
with other nations" and its sense of "national isolation and
irresponsibility" would be consigned to the dustbin of history.[27]

When it became clear, however, that the McKinley administration was truly intent on the acquisition of overseas territories, Atkinson was jarred out of his acquiescent mood.
His belief that expanded trade with Asia and Latin America
did not require annexing territory and his habitual distrust
of colonialism reasserted themselves. In fact, even when he
had been explaining to friends that the acquisition of a few

colonies did not unduly alarm him, Atkinson had been unwilling to concede the same in public, writing to a newspaper on May 26 that if the United States adopted an "imperial policy," it would bring itself "down to the level of the
semi-barbarous states and nations of Continental Europe." [28]
Now, on August 25, he charged in a letter to McKinley
that the United States had neither the right nor the obligation to annex Cuba or Puerto Rico and that territorial expansion was "uncalled for, totally foreign to our system of
government, not within our duty," and likely to produce
calamitous results. Taking Cuba in defiance of the Teller
Amendment would be a moral outrage.[29] He wrote an English friend the next day that the United States, instead of annexing the island, should at the very most establish a protectorate over it and have it "pay its own expenses." [30] By January, 1899, he had formulated a concrete plan for the han-
dling of the Philippines: "These islands can be neutralized;
their commerce can be extended; the peace of God can be
kept in all their ports"; and order can be maintained, "if
necessary by foreign officers serving by agreement among nations." [31] Here again in full flower was Atkinson's anti-
colonialist program for economic expansion, a plan which
included the neutralization of the territory in question, international supervision of the territory's internal stability,
and an open door to the commerce of all nations.

Later in January, shortly before the Treaty of Paris was
put to a vote in the Senate, Atkinson offered McKinley a detailed outline of his scheme which, although restricted in its
illustrative remarks to the Philippines. referred to all "the
tropical islands from which we have removed the oppression
of Spain." Atkinson declared at the outset that the people of
the United States did not want the Philippines but would
not consider returning them to Spain.

> The alternative is an agreement among the great powers to
> neutralize these islands. We have precedents in the neutral-
> ization of Belgium by agreement; in the neutralization of

Switzerland by agreement. . . . We have a precedent in the neutralization of the Suez Canal. Why should we not continue on these lines? England does not wish and will not risk her soldiers in taking possession of the Philippine Islands, even if the opportunity were offered. Germany will not take them; Japan might not take them; no other nation desires to take them; each nation desires that the other shall not; each nation desires a coaling station; the open door to commerce, the development of the wants of the Filipinos through commerce to the end that their demand for manufactures may increase; the development of their own products correspondingly. The necessities of war, of military occupation, of defense against aggression, increase the burden and diminish the commerce; and whereas if by agreement it were ordained that all fortifications should be destroyed, that no naval warfare should be permitted within the waters of the Philippine Islands, that all nations might buy coaling stations, land commodities and enjoy commerce under the same system of collecting the revenue, called the open door,—all interests would be promoted, oppression would end; the Philippine Islands would become first in the history of the world a sanctuary of commerce, like the Cathedrals of old where God's peace was kept while all around was violence, rapine and war.[32]

In an interesting memorandum written three days later (and possibly sent to the President), Atkinson added that the people of the Philippines would themselves have to maintain order, ensure that property rights were fully protected, and perhaps submit for a time to the establishment of a set of extra-territorial courts for the "protection" of resident foreigners. This plan was clearly in the interests of the "Powers," not of the Filipinos, and if fully enacted,

it will be the greatest step toward maintenance of peace, commerce, order and industry that has ever taken place in the world and . . . the administration which may accomplish such an act will go down in history eminent for all that is right and redeem itself from the danger of doing all that is wrong in undertaking conquest and the effort to govern a vassal colony.[33]

During this same period Atkinson launched a virulent letter and pamphlet campaign against the administration's policy of annexation, warning the nation that imperialism was a further descent into "the hell of war." On November 14, 1898, he wrote McKinley a remarkable letter which, in tasteless detail, predicted the wholesale decimation of American forces in the Philippines by the ravages of venereal disease. Already, he alleged, large numbers of soldiers and sailors had been infected in their American training camps and embarkation ports. Once "they had been exposed to the greater hazard" in Cuba, Puerto Rico, and the Philippines, Atkinson forecast that a moral disaster of national proportions would inevitably occur. Thousands of American boys, killed by dread Asian varieties of venereal disease, would never return to their families; additional thousands would return crippled and deformed, useless and disgraced for life; thousands more would return only to pass on their physical corruption to the third and fourth generation. All this would ensue if the administration refused to abandon its new tropical acquisitions. No "false sense of delicacy," Atkinson warned, should conceal the frightful horrors the President would bring on the American people if he persisted in his present course. It was clearly "no time to mince words":

This danger must be publicly named and these facts must be widely known and the exposure to the corruption of the young blood of this nation must be stopped. It is not a pleasant duty but I shall assume the responsibility. The final responsibility will rest upon yourself and all who have authority. Unless you would invite the execration of the mothers of our land and cause your administration to stand recorded in history with utter condemnation, you cannot ignore or slight these facts and this danger which is an evil worse than death, worse than war; to try to ignore it and not to provide against it in every possible manner by avoidance will be to the disgrace of those who shall bring this danger of corruption of the blood upon our country,—a greater disgrace than all other losses of honor combined.[34] *

On November 19, 1898, just five days after sending this extraordinary letter to the President, Atkinson presided over the founding of the Anti-Imperialist League, the event occurring in his own office in Boston. Selected as one of the League's honorary vice-presidents, he immediately began to issue a stream of impassioned anti-imperialist manifestos bearing such titles as "The Cost of a National Crime" and "The Hell of War and its Penalties." In an attempt to stir up enough anti-imperialist sentiment to defeat the peace treaty, he mailed his broadsides to influential citizens throughout the country, compiling an ingenious mailing list that included all members of Congress, the chief clergyman in every American town numbering from 1,000 to 2,500 inhabitants (2,300 pamphlets), the principal Catholic, Episcopalian, Congregationalist, Baptist, and Methodist pastors in every town or city numbering more than 2,500 inhabitants (about 8,500 pamphlets), the mayor or "chief officer" of each of these towns or cities (another 4,000 pamphlets), all officers of boards of trade and commercial associations (3,000 organizations), members of national, state, and local agricultural associations (5,000 in number), the governors and secretaries of agriculture of each state, the directing officer of every agricultural experiment station in the coun-

* For a sharp attack on Atkinson and especially on this phase of his anti-imperialist campaign, see Fred C. Chamberlin, *The Blow from Behind*, Lee and Shepard, Boston, 1903, pp. viii–ix, 53, 55–68, 70, 74–80, 83, 86, 90–91, 123–24, 126–27. Chamberlin effectively demonstrates the highly exaggerated nature of Atkinson's alarming predictions regarding venereal disease and, in a chapter entitled "The Venereal Disease Libel," blisters him for his ungentlemanly behavior and lapses in taste, asking him "for any statistics he may be able to furnish of the prevalence of these diseases among men, without excepting anybody at all, engaged in Mr. Atkinson's business, that of fire insurance—if I may so ask without prying too far into his personal affairs."

try, the officers of all workingmen's associations, and "finally a copy to each of the Granger Associations." [35]

But despite this display of organizational energy, the treaty passed and insurrection broke out in the Philippines. Undismayed, Atkinson churned out more pamphlets, accusing the American government of committing "criminal aggression" in the Philippines, predicting that battlefield casualties and disease would shatter American forces within a few months, and forecasting that 8,000 Americans would die in the first year of fighting. He urged young men at home not to enlist and advised those already in the Philippines not to re-enlist when their current terms of service were over.[36]

As Atkinson's prophecies grew more alarming and his words more careless, the Anti-Imperialist League grew less willing to acknowledge responsibility for them. Spokesmen for the League explained that the honorary vice-president was acting on his own, not in his capacity as a League officer. The League moderates were about to suffer still more at the hands of their zealous associate, for Atkinson was already setting the stage for the most melodramatic incident of the anti-imperialist movement. On April 22, 1899, he wrote the War Department requesting the names and addresses of five or six hundred officers and soldiers stationed in the Philippines, explaining that he wanted to send copies of his pamphlets to them.[37] He was openly testing his right to send pamphlets to fellow Americans directly on the scene in the Philippines —reading matter calculated to produce discouragement and dissension among the troops. Receiving no answer from the War Department, he then proceeded to mail the pamphlets to Admiral Dewey, to three American generals, to two civilian members of the United States Philippine Commission, and to a war correspondent for *Harper's Weekly*—all of whom were in the islands. He had thrown down the gauntlet.[38]

The McKinley administration was unnerved by this challenge. Attorney-General John W. Griggs was reported to have said that "Atkinson could be prosecuted and sentenced to a large fine and ten years of imprisonment because of his seditious writings." Postmaster-General Charles Emory Smith promptly ordered the outright seizure of the pamphlets, which were removed from the Manila mail sacks by the San Francisco postmaster. Although Atkinson's action was disavowed by the Anti-Imperialist League,[39] he took great satisfaction from the incident. In the first place, it proved that there was nothing academic about the fear that imperialism abroad would endanger liberty at home. The administration's seizure of his pamphlets, Atkinson told a reporter, was a brazen attempt "to suppress free speech and forbid free mails to the people of the United States in their correspondence with the citizens of the United States who are now in the Philippines." Another thing which delighted Atkinson was the wave of publicity he received as a result of the pamphlet seizure. It was "a gigantic joke," he wrote Andrew Carnegie, "that such feeble minded persons as those in the Cabinet" had unwittingly stimulated the demand for his pamphlets. The administration had turned a "comparatively unknown" Massachusetts mugwump into a national figure overnight and vastly increased public interest in his activities—eventually over 130,000 of his pamphlets were distributed. The administration had blocked a trickle only to release a torrent.[40]*

Atkinson pressed the attack in his own bulletin, *The Anti-Imperialist*. For about a month the administration newspapers responded in kind, focusing great attention on his

---

* In the wake of the incident, the *Boston Journal* remarked: "The Journal appeals to the United States Government to be lenient with our Mr. Atkinson. He is too old for punishment and not young enough for reformation. He would regard imprisonment in any cause as the crowning glory of his life, but this fine old gentleman of seventy-two is neither a Vallandigham nor an Aaron Burr, and would be as much out of place in a Federal jail as a baby on a battlefield." Quoted in *Boston Evening Transcript*, May 3, 1899. Atkinson never took his case to court and was never prosecuted by the government.

pamphlets and magazine and the anti-imperialist movement in general. Then press attacks on him suddenly ceased as if by order from above, convincing the disappointed Atkinson that "the members of the Cabinet have graduated from an asylum for the imbecile and feeble-minded." He continued to make charges, "trying to stir them up to provoke another attack." [41] He accused the administration of spending huge sums of money on the suppression of Aguinaldo's rebellion, re-establishing slavery, condoning polygamy, and other sins including the operation of a large Manila brothel, "guarded by United States soldiers, and under the supervision of United States army surgeons, over whom Wm. McKinley is Commander-in-Chief." This time the administration wisely chose not to reply.[42]

McKinley and his cabinet members never showed any interest in Atkinson's suggestion of an Anglo-American entente or his scheme for the neutralization of the new territories. On occasion Atkinson returned to the theme of informal empire, as he did in May, 1899, when he recommended that an American official be sent to manage the affairs of a neutralized Philippines, just as "Lord Cromer administers the affairs of Egypt under the Khedive." [43] With the passing of time, however, his thinking underwent a fundamental change on the pivotal question of the needs of the American economy. He came to look upon the internal economic development of the United States as the proper focal point for the use of the nation's surplus resources and energies. Many areas of the country, he wrote, were impatiently awaiting the "brains, industry, and capital" that would make them an integral part of a modern industrial economy. Their development would produce more wealth "than all the commerce of Asia will yield in a generation." Foreign markets would continue to be important, of course, especially since the prices of American goods on the world market determined in part the prices of these same goods at home. Thus foreign demand for American products would remain "the balance wheel of the whole traffic of this country." [44]

But—and this represented an important shift in attitude—Atkinson now maintained that it would be the purchases of Canada and the "machine-using nations" of Europe that would operate the balance wheel. As early as January 18, 1899, in a letter to the *Manufactures Record* of Baltimore, he declared it a "delusion" to believe that the United States could profit appreciably from "the traffic of the Philippine Islands and other eastern countries of very low purchasing power . . ." [45] In the summer and fall of 1899, with guerrilla war raging in the Philippines, he became increasingly skeptical of the value of "the entire export [trade] to the whole of Asia as compared to our markets in Europe." [46] Finally, in February, 1900, in the *North American Review*, he discussed the issue at length under the title, "Eastern Commerce: What Is It Worth?" Although the day might come when the issue would have to be reopened, Atkinson believed that for the indefinite future American manufacturers and farmers would be wasting their time seeking markets in the primitive lands of the East. Only Europeans, Canadians, and the inhabitants of some of Britain's colonial possessions—people who, like Americans, possessed railroads, steamships, factories, and machine shops—had the necessary purchasing power to buy large quantities of American goods. With a barrage of statistics this onetime enthusiast for trade with the East demonstrated that the annual increase in American trade with Europe was, in itself, far larger than the total traffic with all of Asia. If United States exports to the Philippines had quadrupled in the past four years the increase was owing almost entirely to the sale of liquor and other supplies to American troops pacifying the islands. And what of trade with China? Perhaps American exporters could hope to sell a few more steel rails and cotton shirts by trafficking with the Chinese, but as long as "masses of the people are on the edge of starvation," it was highly unlikely that American merchants would do a brisk business.[47] Writing later in the year in *The Anti-Imperialist,* Atkinson concluded that it would be "many generations" before the "hordes of Asia, Africa, and Oceania" could pay for the modern wares produced by American machines.[48]

The idea of informal empire had lost its appeal. British alliances and Oriental trade seemed unimportant. With the commercial issue settled in his own mind, Atkinson assumed with characteristic optimism that the days of American imperialism were virtually over. He directed his attention to other matters, and the flood of letters and statements that he had been sending forth regularly almost ceased by the spring of 1900. By summertime he had persuaded himself that McKinley would soon perform a characteristic "wobble" and pull American troops out of the Philippines, justifying his action by announcing that the rebellion had been effectively suppressed (whether it had or not). The United States could then grant the Filipinos the independent status it had always intended for them, first arranging with other powers to guarantee the islands' independence and neutrality.[49] McKinley, of course, had nothing of the sort in mind, but Atkinson persisted in his belief that American military undertakings of recent months were only a "temporary aberration." Convinced that the national economy was ripe for a renewed internal expansion and that trade with Europe would continue to absorb America's productive surplus, he wrote on December 14, 1900: "I think the world is more interesting than it ever was before, and I have greater confidence in progressive human welfare." [50]

Edward Atkinson was but one of a number of mugwump anti-imperialists who at some point were receptive to some kind of "informal" imperialism. With far less enthusiasm but in very similar terms, Carl Schurz had been pointing out since 1893 that the United States could have all the commercial advantages, coaling stations, and harbors it wanted without assuming the expense and opprobrium of formal empire.[51] David Starr Jordan maintained that trade passed through the open door instead of following the imperial flag. Noting the example of America's "peaceful conquest of Mexico," which he deemed "a legitimate form of expansion," he argued that the tropics could be best controlled not by conquest but by the "permeation" of American business:

> Permeation is cheaper than war. . . . We could fill all tropical countries with consular agents and commercial agents, men trained to stand for good order and to work for American interests, for less than it costs to subdue a single tropical island. . . . In peace, not in war, in commerce, not in force of arms, is found the key to our problem—if any solution be ever possible.

But Jordan had reservations about the ultimate effectiveness of a "permeation" policy, since he believed that "the tropics are stronger than we at last. They will control and swallow up whatever we put into them." [52]

Yale's renowned Social Darwinist, William Graham Sumner, made a strong case for a "non-imperialist" extension of American commerce. Intrigued by the drive for expansion which he termed "Earth Hunger," he suggested that nations could satisfy this craving through pacific and commercial means. There was no longer any need for the kind of colonial methods that had been employed by Spain in the conquest of territories solely for her own economic purposes. In 1896, when proposals for the annexation of Hawaii were in the air, Sumner stated that if the United States "could have free trade with Hawaii while somebody else had the jurisdiction, we should gain all the advantages and escape all the burdens." In January, 1899, when he saw that the United States was determined to follow the "old-fashioned" method of expansion, he caustically described it as "The Conquest of the United States by Spain." Only an open door policy, which America's protection-minded officialdom was unlikely to countenance, could possibly justify the "irksome necessity" of annexing distant territories. And even this justification was insufficient to one who believed that any form of imperialism represented a basic departure from American traditions and from the isolation "which the other nations of the earth have observed in silent envy." [53]

All these men—Atkinson, Schurz, Jordan, and Sumner—regarded themselves as anti-imperialists, and in their advocacy of free trade and their opposition to direct control over foreign territories they were indeed that. But it is also true that they favored subtle forms of American domination and looked on the world as a society in which some nations were more equal than others, in which American commercial agents were granted special privileges, American government officials were treated with special deference, and the American navy was allowed special access to harbors and coaling stations. In short, they did not object to the peaceful yet masterful use of superior American power in pursuit of economic goals. In this phase of their thinking, they shared some of the assumptions of the McKinley administration and compromised their claim to full anti-imperialist status.

In shifting his attention from the potential markets of Asia to the already established and rapidly expanding domestic and European markets, Edward Atkinson more accurately appraised the direction of future economic trends than did most exponents of empire, whether formal or informal. Julius Pratt has observed that the actual colonial acquisitions of the United States, though "valuable" as markets and areas for investment, "were by no means a major factor in its economic prosperity." Commerce between the United States and the unindustrialized areas of Asia and Latin America increased sharply in the years following 1900, but Europe and Canada continued to purchase the great bulk of American exports. Manila, which some had hoped would be America's Hong Kong—its commercial gateway to China and the rest of Asia—never developed into such a trade depot, and, as late as the 1930s, China ordinarily purchased no more than 2 or 3 per cent of America's exports. Americans did not provide oil for hundreds of millions of Chinese lamps; nor was their Open Door policy as enunciated in 1899 and 1900 effective in protecting the Chinese from the depradations inflicted by European and Japanese imperialism.[54]

Ironically, America's colonial possessions made their greatest economic impact on the home country through the sale of tropical goods to the United States. In fact, the end of American rule in one of these possessions, the Philippines, eventually came not because of widespread moral repugnance in the United States to continued imperialist rule nor because of disappointment in the relatively small volume of American exports to the islands (although these were important factors to some), but rather because American sugar, cotton, and dairy producers insisted on building protective walls against Philippine sugar and coconut oil imports. Free trade between the United States and its Asian colony, established in 1913, paved the way for the eventual granting of Philippine independence. It was not the American Anti-Imperialist League but such organizations as the Beet Growers' Association, the Oklahoma Cottonseed Crushers' Association, and the American Farm Bureau Federation which finally helped rid the United States of her Far Eastern empire.[55]

CHAPTER SIX

Charles Francis Adams and the Election of 1900

As the son of a prominent diplomat, the grandson of one President, and the great-grandson of another, Charles Francis Adams, Jr., had more reason than most men to feel confident of his place in nineteenth-century America. But like his brothers Henry and Brooks Adams he lacked the assurance of his forefathers. Introspective in the family mold, at times painfully self-conscious, he was ambivalent about the changing world around him; he was critical of it but wanted to be part of it. Adams hated Wall Street speculators and real estate developers, yet was himself a stock market plunger and heavy land investor who wanted wealth "as the spring-board to influence, consideration, power, and enjoyment." He tried to be both railroad reformer and railroad executive. He was an army officer who was contemptuous of the soldiers under his command; he was a businessman who detested his associates. He was a mugwump who considered most mugwumps fools; he was an opponent of imperialism who tried to destroy the anti-imperialist movement. As a mugwump he was forever restive, forever skeptical of the mugwump line. As an anti-imperialist he was one of the movement's most severe critics. For Adams and for many others, the confusion and uncertainty implicit in the union of mugwumpery and

anti-imperialism were demonstrated in the election campaign of 1900, the climax of the mugwump assault on imperialism.[1]

A Mugwump Faces the Strife of the World

Adams was born in 1835. In the course of his long life he
was an army officer, muckraker,[2] lawyer, government commissioner, civic administrator, corporation president, educational reformer, mugwump, and historian. Adams led a Negro cavalry regiment during the Civil War, and although he
had many reservations about his troops, he felt that the man-
ly rigors of military service had given him the "most beneficial" experience of his life; in fact, he seriously considered
making a career of the army. But he decided, instead, to enter "the most developing force and largest field of the day,"
that of railroads, and held a leading post on the pioneering
Massachusetts Board of Railroad Commissioners throughout
the 1870s before joining the Union Pacific Railroad, first as
a government director and then, from 1884 to 1890, as president. This giant western firm was in great financial difficulty in the 1880s, and Adams could neither get it out of
trouble nor maintain his own ethical standards in the attempt. He considered his business associates an uncongenial
lot, finding none "whose acquaintance [he] valued. They
were a coarse, realistic, bargaining crowd." After being un-
ceremoniously dumped as Union Pacific president, Adams
willingly retired to his "vocation," the writing of history.[3]

Adams' social and political views were generally consistent
with the mugwump pattern. He favored civil service reform,
the reduction of tariffs, and electoral reforms designed to
increase the voting weight of society's "better elements." Although never an avowed enemy of either democracy or
free immigration, he nonetheless disliked the "ignorant and
credulous" Irish who had invaded the Yankee reserve of
New England in such large numbers and remarked in 1869

that universal suffrage in the United States meant "a European, and especially Celtic proletariat on the Atlantic coast, an African proletariat on the shores of the Gulf, and a Chinese proletariat on the Pacific." [4] He never pretended to be an egalitarian. Adams wrote in his *Autobiography*:

> The common-schools my father did not care to send his children to; and I have always been glad of it. I don't associate with the laborers on my place, nor would the association be agreeable to either of us. Their customs, language, habits and conventionalities differ from mine; as do those of their children. I believe in school life; and I believe in the equality of men before the law; but social equality, whether for man or child, is altogether another thing. My father, at least didn't force that on us.[5]

For years he and his brother John Quincy II exercised a kind of patrician control over the town meetings of old Quincy, Massachusetts, liquidating the town's debt, lowering its tax rate, and improving its schools, library, and parks. In national politics he followed the zigzag path of mugwumpery, taking an active part in the anti-Republican revolts of 1872 and 1884 and voting for McKinley and hard money in 1896.

But behind Adams' mugwump façade were several factors which constantly pulled him toward a more conventional stance on contemporary issues. His innate contrariness made him a man who could be counted on to disagree periodically with just about everyone, and this included his fellow mugwumps. A lover of controversy despite his protestations to the contrary, Adams was, in his own words, "otherwise-minded." [6] He often took mugwump friends to task for their negativism and pessimism, privately judging them to be hopelessly vacillating, impractical, and tradition-bound. In the hope of avoiding the peculiar grooves of mugwump life, he made a conscious effort to immerse himself in the main currents of modern American life. This consideration prompted him to volunteer for military service in the Civil

War and face enemy gunfire at Antietam and Gettysburg.
Alone among the members of his family, he undertook a
career in the dominant institution of post–Civil War America, the business corporation. He resisted the easy with-
drawal into nostalgic detachment, preferring to participate
in America's busy new life. His brother Henry put his finger
on this fundamental difference between them when he wrote
Charles in 1869:

> Your ideas and mine don't agree, but they never have
> agreed. You like the strife of the world. I detest it and de-
> spise it. You work for power. I work for my own satisfaction.
> You like roughness and strength; I like taste and dexterity.
> For God's sake, let us go our ways and not try to be like
> each other.[7]

Adams' determination to make a place for himself in the
Gilded Age influenced his attitude toward a whole range of
what he considered outmoded institutions and practices.
Boston society, for instance, struck him as ingrown, provincial, and frivolous, a "boy-and-girl" affair divorced from
the realities of the world at large.* As an alumnus and overseer of Harvard, he waged a personal campaign for the adoption of a curriculum that would better prepare graduates for
the real conditions of American life. He attacked the continued emphasis on the classics, which he called "A College
Fetish" in his Harvard Phi Beta Kappa address of 1883. To
Charles Eliot Norton, a traditionalist who could scarcely
have agreed with him, Adams wrote:

> I think we've had all we want of "elegant scholars" and
> "gentlemen of refined classical taste," and now I want to see
> more University men trained up to take a hand in the
> rather rough game of American nineteenth-century life. To
> do that effectively they must, I think, be brought up in

---

* In his memoirs Adams wrote: "In fact, I may say that in the course of
my life I have tried Boston socially on all sides: I have summered it and
wintered it, tried it drunk and tried it sober; and, drunk or sober, there's
nothing in it—save Boston!" Adams, *An Autobiography*, p. 39.

communication with that life. At least they should comprehend the tongues in which it talks. The fact is I don't admire Greco-Yankee culture in action, in art, or in literature. I prefer Hawthorne to Everett.[8]

When he turned to the writing of history Adams brought to his work a brusque contempt for historians who catered to a "filiopietistic" view of the past. In several of his works on Massachusetts history he sharply criticized this band of whitewashers, dismissing their local patriotism as mere provincialism, and as president of the Massachusetts Historical Society after 1895 he tried to divert the attention of chroniclers from colonial origins to the study of modern, nineteenth-century America.[9] He refused to view the past as a lost golden age:

> It ever has been, and probably always will be, the custom to look back upon the past as a simpler, a purer, and a better time than the present; it seems more Arcadian and natural, sterner and stronger, less selfish and more heroic. . . . The growing laxity of morals, the decay of public spirit, the vulgarity of manners and the general tendency of the age to deteriorate, have from the very beginning of New England been matters of common observation. . . . Each generation has observed these symptoms with alarm; and each generation has in turn held up its fathers and mothers before its children as models, the classic severity and homely simple virtues of which a plainly degenerate offspring might well imitate, but could not hope to equal. . . .
>
> Yet a careful study of the past reveals nothing more substantial than filial piety upon which to base this grateful fiction. The earlier times in New England were not pleasant times in which to live; the earlier generations were not pleasant generations to live with. One accustomed to the variety, luxury and refinement of modern life, if carried suddenly back into the admired existence of the past, would, the moment his surprise and amusement had passed away, experience an acute and lasting attack of homesickness and disgust.[10]

Although he shared many of the mugwumps' misgivings about American society and politics, Adams did not mistrust the present or fear the future as much as they did. He had little use for nostalgia and was impatient with those who hankered for the past. Though grievously disappointed at times with certain aspects of American life, he was not a pessimist. His granddaughter once remarked: "Grandpa was full of virility and *élan* and optimism. He was always sure everything was coming out right." [11] This was not the exuberant optimism of William James, but a restrained and unemotional conviction that the future offered some promise and that it was important to discover what it was. America's problems would have to be met with realism and a readiness to face the future, not with head-shaking and clucking tongues. "We cannot sit still and grumble," he wrote Carl Schurz in 1873; "we must go forward to the country with something positive, or give up any pretense of directing public opinion." [12]

"We Must E'en Lie in It as Best We May"

There is no doubt that at bottom Charles Francis Adams considered the Spanish-American War a terrible mistake and American imperialism a regrettable break with the best of the nation's past traditions. He had great difficulty, however, in deciding what course he should take in opposing these developments. All the complexity and ambivalence of his nature welled up to prevent him from making a straightforward and unequivocal protest against imperialism. He was tormented by a genuine skepticism about the accuracy and relevance of his dissenting viewpoint and by the fear that, in publicly opposing expansionism, he would make a spectacle of himself in the eyes of the world. His doubts finally became too much for him, and little more than a year after President McKinley sent his war message to Congress, Adams veered around and launched an attack on the anti-imperialist movement itself.

It was with alarm that Adams viewed the onset of war in the spring of 1898. His debt-ridden fortune, battered by the depression of the mid-nineties, was in no condition to withstand the economic dislocations that he anticipated war would bring.[13] But he dreaded war for other than personal reasons. He saw no excuse for a "Roman-candle foreign policy" at a time when "popular discontent" was widespread, cities were misgoverned, and Bryan and other malcontents were on the loose.[14] War would almost automatically lead to the annexation of Cuba, an action that would fly in the face of America's historic purpose, which he defined in December, 1898, as "one long protest against, and divergence from, Old World methods and ideals." [15] Throughout the many months of debate over imperialism Adams found the rhetoric of the expansionists impossible to stomach. The everlasting "Expansion, World-Power, Inferior Races, Calvinization, Duty-and-Destiny twaddle and humbug" were too much to bear. In his private journal he confided:

> The clergymen have all got hold of the idea of Duty; we have a Mission; it is a distinct Call of the Almighty. They want to go out, and have this Great Nation import [*sic*] the blessings of Liberty and the Gospel to the Inferior Races, who wait for us, as for their Messiah;—only we must remember to take with us lots of shot-guns to keep those other Superior Races,—all wolves in sheep's clothing,—away from our flock. They would devour them;—but we won't. Oh no! —such ideas are "pessimistic"; you should have more faith in the American people!—Such cant!—It does make me tired.[16]

But even as Adams grew tired of the sanctimoniousness of the expansionists he had grave doubts about the advisability of making a public protest against them. He held his peace during the actual period of warfare with Spain, and in September, 1898, as he journeyed home from a summer visit to Europe, he was continually nagged by the fear that his initial distrust of imperialism was misplaced. If he aired his critical opinions in public it would only prove that he was "out of touch":

> I am "out of touch";—most probably I am wholly wrong; certainly I am partly so. The world is not going to come to an immediate end because things do not go exactly as I want them to go, and the unexpected will continue to occur.

For the moment he concluded that there was no "good and sufficient reason, quite yet, to wholly despair of the republic." [17] Once home he felt his way gingerly, appalled by the fiery rhetoric of the expansionists but unconvinced by the gloomy predictions of the anti-imperialists. Despairing forecasts had been made half a century earlier when Texas was annexed, but time had proved them unfounded. America was too strong, too sound in its foundations, to be seriously damaged by the acquisition of some new territory. Like a healthy human body, the nation possessed "a self-curative force which enabled it to throw off disease which would destroy a similar power in a condition of decadence." There was still no reason, he wrote in October, to abandon hope of "some practical outcome." [18]

But in December, 1898, Adams began to move toward an open expression of dissent. He took the first step early in the month in the semi-private confines of the Massachusetts Reform Club. There he attacked the administration's annexationist plans in outspoken terms and implored his audience to resist "the tendency . . . to give up the fight in advance, on the ground that you are plainly going to be beaten. Battles are not won that way." [19] But the next day Adams wrote in his journal: "I can't make it out. Am I old and out-of-date,—tied up with the ideas of the past,—wedded to traditions . . . ?" [20] Again, however, he suppressed his recurrent doubts, convinced that it was not he but his fellow Americans who had gone "crazy" and thrown over the traces. At last he decided to state his views openly, choosing as a platform a meeting of the Historical Society of Lexington, Massachusetts, on December 20, 1898. Using as his text Edmund Burke's remark, "I put my foot in the tracks of our forefathers, where I can neither wander nor stumble," he told the gathering that it was imperative that Americans follow in the footsteps of their forefathers by resisting all efforts to launch their nation on a course of aggression and imperialism in the European manner. The address was a thoroughgoing, vigorous, and unequivocal assault on United States policy.[21] Although still concerned that he might have appeared foolish or eccentric in his remarks, Adams felt considerable pleasure and relief at having spoken his mind:

> I have said my say in a great issue. I have borne my evidence against cant and political sophistry. My voice may not,—I know it will not, go far; but it has been lifted up. I am on the record; and, for my own satisfaction, I want to be there.[22]

Even before his Lexington speech, however, Adams felt some discomfort in the company of other anti-imperialists. At an early date he urged them to be more constructive in their criticism and to select leaders who could command national respect. He wrote Carl Schurz in November, 1898, to criticize current anti-imperialist strategy and to declare his lack of confidence in such leaders as Edward Atkinson and Gamaliel Bradford whose approach he considered too negative. Instead of persuading the public to recognize its own interest in opposing imperialism, they were making violent "headlong" attacks on the administration. Instead of winning over the public, they were alienating it. While denouncing American possession of the Philippines as immoral and unconstitutional, these anti-imperialists were failing to offer any realistic alternatives to the policies of the administration. He warned Schurz that unless they could come up with a positive program they "must abandon the field." [23]

Adams was never one to weep over lost causes, and as soon as it became apparent that the Senate would ratify the peace treaty and the United States would become a colonial power in spite of his or anyone's objections, he made an effort to be constructive and turned his attention to the question of how the colonies could best be governed. In a letter to Schurz on January 17, 1899, he outlined the principles upon which he thought American colonial policy should be based, putting particular emphasis on equal trade opportunities for all nations in the Philippines, respect for traditional Filipino institutions, a wide degree of Filipino autonomy, and a firm commitment to govern the islands for the benefit of their inhabitants rather than for the advantage of American politicians and businessmen.[24] In February not only was the peace treaty ratified but insurrection erupted in the Philippines, a turn of events that caused Adams to question whether a policy as moderate as the one he had recommended could ever be implemented. It was no longer realistic to insist that the United States relinquish all control over the Philippines. But this was precisely what leaders of the anti-imperialist movement were doing, and Adams became increasingly exasperated with their tactics and over-all policy. Convinced at length that the United States could not avoid some kind of continued involvement in the Philippines, lacking sympathy for a campaign of opposition that seemed to him more and more peevish and unconstructive, and having no wish to be part of a marginal protest movement, he finally concluded that he and the rest of the movement must come to a parting of the ways.

But not quietly. The departure was public and Adams minced no words in explaining it. Only a few months after attempting to stiffen the resistance of his anti-imperialist friends at the Massachusetts Reform Club, Adams now acknowledged defeat and resolved to undermine and destroy the campaign of those who continued the fight. An opportunity arose in May, 1899, when he was invited to an anti-imperialist rally at Cambridgeport, Massachusetts. He declined the invitation in a long letter addressed to Thomas Wentworth Higginson, who was to preside at the meeting, and published in the May 18, 1899, edition of the *Springfield Daily Republican*. Adams explained that he could not attend any more meetings devoted exclusively to faultfinding. The public was growing impatient with nothing but criticism and was demanding some "tangible" alternatives. The ratification of the peace treaty and especially the insurrectionary actions of Aguinaldo's forces in the Philippines had made it impossible to carry out a program that would satisfy the anti-imperialists. There had earlier been a unique opportunity for Americans to choose between a policy of outright colonialism and one that would have allowed the Filipinos to develop an independent and self-sufficient government with a minimum of American protection and advice. But the administration had fumbled this chance by first insisting on an "acceptance of our sovereignty," promising in return to give the islanders "sugar plums" if they were "good and obedient." This blunder had made armed conflict inevitable and had wiped out any hope for a policy consistent with American political traditions.

It was fatuous to think that everything that had happened since April, 1898, could be reversed, and Adams knew it. The administration was now faced with the problem of setting up a system of government and administration for the Philippines, and Adams believed that McKinley would draw on British examples in establishing a "stable" and "beneficent" regime headed by a governor-general, supported by a powerful military force, and dedicated to advancing the prosperity and autonomy of the Filipinos. The only thing left for the anti-imperialists to consider was "what objection exists to such a form of government, and what we, who were not primarily in favor of it, have to propose in its place." He

for one had nothing to offer: "I must frankly confess that I
. . . am here brought to a halt." He found little pleasure in
the prospect of an "almost servile imitation of the English,"
but neither his dissatisfaction nor that of the anti-imperialists could alter the fact that the administration had irrevocably chosen to pursue such a policy. The die was cast: "Instead of being originators, we have accepted the role of imitators. So, having had our bed made for us, we must e'en lie
in it as best we may."

But the anti-imperialists could still be useful if they acted
swiftly. If they were prepared to accept the facts as they
existed there was still time to urge the administration to
guarantee a maximum of Filipino home rule with a minimum of American interference. Adams conceded that it
would be difficult—perhaps impossible—to achieve this goal
because of the inclination of politicians to use the islands as
a patronage refuge for "statesmen out of a job." But he believed that the leaders of the administration sincerely wished
to prevent such an outcome themselves and should be supported in this effort by all genuine anti-imperialists. As for
himself, he no longer wanted "to protest, or to indulge in
harsh or unnecessary criticism." "In this life," he concluded,
"we can rarely have our own way; but when the course of
events has made it clear, as now, that our way is no longer
open, it is the course of wisdom to do what is in our power
to eliminate so far as may be the evil we fancy we see in the
policy imposed upon us, however originally mistaken." [25]

Adams' manifesto came as a shock to other anti-imperialists. Moorfield Storey wrote, "I could wish that you had
found it in your heart to throw up the sponge quietly,
without squeezing it down the backs of your late allies."
Samuel Bowles's *Springfield Daily Republican,* which had
published the offending letter, accused its author of abandoning principle and "bartering essentials" and reminded
him that "God hates a quitter." The editorial writer for the

Hartford Times upbraided him for having offered "precisely the sort of advice that will give all the jingoes . . . exactly the encouragement they desire" and—in a thrust that hit close to home—charged that Adams had "made up his mind in the case of the Philippines to be one of the crowd." Higginson, to whom the letter was addressed, was scornful and reminded Adams of John Brown's utterance in another time of trouble: "Don't talk about surrendering; we can surrender any time." Winslow Warren and Charles Codman, both prominent Boston anti-imperialists, insisted that it was indefensible to show any hint of submission to the imperialists until after the Presidential election of 1900, which would give the people an opportunity to express their opinions on the subject. Codman, who had heard Adams' fighting speech at the Reform Club five months earlier, tauntingly recalled the ringing words he had spoken on that occasion: "The battle has only just begun." [26]

Adams, however, was grimly satisfied with what he had done. Two days after publication of his letter, he wrote in his journal:

> I am called a "quitter" &c. The fact is, much worked up as I have been over this Philippine business I wrote this letter at this time intentionally, and on full consideration. In my judgment, the course of events had made our position hopeless, and we were rapidly becoming ridiculous, as well as odious and tiresome. The issue was decided in the Philippines and by the Filipinos [when they killed Americans]. Our position was made impossible . . .
>
> Those here,—preserve us from our friends!—They were a parcel of cranks! Edward Atkinson, Erving Winslow, . . . Gaml Bradford . . . —a crowd wild and ill-balanced enough to sink any cause. Such an absence of judgment, —such lack of weight!—So I considered that the best thing I could do was to put a stop to the whole thing before a really great cause was run hopelessly into the ground, —made odious as well as absurd. I hope I have done it.[27]

Although Adams did not succeed in his wish to "put a stop to the whole thing," he had hit the anti-imperialists where they were most vulnerable by exposing their unrealistic demand for a return to the *status quo ante bellum*. Still smarting from his attack, his erstwhile allies would have been even more vexed to learn what Adams really thought of the President he was urging them to support:

> What will now be the outcome passes all my powers of divination. I have no confidence in McKinley. He seems to me a poor, weak, flabby [figure?]-of-wax, unctuous and canting. A well meaning, weak, Methodist "statesman." The country is drifting, wholly without direction.[28]

"The Difficult Feat of Voting against Both Parties"

Adams could not really force himself to abandon all interest in the anti-imperialist cause, and from time to time over the next few years he agreed to lend his name to various proposals urging a cessation of fighting between American and Filipino forces or a reduction of American involvement in the Philippines. For the most part, however, he sat out the rest of the campaign in public silence. All that remained was to decide how to vote in the Presidential election of 1900. Adams was able to make his decision with relative ease well in advance of election day, but for most mugwumps the choice was an excruciating one. Thomas A. Bailey's study of the election indicates that McKinley's reelection represented neither a "mandate" for, nor a repudiation of, imperialism. The nature of mugwump anti-imperialist involvement in the campaign strongly confirms his thesis.[29]

It was nearly impossible for any American to leave the polls on election day, 1900, with confidence that he had taken a clear-cut stand on the question of imperialism. The sheer lapse of time had diminished the importance of the issue in the minds of many voters: more than two years had passed since the end of the war with Spain and twenty-one months had elapsed since the ratification of the peace treaty and the beginning of the Filipino rebellion. To others imperialism already seemed an established and unalterable part of the political landscape. The continuing Filipino rebellion further complicated the issue, since many voters agreed with McKinley that the insurrection had to be suppressed in order to vindicate the national honor and the death of American soldiers. Furthermore, the McKinley forces did not campaign as unbridled imperialists, for the Republican platform, while pledging the government "to put down armed insurrection," also promised independence and home rule for Cuba and, in the case of Puerto Rico and the Philippines, "the largest measure of self-government consistent with their welfare and our duties." [30] By 1900 Charles Francis Adams and like-minded anti-imperialists believed that such a promise represented the best terms they could get.

The Democrats, who had provided virtually all the votes cast against the Treaty of Paris in 1899, confidently expected all anti-imperialists to flock to their banner in 1900. They did in fact draw the support of many mugwump anti-imperialists, but they entered the campaign with several handicaps that prevented them from receiving the overwhelming anti-imperialist vote they expected. Their platform hedged on the crucial Philippines issue, confirming the impression of some anti-imperialists that little would be gained by turning McKinley out of office. Although the Democrats denounced the administration's past actions and referred to imperialism in their platform as "the paramount issue of the campaign," there was little in their discussion of future policy to differentiate them from the Republicans. By promising to "give" the Philippines "a stable form of government," they implicitly endorsed the administration policy that made it the first order of business to crush the Filipino rebellion by force of arms. By promising "independence" but failing to offer any timetable for its realization, they disappointed those who wanted a pledge of immediate independence. And by promising the Philippines "protection from outside interference such as have been given for nearly a century to the Republics of Central and South America," the Democrats fell between two stools, disappointing anti-imperialists by tacitly acknowledging the need for continued American involvement in the affairs of the Far East while failing to answer the expansionists' charge that a protectorate was an inadequate form of involvement.[31]

The Democrats' greatest handicap was their candidate, William Jennings Bryan, whom few anti-imperialists trusted. They remembered all too vividly that he had urged his Democratic and Populist allies in the Senate to vote for the peace treaty despite his numerous declarations that he was a firm opponent of imperialism; since two additional votes against the treaty would have defeated it, his intervention had been crucial and still rankled in many memories. The *Boston Herald,* a major anti-imperialist newspaper, declared on August 23, 1900, that "no individual, certainly no unofficial individual, is more responsible than William J. Bryan" for the ratification of the peace treaty.[32] Ex-President Grover Cleveland asked his former cabinet officer Judson Harmon, "How certain can you be that [Bryan] would save you from imperialism? What did he do towards that end when the treaty of peace was before the Senate; and how do you know what such an acrobat would do on that question if his personal ambition was in the balance?"[33] Bryan's conduct of the campaign did nothing to restore confidence in his leadership. After a ringing speech denouncing imperialism on August 8, 1900, he played down the issue in favor of the old free silver and reformist themes of 1896, a decision that undoubtedly cost him thousands of anti-imperialist votes. Conservatives within the anti-imperialist ranks squirmed at the thought of endorsing a candidate who repudiated the Gold Standard Act of 1900, condemned protection, attacked big business, cast aspersions on the Supreme Court, and backed a host of other progressive measures.

As the election approached, mugwump anti-imperialists were compelled to pick and choose among issues and between candidates. What would Bryan do that McKinley had not done? What if anything could be undone of all that had been done? Was it right to give indirect encouragement to the Filipino rebellion by casting a vote for the party which, however vaguely, favored Philippine independence? Was it right simply to abandon the Philippines to whatever fate might await them? If so, was it possible? Was it prudent? Was there any way of knowing that the ballot that one cast would be a vote for freedom?

As early as March, 1899, Charles Francis Adams decided that the Democratic Party would have to dump Bryan and shelve free silver before it could hope to gain the support of mugwump anti-imperialists.[34] He momentarily entertained the hope that an independent anti-imperialist candidate could be found to run against both McKinley and Bryan,[35] but with no independent candidate in sight and the Democratic Party regrettably saddled with the Commoner and free silver, he settled on McKinley, although he found him "peculiarly repulsive": "He is a musty, jokeless, well-meaning undertaker,—unctuous and canting. His 'beneficent assimilation'— (lo! the poor Indian!),—his 'Duty and Destiny' twaddle stirs my bile." Five months before the election, Adams wrote:

> I have some difficulty in finding words adequate to express the contempt I feel for this political invertebrate. . . . He seems to me to be a well-meaning man,—an Ohio man; —no leader, no thinker, no convictions.[36]

Despite the contempt he felt for McKinley, Adams considered his re-election essential.[37] He argued that the anti-imperialists were on the wrong track in seeing imperialism as the greatest threat to American institutions; machine politics, boss rule, and civic corruption represented the true danger. And the responsibility for this state of affairs could be traced primarily to Democratic hands, to such bosses of the party as Tammany Hall's Richard Croker. Adams wrote Carl Schurz on March 25, 1900:

> What is the danger you and [other anti-imperialists] apprehend?—It is, as I understand it, the drifting away from our traditions,—the decay of republican principles. Well!—we will not dispute over the danger. It is grave enough; as well as imminent. My apprehension is not less great than yours. It is as respects the source of danger we differ. You see it externally, in the Philippines; I see it internally, in New York city and Pennsylvania,—in Croker, and Quay, and Platt [the latter two were Republicans]. Nations and communities don't die from disorders external to them; dangerous decay is internal. The trouble with Rome wasn't in the colonies and the empire; it was in the Senate and the forum.
>
> You are [looking?] for the decay of our system in the Asiatic horizon, while the real seat of disease is right at your own door. We could slough off the Philippines;—can you slough off New York city?—It isn't a case of excresence, —that we could manage easy enough;—it's a case of cancer. . . . We cant about imperialism, and look for the "man-on-horseback," and all that nonsense. Our Emperor is here now, in embryo; even we don't recognize him, and we scornfully call him a "boss." Just exactly as in Rome, before the Caesars systematised the [thing?], a succession of Tweeds, and Crokers, and Quays had their day, replacing each other; so now our system is evolving its natural result. . . . The system is working itself out to its natural results, not in the Philippines but right here at home.

In the face of such developments, how could one vote for Bryan?

> I see Bryan,—the evidence of a sick state,—come East, and go direct to New York,—not to confer with Grover Cleveland or with David B. Hill even, but with Croker. He

strikes hands with Tammany; and now you propose to me to remedy the external danger by installing in power the municipal cancer. I can't see it! [38]

Adams offered a variety of other reasons for opposing Bryan. If elected he would probably accept the existing status of the new territories and proceed to use them as a source of party spoils, an unending supply of tropical grease to lubricate the wheels of the Democratic machine.[39] If McKinley was unctuous and commonplace, Bryan was "a hydrant of words," a man who "never conceived an idea except from the columns of a newspaper."

> He is in one sense scripturally formidable, for he is unquestionably armed with the jaw-bone of an ass. He can talk longer, and say less, than any man in christendom. . . . Wm J. Bryan seems a natural product of a half-baked civilization and the freshwater college. A talking machine, he can set his mouth in action, and go away and leave it, sure that it will not stop until he returns.[40]

When Bryan, in a speech in August, made a spirited attack on imperialism, Adams was pleasantly surprised and momentarily regarded him with more charity, but as soon as the candidate turned his attention to other issues, Adams promptly reverted to his original opinion that Bryan was a "demagogue," a "mountebank," a "half-baked" opportunist with the "jaw of a jackass." [41]

Adams privately believed that Bryan would be a poor President, but not a dangerous one. For one thing, the gold standard was "too firmly fixed to be disturbed." This campaign would not threaten Adams' fortune as Bryan's unsettling talk in 1896 had done. "It is different now," he wrote: "I can now philosophize." [42] That Bryan did not represent a serious danger, however, did not alter the fact that he and his party formed a "drunken, reckless crew,—the scum of our political ditch-water." Yet a number of Adams' friends— Schurz, Moorfield Storey, and others—seemed bent on putting him in office, a fact that called more for pity than censure:

> Poor Schurz!—what luck the man has. Here he is at 72, finding himself compelled to lend his voice to the support of this wretched charlatan . . . Well! I did my very best to save him. . . . As to my other anti-imperialist friends,—their chief characteristic is an utter absence of saving commonsense, and I can only wish them joy of their candidate, —the "peerless leader" of the "flute-like" voice! [43]

Adams himself displayed a want of common sense when he came up with a plan that represented the very epitome of involuted mugwump thinking. Ignoring the fact that the executive branch of the government had heretofore been almost solely responsible for setting expansionist policy (and departing somewhat from his previous acceptance of the status quo), he argued that imperialism could be brought to an "ignominious end" by sending to the House of Representatives a Democratic majority which would refuse to appropriate the necessary funds for carrying out McKinley's imperialist programs. The President could propose, but Congress would not dispose. Adams' suggestion was shot through with difficulties, but it had a sure-fire appeal for some of the crotchety corners of the mugwump mind since, as the plan was conceived, by voting for McKinley and a Democratic House or, if one preferred, against Bryan and a Republican House, "we will actually accomplish the *difficult feat of voting against both parties; and making one negative the other in order to bring about the results we have in view.*" [44]

Carl Schurz was following a different tack. As early as October, 1898, he had come out against Theodore Roosevelt's candidacy for governor of New York on the grounds that the election of a man with such "fantastic notions as to the bodily exercise the American people need to keep them from Chinese degeneracy" would fan the flames of jingoism and encourage the imperialist policies of the McKinley administration. Although it might be argued that a victory for Roosevelt's Democratic opponent would benefit the free silver movement and Tammany, Schurz believed that the currency issue had been clearly settled in favor of gold and that, in any case, "there are worse things even than free silver and Tammany, and . . . one of them is the imperialism which in its effects upon the character and the durability of the Republic I consider as pernicious as slavery itself was . . ." [45]

But since Schurz, like Adams, was reluctant to back Bryan and the Democrats,[46] he initially pinned his hopes on another mugwump solution—the formation of an entirely new party that would run an independent anti-imperialist candidate. At a conference at the Plaza Hotel in New York on January 6, 1900, he and a number of other anti-imperialists tentatively decided to undertake the organization of a third party. Schurz hoped to find an "old Republican" to head the ticket, and through the early months of 1900 he suggested various possibilities, including ex-Senator John B. Henderson, one of the "Recusant Seven" Republicans who had refused in 1868 to vote for the conviction of Andrew Johnson; Congressman Henry U. Johnson, an Indiana Republican who had fought in the House against the annexation of Hawaii; author and former general Lew (*Ben Hur*) Wallace; retired Speaker of the House Thomas B. Reed; and octogenarian General William Birney, whose father James Birney had run for President in 1840 and 1844 as the candidate of the Liberty Party.[47]

Schurz was aware that many anti-imperialists were "repelled by the idea of voting for Bryan"; a vote for McKinley, on the other hand, was to his mind a vote for imperialism. A third candidate might provide a way out, not just for a few protest votes, but as an indirect channel of support for Bryan, whom Schurz considered the one anti-imperialist candidate with a real chance to win. How could this come about? The old mugwump's plan was as ingenious and cumbersome as was Adams' design for deadlock. Citing as an example the campaign of John M. Palmer, who had been the candidate of the Gold Democrats in 1896, Schurz claimed that an independent campaign would publicize the anti-imperialist case and bring into the fight many who would otherwise have remained on the sidelines in an open campaign for Bryan. The latter, however, would ultimately benefit because these anti-imperialists would decide at the last moment to make their votes count by casting them for Bryan, the "main anti-imperialist candidate." [48]

But despite the efforts of two separate organizations to name an independent candidate, none was selected, and Schurz—resigned now to openly supporting a man whom he had once denounced as an enemy of all social order—urged Bryan's endorsement by the "Liberty Congress" of the Anti-Imperialist League. With a singular lack of enthusiasm, the congress acquiesced in the endorsement: "While we welcome any other method of opposing the re-election of Mr. McKinley, we advise direct support of Mr. Bryan as the most effective means of crushing imperialism." [49] In a published letter Schurz explained that the circumstances which had dictated his opposition to Bryan in 1896 had changed. At that time the Commoner had run his campaign entirely on the free silver issue, and there had been no legislation on the books to protect the country against his monetary program in the event of his election. But if elected now, Bryan would be "bound hand and foot" on the currency issue by the Gold Standard Act of 1900 and by watchful Republican majorities in both houses of Congress.[50] Thus as the campaign neared its climax, Adams and Schurz, each believing that he had come up with the right design for anti-imperialists to follow, had arrived at totally contradictory plans, Adams favoring the election of McKinley and a Democratic House of Representatives and Schurz supporting Bryan in the anticipation that Congress would continue to be controlled by the Republicans.

In an attempt to influence public opinion the two men published an exchange of lengthy letters reiterating their divergent views. There were few surprises in the correspondence apart from Adams' disingenuous prediction that monetary disaster would follow the election of Bryan, but the spectacle of this solemn exchange of intricate and conflicting mugwumpisms aroused the mirth of Secretary of State John Hay. Sending Henry Adams copies of the letters, Hay appended the following gloss:

> This may not interest you, my beloved pundit, but it will instruct you and that is better. If you refuse to read it, I will give you a brief syllabus of it. S——'s [Schurz's] plan is to elect a lunatic President and trust to a sane Congress to fit him with a straight jacket. A—— [Charles F. Adams] prefers to elect a sane President (not too sane) and give him a lunatic Congress to have fun with. There is much to be said in favor of either plan, but I doubt if one vote in Massachusetts and one in New York will bring either about this year.[51]

Hay was right. It is difficult to believe that many Americans were influenced by the intricacies of the Adams-Schurz dialogue. But the differences between the two men did reflect the confusion and disunity with which the mugwump anti-imperialists faced the election of 1900. Among those leaders whose preference can be determined, there were apparently more who voted for Bryan than for McKinley, albeit with great reluctance in many cases. Some anti-imperialists refused to vote at all, while others searched in vain for an independent candidate. Mark Twain—owing to a recent sojourn in Europe—was at the time ineligible to vote, but he would have stayed away from the polls in any case since there was no independent candidate to support. William Graham Sumner was among those who did stay home. Edward Atkinson, who for a while seemed to subscribe to the McKinley-Democratic Congress formula outlined by Adams, eventually declined to vote at all: "Between two evils choose neither," he said before the election; "I could not swallow Bryan, neither could I digest McKinley," he explained afterward. Horace White, E. L. Godkin's longtime associate and successor as editor of the *New York Evening Post*, wished a plague on both political houses in his editorials although he found Bryan slightly less distasteful than McKinley; it is highly probable that he also refused to vote.

In addition to Schurz, Adams, and Mark Twain, many others at one time or another advocated the formation of a third party, including Godkin, Horace White, editor Samuel Bowles, Moorfield Storey, and Gamaliel Bradford. On the other hand, David G. Haskins and Erving Winslow, both high officers in the Anti-Imperialist League, strenuously opposed any independent nomination on the grounds that, instead of aiding Bryan as Schurz had claimed, it would play into the hands of McKinley by splitting the anti-imperialist vote.

It is an indication of their profound opposition to imperialism that many conservatives who had long reviled Bryan in the harshest terms found themselves casting their ballots for him. Schurz and probably Godkin were among this number, as was Edwin Burritt Smith of Chicago, who urged Bryan to attack McKinley's civil service and tariff policies as well as his imperialist record. Moorfield Storey, who ran unsuccessfully for Congress in 1900 as an independent anti-imperialist, saw no alternative to supporting Bryan. Thomas Wentworth Higginson was one of the few who were able to give unqualified and enthusiastic support to Bryan's candidacy. Others voting for the Democratic candidate were Charles Eliot Norton, Philadelphia civic reformer Herbert Welsh, William Lloyd Garrison, Jr., and Charles Codman; others probably voting for him included William A. Croffut, secretary of the Washington, D.C., Anti-Imperialist League, Samuel Bowles of the *Springfield Daily Republican*, David G. Haskins, treasurer of the Anti-Imperialist League, Winslow

Warren, Erving Winslow, and Gamaliel Bradford. William James, in Europe at the time of the campaign, declared himself "in love with" Bryan's character and disposed to vote for him "with both hands" had he been at home to do so; he nevertheless deplored the Nebraskan's persistent silver talk and wished it had been possible to vote once again for the retired Grover Cleveland.

Among the anti-imperialist leaders who joined Adams in voting for McKinley were president Charles W. Eliot of Harvard, president David Starr Jordan of Stanford (despite his having informed Bryan in the spring of 1900 that he planned to vote for him), Brooklyn clergyman Theodore Cuyler (who could not tolerate the thought of putting a "Populist" in the White House), and Theodore Woolsey Bacon, Professor of International Law at Yale, who asserted that Bryan's support of the Treaty of Paris made him "a ridiculous figure as an Anti-Imperialist candidate." [52]

It is no accident that the mugwumps devised at least six different formulas for expressing their anti-imperialist convictions in the campaign of 1900: some recommended a search for an independent candidate; some preferred a quasi-independent nominee who would act as a cover for support of Bryan; some voted for Bryan and a Republican House of Representatives; some voted for McKinley and a Democratic House of Representatives; some voted for Bryan without any hesitation or qualifications; others stayed home. Voters often have to choose what they consider the lesser of two evils, and to a certain extent this was the mugwumps' dilemma in 1900. But the fragmentation of mugwump sentiment during the campaign also reflected their inveterate hostility to parties as such and their conviction that it was possible for every person to vote in each election strictly according to the issues and candidates, using his vote to express a precise judgment on each discrete political question. American elections have rarely been so tidy, however, and have seldom provided more than the most general of policy "mandates" to the victors. The election of 1900 was no exception. McKinley was defending the "full dinner pail," not just imperialism; the imperialist issue itself was one of many dimensions; and the candidates pitted against each other meant different things to different people. It was typical of the mugwumps to regard the franchise as an instrument so sensitive that anyone could instantly comprehend the rationale behind a particular combination of votes. Over in the Republican ranks anti-imperialist Benjamin Harrison understood better what votes meant. His own voting plans still undecided, he wrote a friend on September 18, 1900:

> There never was I fancy a Presidential Campaign like this. It seems that the men whose votes are to give success to which ever party wins, will be of a mind to protest that the victory is not an approval of some important things for which the successful candidate stands. But there is no place on the tally sheets for these protests and the victory will be taken as a personal vote of confidence. We shall have to be counted for policies that we strongly reprobate.[53]

When all the votes were in and counted the United States still possessed Hawaii, Puerto Rico, and the Philippines, and had not yet relinquished Cuba. Vice-President-elect Theodore Roosevelt, a belligerent expansionist, was soon to be put in the White House by an assassin's bullet. It would have been uncharacteristic of most mugwumps to ask themselves whether they could have accomplished more by working more closely with the party organizations. Such a question did occur, however, to Charles Francis Adams, who reportedly reflected late in life "that if he were to live his life over again he should attach himself firmly to what he considered the best party, and aim at his reforms there, rather than from the outside." [54] But there is no guarantee that this would have made him any happier.

Part Two

Republicans Out of Step

The party of Abraham Lincoln that led the United States to its position as an imperialist power in 1898 did so over the objections of some of its own members. Republican anti-imperialists were important not because of their numbers but because of their prestige and because their dissent afforded conspicuous proof that the war with Spain had raised issues which transcended party lines. Indeed, some of the staunchest members of the McKinley administration, including the President himself, had serious doubts about the wisdom of pursuing what Theodore Roosevelt and Henry Cabot Lodge called the "Large Policy." Postmaster-General James A. Gary quit his office partly because of his anti-war feelings. Secretary of the Navy John D. Long, although eventually reconciled to retaining control of the Philippines, would have preferred to see the United States "rid of the Philippines and of everything else except our own country."[1] McKinley's three Secretaries of State expressed varying degrees of discontent over America's new colonial responsibilities. John Sherman, infirm with age and ineffective in office, resigned and joined the anti-imperialist movement. William Day, Sherman's successor in the State Department, remarked on one occasion that the United States had no choice but to give the Philippines "back to Spain."[2] And his successor—John Hay—while still serving as ambassador to Great Britain, confessed that he was sympathetic to the anti-imperialist views of Andrew Carnegie.[3] The latter, a stalwart Republican industrialist on close terms with many administration figures, threw both money and energy into the anti-imperialist movement. Even the great strategist of expansion Alfred T. Mahan momentarily entertained doubts about taking the Philippines, proposing to Henry Cabot Lodge in July of 1898 that the United States "take only the

Ladrones and Luzon; yielding to the 'honor' and exigencies of Spain the Carolines and the rest of the Philippines." [4]

Congress itself harbored a small but vocal group of Republican recalcitrants. In the House of Representatives, Speaker Thomas B. Reed strewed parliamentary stumbling blocks in the path of House expansionists and eventually took a stand in complete opposition to the administration. Charles Boutelle of Maine, Samuel McCall of Massachusetts, and Henry U. Johnson of Indiana were other House Republicans who resisted their party's lead. In the Senate Shelby Cullom of Illinois held that "we would have been in a better situation than we are now" if Dewey had sailed away from Manila after scoring his great victory there.[5] John C. Spooner of Wisconsin dreaded what would "follow war. . . . I fear Cuba having been rescued from Spain, may more than once demand rescue from the Cubans." [6] Illinois' other senator, William Mason, and George Wellington of Maryland also dragged their heels, while George Frisbie Hoar of Massachusetts, Justin Morrill of Vermont, and Eugene Hale of Maine openly threw over the traces.

In addition to such active politicians as Sherman, Hoar, Reed, Hale, and Morrill, the ranks of Republican anti-imperialists numbered men of past service to the party, including former cabinet member, representative, and senator George S. Boutwell (who became president of the Anti-Imperialist League), ex-senators George F. Edmunds of Vermont and John B. Henderson of Missouri, and former President Benjamin Harrison.

The reasons offered by dissident Republicans to explain their opposition to imperialism varied from man to man; it is noteworthy, however, that a large proportion of these Republicans—like their mugwump counterparts—were elderly men whose earliest political memories were of the heady battle against slavery, the founding of the Republican Party, and the fighting of the Civil War. Imperialism seemed a flat repudiation of the Republican principles to which they had long given their partisan support. They felt, like the mug-wumps, a strong nostalgic pull toward those earlier, simpler, and ostensibly more upright days when America had been a self-contained nation and their party had been on the side of the angels. Secretary of the Navy John D. Long of Massa-chusetts, who despite private misgivings remained loyal to the administration, expressed this sentiment perfectly when he wrote in the fall of 1898: "I really believe I should like to have our country what it was in the first half of this century, provincial, dominated by the New England idea, and merely a natural outgrowth which for two hundred years had been going along in the lines of the Fathers." He added: "But I cannot shut my eyes to the march of events—a march which seems to be beyond human control." [7] It was the wish of the Republican anti-imperialists to call a halt to this partic-ular march.

CHAPTER SEVEN

George F. Hoar:
The Trials of Dissent

When the McKinley administration sought congressional approval for its expansionist ventures it prudently set up defenses against the anticipated attacks from the Democrats. A little sniping from behind the Republican lines was also expected, but no one in the administration was prepared for the full-scale guerrilla campaign conducted by George F. Hoar, Thomas B. Reed, Justin Morrill, and other Republicans. Chief among these campaigners was Hoar, "whose fight against annexation," according to one account, was "a parliamentary classic." [1]

The Anti-Mugwump

George Hoar was a bluff partisan Republican, and if he had had his own way he would have preferred to give the Grand Old Party his constant, unquestioned, and total loyalty. But he was unable to order his political life quite so simply, for he was also a man who took his principles and ideals seriously, and his party and principles unfortunately did not always match as closely as he would have liked them to. One such time was 1898, when Hoar discovered that to defend principle he had to attack party, or to stay with party he had to abandon principle. Since he found neither course acceptable, he tried mightily to have the best of both propositions and defend principle and party equally, no mean task for any man, especially one with Hoar's volatile emotions. The result was a fascinating episode in ambivalence, but fascinating only to the observer since Hoar himself was rendered irritable and miserable by the dilemma. He managed nearly always to conduct himself with dignity and generosity while arguing against his expansionist opponents, but when mugwumps accused him of faintheartedness in the anti-imperialist cause, his calm and reason vanished in the shower of vituperation with which he answered them. In his determination to remain a good Republican despite everything he blamed the Democrats for the expansionism sponsored by his own party. As a friend described the phenomenon, Hoar "terribly weakened his own influence by justifying the robber while he condemned the robbery of the Philippines." [2]

The source of Hoar's principles lay in his New England background. His illustrious ancestors included a president of Harvard, two great-grandfathers, a grandfather, and three great-uncles who fought at Concord Bridge, and another grandfather, Roger Sherman of Connecticut, who signed the Declaration of Independence. Reared "in the pure, noble and simple society" of Concord, where he was born in 1826, young Hoar attended Harvard and then settled in Worcester, Massachusetts, where he practiced law for twenty years.[3] The young attorney became involved at an early date in anti-slavery politics and was named chairman of the Free Soil Committee of Worcester County in 1851. Except for two years of service in the state legislature in the 1850s, however, he did not take too active a part in politics until after the Civil War. In 1868 he was elected to the House of Representatives in the same election that put Grant in the White House. After four terms in the House, Hoar moved up to the Senate at the age of fifty and served from 1877 until his death in 1904. Constitutional legislation in particular engaged his skills, and he had a large part in drafting the Sherman Anti-Trust Act of 1890. He supported civil service reform, high tariffs, international bimetallism, and civil rights legislation. Hoar was never noted for conspicuous or controversial deeds (until 1898) and was never touched by the brush of scandal that tarred so many of his colleagues in the seventies and eighties. A solid and able senator, he worked hard and was rewarded every six years with a new term in office.

Like his colleague from Massachusetts, Henry Cabot Lodge, Hoar was something of a "scholar in politics," a well-informed student of colonial history and friend of education. He was an overseer of Harvard College, a trustee of both Worcester Polytechnic Institute and Clark University, a regent of the Smithsonian Institution, and president of both the American Historical Association and the American Antiquarian Society. He spent his spare time reading poetry or history and translating Thucydides. The owner of an excellent personal library, he could often be found browsing in Washington's used bookstores for items to add to his collection. In the capital he commanded much respect, particularly among those who knew him best. John D. Long found in Hoar "the highest sense of public duty [and the] most chivalrous and unflinching courage of his convictions," and Senator Edward O. Wolcott of Colorado considered him "in many respects the most cultivated man in the Senate . . . head and shoulders the ablest Senator from New England." [4]

Round of feature, always simply dressed, with hair "as white as Boston beans are before baking," Hoar looked on the surface like a genial Pickwickian character.[5] In reality he was pugnacious and cantankerous, quick to take offense and ready to give insult, always convinced of the dishonesty or venality of anyone who opposed him, at times so difficult to get along with that Charles Francis Adams once complained of his "official sensitiveness and bad manners" and described him as "very partizan, and very small," if not "wholly a boor." [6] At the time of Hoar's death Grover Cleveland remarked that "the recording angel is going to have a tough time of it with that old fellow. He has done so many good things, and said so many spiteful things, that I shouldn't know how to deal with him." [7]

Hoar's quick temper was often turned against the mugwumps, who were perhaps his most bitter enemies. There were a number of reasons for his dislike of these independents, many of whom came from his native state. Mugwump academicians especially infuriated him when they criticized American life or cast doubts on the basic good sense of the "common people." These men, with their "white and clean hands," never did "any strenuous work on the honest side" when real moral issues were at stake but instead commented disparagingly on their own country "in excellent English in magazine articles, in orations before literary societies, or at the Commencements of schools for young ladies." [8] In 1884 Hoar attacked President Eliot of Harvard and a little group of Harvard professors ("these gentle hermits of Cambridge") for degrading "the public life of the Commonwealth by teaching our educated youth to be ashamed of their history." [9] In his address as president of the American Historical Association in 1895, he startled the historians assembled to hear him by accusing them of belittling the image of America in their writings. "When I consider the tone of the press, of men of letters, and even some writers of history when they describe [America] I am sometimes astonished that any American youth can love his country at all." As he complained on another occasion, "the history of no people is heroical to its mugwumps." [10]

Hoar's near black-and-white view of American political parties fed his animosity toward the mugwumps. He saw no reason why a person of good sense should have trouble distinguishing the Republican Party from the Democratic Party, since the former had been organized for objects more "great and noble" than those of any other political organization in history.[11] He once remarked in the Senate that "there are some parts of the country where the counting of noses always prevails, where those having white noses are counted as Republicans and those having red noses as belonging to some other party," [12] and on another occasion he attempted to describe to a European the fundamental differences in the membership of the two parties:

> The men who do the work of piety and charity in our churches, the men who administer our school system, the men who own and till their own farms, the men who perform skilled labor in the shops, the soldiers, the men who went to war and stayed all through, the men who paid the debt and kept the currency and saved the nation's honor, the men who saved the country in war and have made it worth living in [in] peace, commonly and as a rule, by the natural law of their being find their places in the Republican party. While the old slave-owner and slave-driver, the saloon keeper, the ballot box stuffer, the Ku Klux Klan, the criminal class of the great cities, the men who cannot read or write, commonly and as a rule, by the natural law of their being, find their congenial place in the Democratic party.[13]

Hoar rejected the mugwump case for political independence. Believing that a political party was more important than any of its individual members, he saw no virtue in voting "for the best man without regard to party." Ticket-splitting was not a commendable exercise in independence but a self-indulgent way of voting "for an individual at the cost of dishonoring [the] country." The man who remained loyal to his party even when he disagreed with some of its policies and candidates acted "according to his own conscience and judgment as thoroughly as the man who refuses to combine with other people for the promotion of public ends." [14] Such a man stood a better chance than the mugwump of improving his party because, by remaining faithful through the most difficult periods, he would be on hand when the time was ripe to regenerate the party from within. From the sidelines he could only snipe away in impotence, to the profit of neither party nor country. In these terms Hoar defended his lifelong devotion to the Republican Party, convinced that only through this loyalty had he been able to achieve anything of worth in American politics.[15]

Hoar did not merely disagree with the mugwumps. He despised them, snarling that they were "the vilest set of political assassins that ever disgraced this or any other country." [16] The peculiar vehemence of his hostility stemmed ironically from his own streak of unorthodoxy. In 1872 he opposed most of his fellow Republicans in wanting to see Grant dumped from the party ticket, and in every subsequent Republican convention through the one held in 1888 he supported candidates who were rejected by a majority of the assembled delegates.[17] In Congress, particularly in the 1870s and 1880s, he often took a line incompatible with that of the party regulars. On other occasions he gave them such grudging support that President McKinley is reported to have called him "the man who furnishes our opponents with their arguments and us with his votes." [18] Hoar himself argued that a measure of independence was all right so long as it was exercised within the confines of party loyalty,[19] but he always felt thoroughly uncomfortable when his own inclination to stray from the party base led him into the camp of the mugwumps. In a moment of unwitting self-revelation he told the Senate in 1896 that mugwumpish critics of American foreign policy "excite my indignation and dislike more when they happen to be on my side than when they are against me." [20]

Hoar's running battle with the mugwumps served a dual purpose: it assuaged the discomfort he felt at his own recurrent departures from the Republican faith and it distinguished his own position—arbitrarily if necessary—from that of the mugwumps. Should the mugwumps happen to agree with him, Hoar felt compelled to discredit their reasons for doing so or, better yet, demonstrate that no real agreement existed. He could never resist the urge to criticize mugwumps on general principles as men who contributed "to public discussions nothing but sneers, or expressions of contempt or pessimistic despair." [21] If his mood was especially belligerent he would flaunt his partisanship in their faces, as he did in 1884 when he declared it "the acme of uncharitableness" for the mugwumps to reprove James G. Blaine or any other politician for dispensing political favors to friends.[22] When it came to railing at his political opponents, Hoar found that any excuse would do.

His unremitting attacks on the mugwumps, coinciding as they did with his own tendency to independence, laid Hoar open to repeated charges of inconsistency and hypocrisy. One critic claimed that the two senators from Massachusetts differed only in that Lodge had "no conscience" while Hoar had one but never obeyed it.[23] The mugwumps themselves took Hoar's behavior as further proof of the evils of party regularity. Difficult times were in store for both Hoar and the mugwumps when the old Worcester partisan prepared to do battle against American imperialism only to discover that his principal allies were none other than his ancient foes.

The Beginnings of Dissent

How Hoar would react to the events of the Spanish-American War was an open question. He had demonstrated a streak of jingoism in the 1890s when he threw his support to Harrison and Cleveland in their difficulties with Chile and Great Britain, backed Harrison's abortive project to annex Hawaii, and wrote into the 1894 Massachusetts Republican platform declarations calling for "Americanism everywhere," "The flag never lowered or dishonored," "No surrender in Samoa," and "No barbarous Queen beheading men in Hawaii." [24] When Turkey began its persecution of Armenians, Hoar responded in December, 1895, by drawing up a set of tough anti-Turkish resolutions and wiring President Cleveland with assurances of support in whatever action the Chief Executive might take against the Turks, who, for all he cared, could be treated "as pirates or common enemies of the human race." [25]

But Hoar also had a less belligerent side. As a freshman representative in 1870 he had opposed the annexation of Santo Domingo. In 1882 he had protested against pressing an "unwilling China" into agreeing to an immigration act that barred its nationals from entering the United States.[26] When debate arose in 1896 over the proper American course in the conflict between Cuba and Spain, he opposed any policy that threatened to bring increased American involvement. A year prior to the outbreak of war with Spain, he wrote: "Neither our institutions nor the temper of our people are adapted to the government of dependencies. We wish for no vassal states, nor subject citizens." [27] Hoar was apparently abandoning his chauvinism of the early nineties.

Although war became increasingly likely Hoar continued to hope that it could be avoided, that the United States would refrain from the unnecessary provocation of Spain.[28] He consistently opposed the Senate's frequent attempts to push McKinley into hostilities. Ultimately, on April 11, 1898, it was the President himself who requested congressional authority to use force "to secure a full and final termination of hostilities between the Government of Spain and the people of Cuba." [29] Hoar, despite his disappointment at this turn of events, decided to support McKinley on the grounds that the war, if fought, would be "the most honorable single war in all history," undertaken without "the slightest thought or desire of foreign conquest or of national gain or advantage." [30]

On April 16 the Senate approved a war resolution that included a section, unacceptable to the administration, recognizing "the Republic of Cuba as the true and lawful Government of that island." Supporting the President's objection to legal recognition of the Cuban rebels, Hoar joined other leading Republican senators in voting against it.* When the House of Representatives also refused to accept the measure, the Senate majority yielded and passed new resolutions in compliance with McKinley's wishes. This arrangement won the approval of the Senate Republican leadership, but Hoar, though present on the floor the day of passage, was recorded as "not voting." [31] He further emphasized his deep reservations about the impending war by failing to appear on April 25, 1898, when the Senate unanimously declared that for four days an actual state of war had already existed between the United States and Spain.[32]

Well before the outbreak of the war Hoar had been wrestling with the problem of expansionism in the form of a new treaty for the annexation of Hawaii signed on June 16, 1897. He had supported annexation four years earlier, but now he worried about the "bad and mischievous" arguments being advanced in its favor [33] and in December, 1897, submitted to the Senate a petition from Hawaii signed by over 21,000 citizens opposing the annexation of their republic.[34] Sensing his feelings, the administration dispatched its big guns to bring him into line. Both Theodore Roosevelt and Alfred Mahan besieged him with annexationist arguments, and the President called him to the White House on the pretext of asking if he thought old Justin Morrill should be urged to vote for the treaty. Hoar interrupted: "I ought to say, Mr. President, in all candor, that I feel very doubtful whether I can support it myself." He complained that the advocates of the treaty were claiming that annexation was essential "in order to help us get our share of China." McKinley quietly

---

* Hoar was in the company of such powerful Republicans as Nelson Aldrich, William Allison, Stephen B. Elkins, Eugene Hale, Mark Hanna, Justin Morrill, Orville H. Platt, Thomas C. Platt, and John C. Spooner. U.S., *Congressional Record*, 55th Cong., 2d Sess., 1898, p. 3993.

assured Hoar that such talk did not represent administration thinking. Hawaii was needed, he emphasized, for reasons of military security; Japan would seize the islands by force if the United States did not move first.[35]

Although Hoar was still uncommitted at the conclusion of his talk with the President he decided shortly thereafter to go along with McKinley on Hawaii, reluctant to make these islands the "battleground" in a fight against expansionism.[36] He must also have recognized how little chance there was of defeating the Hawaiian project after the administration abandoned annexation by treaty in favor of annexation by joint resolution of Congress, which required a mere majority in each House for approval. Trying to make the best of a bad situation, he contended that a vote for Hawaiian annexation in no way represented an endorsement of a general program of expansion. But during the Senate debate on the joint resolution this argument was explicitly rejected by the opponents of the resolution, who insisted that it must be defeated for the very reason that the administration looked upon Hawaii as merely the appetizer in an upcoming expansionist banquet. Hoar was especially discomfited when his old friend from Vermont, Justin Morrill, linked Hawaii with other imperialist projects in condemning the resolution as a step toward joining the "expensive and furious" European "catch-as-catch-can naval hunt to seize ports and harbors, or any tidbits of the Chinese Empire." [37]

Hoar's speech came at the very close of the Senate debate over Hawaii. It was a curious performance. He was troubled, he explained, that he and Senator Morrill could not agree on the significance of the Hawaiian issue. He was even more disturbed to hear how many of those who were planning to vote for the joint resolution had couched their arguments in the rhetoric of expansionism. Whatever their intentions might be, Hoar wanted to make it clear that he was opposed to the acquisition of Cuba or the Philippine Islands. He disputed the view that a powerful navy was "the best instrumentality of a friendly intercourse with mankind" and rejected the notion that the United States had entered "a struggle, lawless and barbarous, for the plunder of dismembered China." He then discounted the importance of all he had said—"All this is a needless alarm"—and argued instead that, despite all the imperialist rhetoric, the annexation of Hawaii should be viewed as an isolated measure carried out solely to protect the islands from Japanese aggression and strengthen America's military position in the Pacific Ocean. In a vain attempt to make the transaction sound utterly insignificant, hardly worthy of discussion, he defined the issue before the Senate as a question of "whether we shall add thirteen hundredths of 1 per cent to our population and eighty-four one-thousandths of 1 per cent to our domain." He even likened the native Hawaiians to "children in an orphan asylum or an idiot school," explaining a few years later that their "only hope and desire and expectation" had been that "they might lead a quiet, undisturbed life, fishing, bathing, supplied with tropical fruits, and be let alone." But, unable completely to banish his own fears of the repercussions of Hawaiian annexation, Hoar gave notice to the McKinley administration that Hawaii was as far as he would go, insisting again that the United States should "acquire no territory," "annex no people," "aspire to no empire or dominion . . ."[38]

The shakiness of Hoar's position was not lost upon his listeners. He had hardly taken his seat when Democratic Senator William Lindsay of Kentucky branded his speech "a poetical apology for an act about to be committed," and the next day Silver Republican Richard Pettigrew of South Dakota pounced on it with heavy sarcasm:

> The Senator from Massachusetts says that this is wrong; that it is a sin; that it is wicked; but the islands are so little that if we will forgive him for taking that country, he will sin no more; he will be virtuous and resist a like crime if it involves a larger acquisition of territory.[39]

When the Senate roll was called the annexation of Hawaii was approved by a vote of 42 to 21. Of the Republicans only the eighty-eight-year-old Justin Morrill had joined the Democrats to vote "nay." Hoar had given his approval to an act of expansion and once more was confronted with charges of "speaking one way and voting another." [40] *The Nation* stated that because Hoar had not wanted "to cut loose from his party," he had again made "a characteristic exhibition of himself . . . getting up a lot of excuses for surrendering his convictions when the pinch comes." [41] Under these attacks, especially those from the mugwumps, Hoar grew increasingly sensitive and for months thereafter wrote testy letters defending his vote and emphasizing that the anti-imperialist cause could only be harmed by continued condemnation of the Hawaiian resolution.[42]

Just a week after the Senate's action Hoar, his conscience still troubled by his vote and his nerves jangled by the barrage of criticism directed against him, lashed out in a fierce attack against a mugwump. The unfortunate victim was Charles Eliot Norton, who was innocent of criticizing Hoar, but who had been vigorously attacking America's decision to go to war with Spain, a decision to which Hoar had become fully reconciled. Here was an irresistible opportunity to vilify a mugwump, assault a Harvard professor, and discharge some tension all at the same time. Thus, in a public address, Hoar declared:

> I see that Professor Norton of Harvard is quoted as telling the youth of the University that it is characteristic of the American people to be trifling. . . . The professor, a little later, gives us his opinion that the war is unjust and dishonest, and advises the youth who look to him for counsel that it is not their duty to enter it. The trouble with Professor Norton, who thinks his countrymen are lacking in a sense of honour, is that there are two things he cannot in the least comprehend—he cannot comprehend his countrymen, and he cannot comprehend honour.

Deeply hurt by this assault, Norton wrote Hoar a letter of protest, only to receive a peevish and ill-mannered reply (which Hoar made public). "All lovers of Harvard," wrote the Senator to his classmate of 1846, "and all lovers of the country, have felt for a long time that your relation to the University made your influence bad for the college and bad for the youth of the country. It was high time that somebody should say what I have said." Still not content, he rubbed salt even deeper into the wound. "I am afraid," he continued, "that the habit of bitter and sneering speech about persons and public affairs has so grown upon you that you do not yourself know, always, what you say." [43]

Although Hoar was congratulated by a number of friends, including Edward Everett Hale,[44] for his attack on Norton, many were shocked and regarded it as a demonstration of petulance, ill temper, and cowardice in the face of a grave public issue. A leading Boston anti-imperialist, attorney David G. Haskins, Jr., wrote Hoar that Norton was "more true to the motto and the principles of the College, than you have been, in your hasty and impulsive attack on him." And *The Nation,* referring once more to the Senator's ability to give "such excellent reasons for voting otherwise than he does," observed that the abuse of Norton, a man of principle, came from one whose "convictions are subordinate to the requirements of voting straight." [45] Yet this incident was misleading. Hoar's emotional explosion only distracted attention from the fact that he was already moving toward a break with the administration, a break that would cause many to remember him as the foremost of all anti-imperialists.

The Fight against the Treaty

Hoar was disabused of his hope that the administration had no interest in imperialist policies when it became clear that the peace negotiations would result in fresh annexations. He passed forthwith into the ranks of the opposition. On November 1, 1898, he told a Worcester audience that only at the time of the Civil War had the United States been confronted by dangers as great as those now posed by imperialism. A republic conceived in the spirit of liberty was in peril of being transformed into "a vulgar, commonplace empire founded upon physical force, controlling subject races and vassal states, in which inevitably one class must forever rule and other classes must forever obey." [46] Asked by McKinley, his friend and fellow Republican, what kind of mood he was in, Hoar answered: "Pretty pugnacious, I confess, Mr. President." Whereupon McKinley reached for his hand and remarked, "I shall always love you, whatever you do." [47]

But this was one of those occasions when a compatriot's affection could not stand in the way of devotion to principle. Hoar believed that the United States had no right to buy the "sovereignty" of any people and that neither the Constitution nor the laws of morality sanctioned the undemocratic control of the Philippines.[48] He accused the expansionists of asking their countrymen to forsake the Declaration of Independence, Washington's Farewell Address, the Monroe Doctrine, and the nation's traditional distrust of a standing army. They proposed to throw America into the thick of the "struggles and squabbles" that forever boiled around the European contest for "dismembered countries and plundered States"—a competition that the American people loathed and for which their constitutional system rendered them unfit. If America were to follow this expansionist path, she, who had won imperishable honors by risking her very existence in order that slavery might be destroyed, would proceed to

> apply on a larger scale the old doctrine and apology of the slaveholder, that it was right to bring human beings into slavery and to hold them and own them in slavery, for their good, by conquering, buying and subjecting a whole

nation,—ten million people,—and owning and governing them for their good—for their good, as we conceive it—not as they conceive it.[49]

Not that Hoar thought that the new possessions could be returned to Spain or simply left in a state of "confusion and anarchy." But he did believe that Cuba, Puerto Rico, and the Philippines could be granted complete independence after a short period of American or international protection. "Turbulence and revolutions" might disturb the new states for many years, but this would be of no more moment to the United States than the unrest and confusion which had been a permanent condition of Latin America for three-quarters of a century.[50]

So armed with arguments and an alternative policy, Hoar prepared to fight against the Paris peace treaty. McKinley was apparently concerned about the impact Hoar's opposition might have on the Senate, for in a transparent move to get him out of the country, he asked him on September 13, 1898, to take John Hay's post as ambassador in Great Britain. It was an alluring offer, but Hoar politely rejected it.[51] He was busy plotting his strategy. First he hoped that enough Republicans would join the Democrats to defeat the treaty as it stood. It could then be rewritten to grant independence to all the former Spanish possessions and be ratified in this amended form. Hoar recognized that McKinley in all probability would refuse to assent to any amendments and reintroduce the original treaty at the opening session of the Fifty-sixth Congress (in which there would be an increased number of expansionist senators), but he was confident that after once carrying the day the anti-treaty forces would have sufficient momentum to defeat the pact a second time.[52]

The anti-imperialists would have to act quickly, however. This was not like the long struggle against slavery, a comparison mugwumps were fond of making, where repeated defeats had been sustained without lasting damage to the cause. This was a contest that would have to be won immediately to be won at all: "if these Spanish possessions and perhaps a part of China and St. Thomas get annexed to the country during the present administration we can never get rid of them." [53] And since careful timing and concerted action seemed of the highest priority, Hoar was annoyed when mugwumps began to rake up past mistakes (including the sore point of Hawaii) instead of concentrating single-mindedly on the issues still awaiting resolution. This preoccupation with the past, he informed Charles Francis Adams, was "a great mistake":

> They are counting up to the American people their mistakes in the past. They say: "You have treated the Indians badly; you have treated the negroes badly. You made a great blunder and mistake in annexing Hawaii. You are generally base and unfit for government. For that reason do not undertake this." It is very much as if a lawyer should address a jury late in the term of the court, and say: "Gentlemen, every verdict so far you have rendered has been stupid and against the evidence. You are utterly unfit for your function of jurymen. But do now show yourselves a little more sensible and give my client a verdict this time." I do not imagine such an appeal would be likely to result favorably to the man who made it.

The way to halt the annexation of the Philippines was to "take that case by itself, say nothing about the past and make a vigorous opposition." [54]

Senate consideration of the peace treaty was scheduled to be conducted behind the closed doors of executive session, but Democratic Senator George G. Vest of Missouri opened the subject to public debate by introducing a resolution in regular session which declared that the federal government had no power to acquire and rule colonies unless they were ultimately to be made states of the Union. Hoar defended the motion in a passionate speech on January 9, 1899. After denouncing the arbitrary imposition of American authority over the Philippines as immoral and unconstitutional and exposing the hypocrisy of the plea that the Filipinos had to be subdued for their own good, he warned that American intervention in Asia would invalidate the Monroe Doctrine, encourage "every European nation, every European alliance" to "acquire dominion in this hemisphere," and forever poison the whole American system, transforming America into "a cheapjack country, raking after the cart for the leavings of European tyranny." Hoar made a point in his speech of reaffirming his loyalty to the Republican Party—"I do not mean, if I can help it, to follow its hearse"—but he also made an unusual thrust at its leader. Disputing the dogma that America could not "haul down the flag" once it had been raised, he quoted McKinley's own statement that forcible annexation would be "criminal aggression" and asked: "Who shall haul down the President?" In conclusion he declared: "I thank God I have done my duty, and that I have adhered to the great doctrines of righteousness and freedom which I learned from my fathers, and in whose service my life has been spent." [55]

The final vote on the treaty was still a month off. Hoar's hope of defeating it plummeted when he learned that William Jennings Bryan had urged his followers to vote for it and that the administration was "moving Heaven and earth, to say nothing of some other places," to get it approved.[56] Late in January in executive session he frantically avowed that "if he could only prevent the ratification of that Treaty, he would willingly lay his head upon the block before the Vice-President's chair." [57] Although he was aware that virtually no other Republican would join him in voting against the pact, Hoar turned down the request of a fellow party member to support McKinley. Invoking the name of his ancestor Roger Sherman, a signer of the Declaration of Independence, he replied that he would "not consent to disgrace my lineage by trampling upon it now." Even if "the people" favored expansion, he would stand firm in the belief that defending "righteousness," "truth," "justice," and "freedom" was more important than heeding the popular mood. But what of party loyalty? Hoar's answer would have amazed a generation of mugwumps: "Am I bound by the Constitution and my oath to vote upon the merits of the question as I see it, or have I a right, violating my oath and violating the Constitution to surrender my opinion to that of a majority of the party, and act against it?" [58]

The day of the crucial vote, February 6, 1899, finally arrived. The first confused reports of insurrection in the Philippines were trickling in as the Senate made ready for the tally. First up for decision was the Vest-Gorman Amendment, providing that the United States should wield control over the Philippines only until such time as the Filipinos could "establish a form of free government suitable to their condition and securing the rights of life, liberty, and property and the preservation of order and equal rights therein." This was the sort of amendment that would have made the treaty acceptable to Hoar, but it was defeated 53 to 30, with only Hoar and Eugene Hale of Maine favoring it among the regular Republicans in the Senate.

Then came the vote on the Paris treaty itself. It was approved by a vote of 57 to 27—just two additional votes in opposition would have killed it. Hoar and Hale were once again the only Republicans to vote against it.

In order to mollify the anti-imperialists, friends of the administration offered the McEnery Resolution, a vague statement filled with benevolent intentions but promising nothing more precise than that the United States "in due time" would dispose of the Philippines in a way that would "best promote the interests of the citizens of the United States and the inhabitants of said islands." Hoar immediately proposed an amendment to the resolution which would require the consent of the Filipinos as a prerequisite to the establishment of a government in the islands. This and a

similar proposal were defeated by solid majorities, whereupon Democrat Augustus O. Bacon of Georgia offered another amendment to the McEnery Resolution, stipulating
that the United States would not exercise "permanent"
control over the Philippines but would set the islands free as
soon as "a stable and independent government shall have
been erected therein . . ." Although moderate enough, Bacon's amendment did provide a vehicle for the views of those
who disapproved of expansion for its own sake but who
nevertheless wanted to end the war and eliminate Spain
from any future influence in the Philippines. On February
14 a vote was taken on the amendment; the Senate locked in
a 29-to-29 tie, with 32 members abstaining and with Hoar,
Hale, and Pennsylvania's Matthew Quay the only Republicans casting affirmative votes. Vice-President Garret Hobart
broke the tie with a "nay" vote to defeat the amendment,
thus clearing the way for a decision on the original McEnery
Resolution which passed by a count of 26 to 22. George
Hoar was the only Republican to vote against this meaningless sop offered to the anti-imperialists.[59]

The full significance of the vote on the Bacon Amendment is difficult to determine, owing to the large number of
abstentions. The final tally did reflect the presence of considerable anti-imperialist strength, and only thirty votes (including the Vice-President's) could be rounded up for a specific rejection of early independence for the Philippines.
Had the Senate been allowed to vote on the single issue of
holding on to the Philippines (instead of having also to decide whether to put an official end to the war with Spain),
the anti-imperialists almost surely would have won. As it
was, the administration forces were astonished at the determination of their opponents even in the face of news of insurrection in the Philippines. Henry Cabot Lodge wrote
Theodore Roosevelt: "It was the closest, hardest fight I have
ever known." In such a close contest Bryan's intervention
had been crucial: among the ten Democrats, four Populists,

one "Silver Republican," one "Silverite," and one "Independent" who supported ratification of the peace treaty, there must have been several who would have joined the opposition and defeated the treaty had Bryan either remained neutral on the question or made its defeat a party issue.[60]*

Having stood with Democrats and Populists in a manner applauded by mugwumps, Hoar quickly set about establishing that he was still one of the Republican faithful. First he rushed to reassure McKinley of his fealty. Henry Adams (who had no love for Hoar) described the scene as it was related to him by Lodge:

> Last Tuesday morning, just the morning after the Senate vote, Hay, walking into the President's room, stood agog to see sitting by the President's side, with arms about his neck as it were, unctuous, affectionate, beaming, the virtuous Hoar! Cabot Lodge, entering at the same time, was struck dumb by the same spectacle. Only a few hours before, in the full belief that his single vote was going to defeat and ruin the administration, Hoar had voted against the Treaty, and there he was, slobbering the President with assurances of his admiration, pressing on him a visit to Massachusetts, and distilling over him the oil of his sanctimony.[61]

On this occasion McKinley might well have been thinking that Hoar was "the man who gives both his arguments and his votes to our enemies but his love to us." Easing back into the security of the Republican fold, Hoar began telling anyone who would listen that in truth Bryan and the Democrats were responsible for saddling America with imperialism and that the cause of anti-imperialism could not be served by repudiating the leadership of the Republican Party. He wrote George S. Boutwell that Bryan was "the most thoroughly guilty man in the United States of the wrong of this whole Philippine business." When Boutwell raised his eyebrows at this version of recent events and reminded him that McKinley had not only drawn up the treaty with Spain but urged

* The House of Representatives never acted on the McEnery Resolution.

its passage, Hoar answered lamely that Bryan was nonetheless the guiltier of the two because he knew "the whole thing to be wrong" while McKinley "believed what he was doing to be for the best interest of his country." [62]

Finally, in his eagerness to refurbish his tarnished Republican credentials, Hoar made a conspicuous display of his refusal to cooperate with non-Republican elements in the anti-imperialist movement. He pleaded, and not without logic, that the mugwumps and other renegade Republicans who ran the various anti-imperialist leagues were accusing McKinley of such heinous crimes that they could never hope to enlist the Republican support essential to any success in restraining the expansionists. When invited to anti-imperialist meetings at which the President was likely to come under attack, he declined to attend. When asked by the Anti-Imperialist League for permission to print one of his speeches in a pamphlet containing remarks by other anti-imperialists, he refused the request. He would serve the cause "by speaking to Republicans," not by associating himself with diatribes against his President and party.[63] He believed that the mugwumps could never win wide public support because they "have been opposed to nearly everything the American people have believed in and have done for the last twenty years . . ." Only a movement of loyal Republicans could "extricate us from this terrible condition of things . . ." [64]

After the Treaty

The pattern of Hoar's involvement with anti-imperialism remained fixed despite the passing of time and the shifting of circumstances. He kept up both his stern denunciations of imperialism and his relentless vendetta with the mugwumps. Even after the passage of the peace treaty Hoar continued to hope for an autonomous Philippines, whether under some kind of protectorate or completely independent.[65] His attacks on imperialism increased in eloquence and fury when the suppression of the Filipino rebellion began. "I can see no difference," he told the Massachusetts Club of Boston on April 29, 1899, "in the lynching of a Southern [Negro] postmaster and lynching a people because they think a government derives its just powers from the consent of the governed, and got those ideas from the Constitution of the United States." Expansionists failed to appreciate, he told the Senate on January 9, 1900, that "the God who made of one blood all the nations of the world had made all the nations of the world capable of being influenced by the same sentiments and the same motives, and that the love of liberty does not depend on the color of the skin, but . . . on humanity." [66]

Unlike most anti-imperialists, who were as disdainful of "inferior races" as the expansionists, Hoar frequently praised the Filipinos as a people of great ability and integrity. He found Emilio Aguinaldo and his cohorts worthy of comparison with America's founding fathers. Although Hoar was not entirely free of the racist assumptions of his age, he had long shown an unusual degree of sympathy for the troubled minorities of America. He wrote in his memoirs:

> The Indian problem is not chiefly how to teach the Indian to be less savage in his treatment of the Saxon, but the Saxon to be less savage in his treatment of the Indian. The Chinese problem is not how to keep Chinese laborers out of California, but how to keep Chinese policies out of Congress. The negro question will be settled when the education of the white man is complete.[67]

Hoar believed that the white man was wrong in adjudging the Filipinos incapable of governing themselves. Noting the skill with which Aguinaldo's rebels had organized their own government, he recited in the Senate their qualifications for nationhood:

> That is a people, that is a power of the earth, that is a nation entitled as such to its separate and equal station

among the powers of the earth by the laws of nature and of nature's God, that has a written constitution, a settled territory, an independence it has achieved, an organized army, a congress, courts, schools, universities, churches, the Christian religion, a village life in orderly, civilized, self-governed municipalities; a pure family life, newspapers, books, statesmen who can debate questions of international law, like Mabini, and organize governments, like Aguinaldo; poets like José Rizal; aye, and patriots who can die for liberty, like José Rizal.[68]

Indeed Hoar praised the Filipinos so warmly and often that he was accused in some quarters of treason—of aiding the Filipinos in their rebellion and their killing of American soldiers. Aguinaldo and his followers did in fact take comfort from the anti-imperialists' campaign, but Hoar refused to apologize on this account. His protest was legitimate, and so was the rebellion in the Philippines. If the administration truly wished to put an end to the loss of American lives, it would have to look to itself for a solution; its insistence upon American sovereignty over the islands had provoked the violence, and only a reversal of that policy could end it.[69]

No one doubted for a moment that Hoar would elect to stick with the Republicans in 1900. His entire record pointed in that direction. He backed Roosevelt's run for the governorship of New York and wrote Lodge that the differences between them were merely those "of emphasis and not . . . of principle or of grave and serious policy."[70] He ostentatiously avowed his continuing high regard for McKinley even while asserting in his peculiarly partisan manner that the annexing of the Philippines was "the only grave mistake the Republican party has made for fifty years."[71] He asked McKinley to campaign on a specific promise of early Philippine independence but gave him full allegiance even when his request was flatly rejected. He won his own re-election with ease and proved himself one of McKinley's "most effective campaigners."[72]

To the end Hoar was torn by the often conflicting demands of anti-imperialism and party loyalty. He remained loyal to the administration during and after the election of 1900 and voted in 1901 for the Platt Amendment, which closely linked the fortunes of "independent" Cuba to the future whims and wishes of the United States. When an occasion arose to award McKinley an honorary degree from Harvard, Hoar battled the mugwumps on the Board of Overseers who sought to deny the President his accolade.[73] Yet after McKinley's assassination it was the grieved Hoar who refused to deliver a eulogy in Worcester because he felt unable to deal with the Philippine question without appearing to criticize the dead President.[74] In the Senate, apart from his vote on the Platt Amendment, he did not swerve from his opposition course. He joined the fight to limit American commercial exploitation of the Philippines and sharply criticized the Supreme Court's "Insular Decisions" justifying the extra-constitutional rule of America's colonies.[75] The passage of time only increased the distress he felt at the injustice being wrought in the Philippines. With Aguinaldo's war for independence effectively crushed in 1902, Hoar sadly concluded:

> We changed the Monroe doctrine from a doctrine of eternal righteousness and justice, resting on the consent of the governed, to a doctrine of brutal selfishness looking only to our own advantage. We crushed the only republic in Asia. We made war on the only Christian people in the East. We converted a war of glory to a war of shame. We vulgarized the American flag. We introduced perfidy into the practice of war. We inflicted torture on unarmed men to extort confession. We put children to death. We established reconcentrado camps. We devastated provinces. We baffled the aspirations of a people for liberty.[76]

In his autobiography, which appeared shortly before his death in 1904, Hoar proudly described his defense of Philippine freedom as one of the major accomplishments of his life. The imperialist doctrine that had crushed this freedom was alien to the principles embodied in the Declaration of Independence and defended by "our statesmen of all parties down to a time long after the death of Lincoln." Although his two volumes of reminiscences bristled with the familiar sorties against the mugwumps, they were also tinged with an air of sadness and regret, as if Hoar had been unable in the end to escape the knowledge that it was the party of Abraham Lincoln, his beloved Republican Party, which bore the heaviest responsibility for destroying his dream of freedom for the Philippines:

> When I think of my party, whose glory and whose service to Liberty are the pride of my life, crushing out this people in their effort to establish a Republic, and hear people talking about *giving* them good Government, and that they are better off than they ever were under Spain, I feel very much as if I had learned that my father, or some other honored ancestor, had been a slave-trader in his time, and had boasted that he had introduced a new and easier kind of handcuffs or fetters to be worn by the slaves during the horrors of the middle passage.[77]

When Hoar died in 1904 Thomas Wentworth Higginson, an uncompromising mugwump, was asked by the American Academy of Arts and Sciences to write an "appreciation" of him. The result was a harsh appraisal of Hoar's political career. Higginson observed that Hoar, who had entered political life in the company of courageous anti-slavery men, had somewhere lost his devotion to truth and his willingness to make sacrifices in the name of principle. Citing an occasion when Hoar had argued in one fashion and voted in another, causing a Republican newspaper to comment, "The worthy Massachusetts statesman once more went to dinner when the dinner bell rang," Higginson remarked that this was but a half-truth. It was not that Hoar "cared so much for the actual dinner, but it came hard to him to see his old table mates sitting down without him." Overweening party feeling had prevented him from being the man of principle he could have been. It would "one day be recognized that in an age of great self-devotion and great sacrifices, Senator Hoar made many small sacrifices, but no large ones." Higginson's appraisal was severe but perceptive—and fair enough to recognize and laud the other half of Hoar's record. He wrote generously of the Senator's anti-imperialist efforts: "upon the great national question which dwarfed all others in his very latest years,—that of imperialism as shown in the Philippines,—he held his course with superb courage and was true to the last." [78]

Throughout his political career Hoar's integrity and flexibility were undermined by his inordinate dislike of mugwumps and their principles. Some of his objections were well taken, but his deep antipathy for the mugwumps and his exaggerated sense of party loyalty all too frequently pushed him into boorish and hypocritical behavior. If he had been able to channel some of the energy he used in insulting Charles Eliot Norton and sparring with mugwump anti-imperialists into the construction of a mugwump-Republican coalition, he might have been more effective in advancing the cause of anti-imperialism and championing the Filipinos in their bid for early independence. But he could also have been much less effective than he was. Such a partisan could easily have wrapped himself in the mantle of party loyalty and declared that the administration's policy would eventually work out for the best for all concerned. Instead Hoar defied party leadership and the accusing stares of his colleagues to become one of the country's most determined anti-imperialists—one of the two lone Republicans to oppose their President and vote against the Treaty of Paris. For a man who disliked watching his old table mates sitting down without him this was no easy choice.[79]

CHAPTER EIGHT

Andrew Carnegie: The Primacy of the Philippines

It was fitting that America should produce an anti-imperialist who offered to buy the independence of the Philippines with a personal check for twenty million dollars.[1] Flamboyant gestures of this sort were one of Andrew Carnegie's trademarks, as was his tendency to make sweeping public pronouncements and commitments which failed to square with his private beliefs and practices. Here was a man who bore watching, for, whether deliberately or not, he could frequently and easily mislead the casual observer. He was a magazine-article friend of labor who could recite all the reasons why it was wrong for a worker to be a scab but who knew better than any man how to break a union. He wanted the world to think that he cared little for the protective tariff and eagerly anticipated the coming of free trade, but actually he paid close attention to the details of tariff legislation and helped write the McKinley Tariff of 1890. He is remembered as a vigorous anti-imperialist who threatened his own political party with ruin for its imperialist transgressions. His position on the issue was not really so straightforward but was shot through with inconsistencies in logic and shifts in thought. Nonetheless, Carnegie's uneven protest is significant because its very spottiness reflects not only some quirks of his own character but, more importantly, a major truth about the entire anti-imperialist movement.

A generation of Americans saw in the life of this ebullient Scottish immigrant the embodiment of the national dream of economic opportunity for all. Having arrived in the United States in 1848 as a poor lad of twelve, Carnegie climbed speedily upward: "bobbin boy, telegraph messenger, telegraph operator, assistant railroad superintendent, railroad division superintendent . . . bridge builder, iron maker, steel maker, organizer of industry" [2]—one of the greatest entrepreneurs in American history. Self-made and skilled at self-promotion, he was quick to tell the world that American liberty had made his breathtaking ascent possible. From the time of his youth he was driven by a powerful yearning for culture and the kind of respectability that wealth alone could not provide. He read widely and sought out the company of "literary men," and from one of these, Herbert Spencer, he learned the Social Darwinist ideas that helped to explain his own success. An able writer himself, he popularized Spencer's conception of progress-through-struggle in numerous books and essays and propagated his own beliefs in a free economy and republican government. In 1889 he wrote his famous essay on the gospel of wealth, which defined the stewardship of the rich and offered further and novel justification for his own dazzling financial success. By making such a striking appeal to the rich men of society to use their surplus for "social" purposes he helped to transform the American tradition of charity into that of modern philanthropy.[3]

In gratitude to the country that had welcomed and enriched him Carnegie became an unbridled nationalist. His *Triumphant Democracy*, a paean to the United States published in 1885, opens with the dedication: "To the BELOVED REPUBLIC Under Whose Laws I Am Made the Peer of Any Man, Although Denied Political Equality by My Native Land, I Dedicate This Book With an Intensity of Gratitude And Admiration Which the Native-Born Citizen Can Neither Feel nor Understand." [4] Carnegie liked to think of himself as a spokesman for a radically egalitarian nation and frequently contrasted the virtues of republicanism with the system of "privilege" embodied in the British aristocracy. As a child he had yearned "to get to be a man and kill a king," but as a man he was content to attack monarchy with his pen, asserting that Britain's vaunted parliamentary institutions were nothing but a "sham" to cover the evils of inequality.[5] American institutions, on the other hand, were the hallmarks of a society with "no ranks, no titles, no hereditary dignities, and therefore no classes." [6] In artless cadences he explained that since Britain was the home of a "privileged" aristocracy, justice could not dwell there. Conversely, since no aristocracy existed in America, a just and classless society could take root and flourish. Today the superficiality of the thoughts seems obvious, the style a bit quaint. Even at the time they were made these forays against the British aristocracy appeared hypocritical to those who knew how thoroughly Carnegie enjoyed and was flattered by his frequent contacts with English aristocrats. There is no hard evidence, however, that he was disingenuous when he asserted that republican America had no inequalities or classes or when he wrote that there was "not a privilege possessed by any citizen" that was not available to the Negro. In thinking of classes in purely formal and legal terms, he was naïve, not dishonest.[7]

It was with the same simplicity that Carnegie attributed America's traditional avoidance of the evils of war and imperialism not to fortunate geographic location, nor even to skillful diplomacy, but rather to the nation's republicanism.[8] He was never a complete pacifist, but from his early

youth, when he absorbed the teachings of a favorite uncle
who was an outspoken pacifist, Carnegie was generally opposed to wars of all kinds, with the notable exception of the
American Civil War.[9] After a trip around the world in
1879–1880 he spoke of the terrible social and financial burdens that militarism had imposed upon European life and
pointed in contrast to the happy estate of China where "the
triumphs of peace are held in chief esteem." The journey re-
inforced his conviction that the United States was extremely
fortunate in having "the poorest navy and smallest army" in
the world, since this distinction placed her in an excellent
position to lead the world to peace:

> Favored land, may you prove worthy of all your blessings
> and show to the world that after ages of wars and conquests
> there comes at last to the troubled earth the glorious reign
> of peace. But no new steel cruisers, no standing army. These
> are the devil's tools in monarchies; the Republic's weapons
> are the ploughshare and the pruning hook.[10]

Like his republicanism, Carnegie's commitment to peace
had a certain spurious quality (as illustrated, for instance,
by his company's lucrative sales of naval armor to the
world's "poorest navy"), but he did maintain a lifelong
interest in American and British peace organizations, international arbitration, and "world law," his enthusiasm cul-
minating in 1910 in his gift of ten million dollars to the Endowment for International Peace.[11]

Carnegie wrote in 1880 that, while he found nothing ob-
jectionable in the colonization of uninhabited or sparsely
populated territories, he thought it utter folly to conquer
and attempt to govern "an alien race" as the British had
done in India. The impressiveness of their achievement in
the subcontinent was undeniable; no other nation in the
world could rival Britain's skill in introducing "civilized"
institutions into backward lands. But even though the natives of India had profited from some of the technical progress and order imposed upon them, they had suffered im-

measurably from their inferior status as colonial subjects, which had transformed them into a mob of obsequious and dependent weaklings, bowing and scraping at the sight of their white masters. Britain had destroyed India's "native institutions" and had forced "her views upon an unwilling people wholly unprepared to receive them"; in return she had received nothing of value since, in Carnegie's opinion, trade with colonies was in no way preferable to trade with a free people.[12] By 1885 he had pulled his impressions together to form an anti-imperialist credo for the United States:

> The American people are satisfied that the worst native government in the world is better for its people than the best government which any foreign power can supply; that governmental interference upon the part of a so-called civilized power, in the affairs of the most barbarous tribe upon earth, is injurious to that tribe, and never under any circumstances whatever can it prove beneficial, either for the undeveloped race or for the intruder. They are further satisfied that, in the end, more speed is made in developing and improving backward races by proving to them through example the advantages of Democratic institutions than is possible through violent interference. The man in America who should preach that the nation should interfere with distant races for their civilization, and for their good, would be voted either a fool or a hypocrite.[13]

Carnegie presumably held to this same view when he served as a United States delegate to the Pan-American Conference of 1889–1890. In the course of the meetings, which lasted for several months, he learned much about the interests and hopes of Latin America's representatives and was especially impressed by their "sensitive spirit of independence." As a spokesman for their powerful northern neighbor, he attempted to allay their fears of United States expansionism, trying to persuade them that the conference would be (as he put it to James G. Blaine in accepting his appointment) a "first step looking to a coming brotherhood among the nations of the Western world." [14] The idea of such a family union did not reassure the Latins, and Carnegie was to recall their touchiness when, in the winter of 1891–1892, a crisis in United States–Chilean relations suddenly threatened to erupt in war between the two nations. Appalled at the belligerence of the American government, he dispatched a telegram to President Harrison, imploring him to be patient as befitted the president of a great nation in his transactions with a small, weak, and "sorely tried" country. He afterwards rushed to Washington to urge in person that Harrison keep his temper in such a "paltry dispute." [15]

Harrison considered this solicitude for Chile unpatriotic. Actually Carnegie was the last to think that the United States should play a passive role in the affairs of Latin America. If the hemisphere was a brotherhood, he had no doubts about the identity of the biggest brother. His opposition to imperialism was based at all times on the explicit assumption that the United States would dominate the Western Hemisphere, although the precise nature of this domination was rarely spelled out. When Carnegie was only eighteen years old he had written one of his cousins in Scotland that "we will let Europe manage its own affairs while we take care of the American continent." [16] In the 1880s he supported the Arthur administration's attempts to abrogate the Clayton-Bulwer Treaty—which committed the United States to cooperate with the British in the building of any isthmian canal—on the grounds that the United States should "control anything and everything on this Continent. . . . No *joint* arrangements, no entangling alliances with monarchical, warlike Europe. America will take this Continent in hand alone." [17] Carnegie was not speaking in annexationist terms when he declared that the Western Hemisphere would be taken "in hand," although at one point he did favor incorporating Canada into the United States.[18] He believed, as he wrote in *Triumphant Democracy* in 1885, that the United States should stand as a protector of its neighbors, assuring all of them, from Canada to Chile, that they had nothing to fear from their powerful guardian. He was proud that "the pigmies" of the region could rely on America for help in any "day of trouble." [19]

Carnegie's reaction to the Venezuela controversy in 1895 and 1896 was a perfect demonstration of his conception of the role the United States should play in hemispheric affairs. He agreed with the Cleveland administration that Britain's refusal to arbitrate the dispute with Venezuela was at the root of the crisis. Now London and all the capitals of Europe would learn the long-overdue lesson that Washington must be consulted before any important political or territorial changes could be made in the Western Hemisphere. This was America's own "sphere of operations" where she could "boss things" as she chose. But bossing things did not entail the acquisition of "non-coterminous" territories, and when Secretary of State Richard Olney claimed that the will of the United States was "sovereign upon the American continent," Carnegie, protesting that "every schoolboy" knew better, warned that such a presumptuous declaration would have a "most injurious" effect on "the sister Republics of the South . . ." In its conduct toward the other American republics, the United States should act the part of an "elder brother," protective but not domineering.[20]

Carnegie's own expansionist schemes often revolved around future Anglo-American relations. One of his pet ideas was the union of all Anglo-Saxon peoples under one flag, a notion which he termed "race imperialism" and which came to him as early as 1853 when he spoke of "the Banner of St. George and the Stars and Stripes" working "side by side" for "Liberty" against "Despotism." [21] This vision of Anglo-American unity was especially fixed in his mind in the 1880s and early 1890s. After first urging the two countries to negotiate an arbitration treaty that would make war between them impossible, he went on to suggest a formal amalgamation of all English-speaking peoples into one political organization with its capital in America, the natural center of power of the Anglo-Saxon world. Carnegie wrote William E. Gladstone that Britain's only hope for continued independence lay in total emulation of America: she would have to discard her aristocracy and established church, ship her royal family back to Germany, and transform herself into a republic, complete with president, congress, and supreme court. Otherwise the British Isles, outdistanced by America's rising industrial power, were destined to become mere states of the Union, represented in Congress but generally without power, being to the United States what Greece was to Rome—"the headquarters of its culture, its institutions, the place from which great ideas would flow," and "the garden and pleasure ground of the race." [22]

These fancies evoked more amusement than serious attention, but they helped earn for Carnegie the nickname "The Star-Spangled Scotchman," which he probably enjoyed as much as the amazing flag he designed to fly over Skibo, his summer castle in Scotland: "a united flag, the 'Stars and Stripes' on one side, 'Union Jack' on the other, sewed together." [23] In the nineties his sweeping vision of "race imperialism" began to fade, the radical idea of union first giving way to a wish for alliance and then, with the breaking of the Venezuela crisis, paling to a sentimental belief in a brotherly attachment based upon common race. By early 1898 "race imperialism" meant only that the United States would aid Britain if she were ever ganged up on by "a combination of other races." [24]

Carnegie's design for a brotherhood of independent republics in the Western Hemisphere did not include any plans for freeing those still under European colonial rule. Thus, while he was sympathetic to the rebels in Cuba, he did not want the United States to go to war in their behalf. Late in 1897 and in the early months of 1898 he grew increasingly concerned about the deterioration of relations with Spain, fearing that war would damage business prospects and play into the hands of those who wanted to annex Hawaii, a project he opposed.[25] On the eve of hostilities he wired McKinley from Europe, imploring him to submit the Cuban problem to the mediation of the British. When war was actually declared, Carnegie could not at first believe that the situation had reached such a desperate point. Spain would surely back down before any blows were struck. Otherwise the United States would be forced to invade Cuba and might be drawn on by the almost irresistible lure of empire. If she succumbed to this temptation the consequences would be "more serious than the war." Carnegie hoped that the United States would simply expel Spain from Cuba and then, by a "chivalrous act," withdraw herself without delay.[26]

But when Spain did decide to fight, his patriotic impulses surged to the fore. Putting the blame for the war squarely on Spain and proclaiming it America's duty to liberate Cuba from oppression, he even offered strategic counsel, wiring General Nelson A. Miles after the capture of Santiago de Cuba to suggest that American forces seize Puerto Rico before completing the conquest of Cuba, a daring stroke which he believed would deeply impress Spain and the rest of Europe.[27]

As soon as an armistice was reached in August, however, Carnegie proceeded to deluge newspapers, magazines, and public officials with letters of protest and warnings against imperialism. So heavy was this torrent of communications that he rapidly emerged as one of the most prominent anti-imperialists in the country. On November 1, after several weeks of this activity, E. L. Godkin wrote from the *Evening Post*, "You are doing the best work of your life. God prosper you! . . . Keep it up; we will copy you everytime." A few weeks later Carl Schurz, in the belief that Carnegie's actions had made him "the leader of the Anti-Imperialist Movement," suggested that he "take active charge at once." [28] In the same month the steelmaker began making heavy contributions to the Anti-Imperialist League, which had just been founded in Boston, and in return was elected a first vice-president.[29] In his conclusion to a tavern monologue on American policy in the Philippines, "Mr. Dooley" alluded to Carnegie's stand: "So I suppose, Hinnissy, we'll have to stay an' do th' best we can, an' lave Andrew Carnegie secede fr'm th' Union." [30]

In public and in private Carnegie attacked imperialism from both practical and idealistic vantage points. Imperialism was expensive, and American farmers and workers would have to bear the brunt of the cost. It diverted attention from industrial development to the kind of foreign adventures that would deprive the United States of both the energy and military security essential to all economic progress. The glorification of physical force which was always part and parcel of imperialism would damage America's moral fiber, and the use of violence and guile abroad would encourage social instability and unrest at home. An imperialist career would cause the United States to forfeit a great fund of international respect built up through years of dedication to peace and the industrial arts. It would silence the tongue of American justice and make it difficult to protest with a clear conscience against British imperialism in South Africa. Worst of all, imperialism would entail a total abandonment of American democratic principles; it would mark a "parting of the ways." Specifically, America's new course would lead inexorably to an unjust war against the natives of the Philippines, a turn of events Carnegie forecast as early as August, 1898, and to which he alluded again in October when he expressed his concern that American men who had enlisted "to fight the oppressor" would end up "shooting down the oppressed." [31] Over a year later he was invited to a reception honoring the American commission that had negotiated the Treaty of Paris. Whitelaw Reid, the member of the commission who had sent Carnegie the invitation, received a sarcastic reply:

> Unfortunately I shall be in Pittsburgh the evening of your reception to the signers of the *War* Treaty with Spain, not the Peace. It is a matter of congratulation however that you seem to have about finished your work of civilizing the Fillipinos [*sic*]. It is thought that about 8000 of them have been completely civilized and sent to Heaven. I hope you like it.[32]

The war with Spain was the final blow to Carnegie's once grandiose conception of "race imperialism." While John Hay and certain anti-imperialists like Edward Atkinson hoped that the events of 1898 and 1899 would signal the beginnings of an Anglo-American *entente*, Carnegie discounted any but sentimental ties between the two nations. He still believed that "blood is thicker than water," [33] but he now opposed the idea of a formal alliance which, in his opinion, would oblige America to defend British imperial interests in the Far East. Carnegie was suspicious of British advice that the United States retain the Philippines. The novel spectacle of such open solicitude and friendship was clear evidence that Great Britain's leaders were scheming to use American power to rake their own chestnuts out of the fire in Asia. While the Americans should be willing to rescue England from any overwhelming coalition formed to destroy her, they were too devoted to their republican traditions to help her in her wars for foreign trade, her imperialist quarrels with Russia, or her wicked policies in South Africa. The flag at Skibo still flew, but its purpose was now merely decorative.[34]

One reason for Carnegie's opposition to increased Anglo-American cooperation in the Far East was his persistent belief that the United States should "attend to [its] own continent" while other countries attended to theirs.[35] In fact, with the passing of time, he narrowed his opposition to expansion to such a point that it applied only to the Far East. Once Spain was effectively eliminated from the Caribbean and her colonial holdings were safely in American hands, Carnegie began making excuses for those instances of expansion that no longer seemed dangerous to him. In short order he reconciled himself to the annexation of Cuba, which he was certain Cuban sugar interests would request,[36] Puerto Rico, which possessed an excellent naval base that the United States could "never" relinquish,[37] and Hawaii, the only spot in the Pacific from which a potential enemy could successfully mount an attack on the western coast of the United States.[38] He was even prepared to accept the British West Indies as American possessions if Britain would exchange them for the Philippines.[39]

How could an anti-imperialist endorse such wholesale expansion? The explanation lies in the fact that throughout the entire anti-imperialist movement, though not in the mind of every individual anti-imperialist, there was the conviction that by far the most dangerous part of America's suddenly launched expansionist program was the plan to annex the distant Philippines, a project that foreshadowed an enormous increase in the foreign responsibilities of the United States and could not be accomplished without the direct use of force on the native population. Despite his having previously condemned imperialism wherever it appeared, Carnegie now justified the distinction he drew between the Philippines and other territories by simply denying that the issue of "imperialism" was involved in the latter cases. He stressed the indisputable but rather irrelevant fact that Cuba, Puerto Rico, and Hawaii were all quite small and (with the exception of Hawaii) all located close to the United States. He also claimed that the peoples of these islands possessed no "national aspirations," a conclusion he apparently reached because none of them had resisted American occupation. In Puerto Rico and Cuba American forces were greeted as liberators, while in Hawaii, according to his inaccurate account, annexation had been accomplished "by a vote of its people, which robs its acquisition of many dangers." These territories, because of their size and relative proximity to the mainland, would eventually become "American in every sense." The friendly disposition of their inhabitants ensured that they would become true Americans instead of "foreign races bound in time to be false to the Republic in order to be true to themselves." Finally, in an effort to differentiate these territories from the Philippines, Carnegie came close to saying that the acquisition of a new territory was not imperialistic unless it was accompanied by war and violence. Thus he remarked that "Cuba need not trouble us very much. There is no 'Imperialism' here—no danger of foreign wars." [40]

But on the issue of the Philippines he remained adamant, warning McKinley that his policy there would plunge the country "into the vortex of the Far East." [41] More than 6,000 miles separated the Philippines from San Francisco, so by no stretch of the imagination could these far-off isles be considered part of the Western Hemisphere where Carnegie believed the United States should hold sway. The Philippines were neither diminutive nor docile but were instead an archipelago of more than 7,000 islands, almost equal in size to Great Britain and with a teeming population of about 7 million, many of whom had been fighting for their independence long before the Americans had arrived on the scene and were prepared to continue the struggle against any new ruler. [42]

It seemed to Carnegie that there were also irrefutable economic arguments against taking the Philippines. These arguments applied equally to Cuba, Puerto Rico, and Hawaii in almost all particulars. This never disquieted Carnegie, but it does illustrate the double standard he had adopted for determining which territories were acceptable acquisitions for the United States and which were not. Carnegie contended that American acquisition of the Philip-

pines would engender international tension in the Far East
and thereby threaten the "peace and security" necessary for
a flourishing foreign trade. "The waters must be calm, disturbing influences absent." [43] But even assuming international calm, imperialism would bring no economic gains
because trade did not follow the flag of empire. The United
States itself stood as proof that a nation, without imperial
dominions, could export goods at a rate never before
equaled in her commercial history. If America took control
of the Philippines, she would discover to her sorrow that
some more advantageously located nation would dominate
the colony's trade, just as Britain had discovered that "loyal
Canada" traded more with the United States than with the
mother country and bought "her Union Jacks" in New York
rather than in London.[44]

Furthermore, the United States would encounter serious
economic and political problems in any pattern of trade relations established with new possessions. Free trade would
create one set of difficulties, restricted commerce another.
American agricultural interests would be damaged by admit-
ting the colonies' sugar, tobacco, flax, and hemp into the
United States duty-free. Raising a tariff against these commodities, on the other hand, would ruin the economies that
produced them and violate the Constitution.[45]

An even worse dilemma would appear when the time
came to define the colonies' economic relations with other
nations. If, for example, the United States should decide to
place a tariff on European goods shipped to the Philippines
in order to keep the islands' market for itself, Britain,
France, Germany, and Russia might well combine to force a
reversal of policy or simply push the United States out of the
archipelago, just as all but Britain had compelled Japan to
give up Korea after the Sino-Japanese War a few years before.[46] On the other hand, should McKinley resolve to open
the door of the Philippines to the trade of all nations on

equal terms,* American producers would lose out in the competition with foreign producers because shipping costs from the United States would be double those paid by the manufacturers and farmers of such nations as Germany, France, Britain, Australia, and Russia. The "Open Door" policy would mean a closed door to American goods.[47] In December, 1898, Carnegie's predictions seemed to be confirmed when reports arrived that Admiral Dewey's fleet was being provisioned by Australian merchants, who had just shipped from Sydney "6,000 carcases of mutton, 250 of lambs, 125 [tons?] of potatoes, 81 tons of onions, and 22 tons of carrots."[48] The editor of a farm journal also noticed the report and wrote a verse on the subject which came to Carnegie's attention:

> What's this I hear? Australia has the job of
>   selling sheep
> To feed our Yankee boys in blue? That makes my
>   dander creep!
> See here, young man, is this thing true? Is this
>   here sale a fact?
> If 'tis, I'll put my glasses on an' read the
>   riot act.
> What do I hire you for, young man? How do you earn
>   your pay?
> To set and let Australia feed them sailors while
>   you play?
> No, sir, not by a darn sight, you help this
>   country's trade.
> An' Yankee farmers pay the tax with which you
>   fools are paid.

---

* McKinley initially moved in this direction, but by 1913 "colony and mother country were on terms of reciprocal free trade, and tariff barriers thereafter minimized the role of other powers in commerce with the Philippines." Theodore Friend, *Between Two Empires: The Ordeal of the Philippines, 1929–1946*, Yale University Press, New Haven, 1965, p. 6.

> [torn] your big "expansion" an' your darned
>   old "open door,"
> If that's a sample of it, don't you give us
>   any more. . . .
>
> The farmer comes in first, young man, his boot
>   is big and stout
> An' if you give him second place, he'll kick you
>   fellers out.[49]

In Carnegie's mind the Philippines presented the United States with a set of difficult and unique problems. It was specifically because of his concern about these islands that he tried to arouse farm and labor sentiment against the Treaty of Paris and urged William Jennings Bryan to use his influence to this same end.[50] The Philippines question also prompted him to pour money into the coffers of the various anti-imperialist leagues and finance many anti-imperialist publications. He wrote Carl Schurz on December 27, 1898:

> Print your speech in pamphlet form and distribute it and I will be your banker. That is the way in which I can aid the good work. You have brains and I have dollars. I can devote some of my dollars to spreading your brains.[51]

As late as 1901 Mark Twain, who had just published a biting anti-imperialist essay in the *North American Review,* wrote Carnegie:

> You seem to be in prosperity. Could you lend an admirer $1.50 to buy a hymn-book with? God will bless you. I feel it; I know it. . . . P.S.—Don't send the hymn-book; send the money; I want to make the selection myself.

and Carnegie replied:

> Nothing less than a two-dollar & a half hymn-book *gilt* will do for you. Your place in the choir (celestial) demands that & you shall have it.
>   There's a new Gospel of Saint Mark in the *North Amer-*

ican which I like better than anything I've read for many a day.

I am willing to borrow a thousand dollars to distribute that sacred message in proper form, & if the author don't object may I send that sum, when I can raise it, to the Anti-Imperialist League, Boston, to which I am a contributor, the only missionary work I am responsible for.

Just tell me you are willing & many thousands of the holy little missals will go forth.[52]

In the politics of anti-imperialism Carnegie played a double game. While attempting to scare off McKinley from expansion by predicting a calamitous Republican defeat at the polls in 1900, he hinted that he might throw his support to Bryan if the latter would campaign entirely on imperialism and let the free silver issue go. Observers speculated that his open courtship of the Democratic leader might lead to a fusion of "silver and iron." Bryan resisted Carnegie's overtures, however, on the grounds that they would hamstring him on domestic affairs, and when he came out in support of the peace treaty and persisted in his talk of free silver, Carnegie made no secret of his displeasure.[53]

Bryan's reluctance to accept Carnegie's embrace was well founded, for the latter had been a staunch Republican since the days of Lincoln. Blaine had been his close personal friend, and when McKinley was in financial difficulties in 1893 Carnegie was among those who bailed him out. He strongly supported McKinley's election in 1896—at that time he had called Bryan a "light-headed-blathering demagogue." [54] What Carnegie clearly hoped to accomplish in 1899 and 1900 was to intimidate the administration by demonstrating with his own threat of defection that an imperialist policy in the Philippines would put an undue strain on the bonds of party allegiance—"it has proved too great for me," he wrote ominously on November 24, 1898.[55] He closed one of his letters to McKinley with the words: "Your friend personally; but the bitterest enemy you have officially, as far as I know." [56] John Hay, who received many communications in this vein from Carnegie, wrote to Whitelaw Reid:

> Andrew Carnegie really seems to be off his head. He writes me frantic letters signing them "Your Bitterest Opponent." He threatens the President, not only with the vengeance of the voters, but with practical punishment at the hands of the mob. He says henceforth the entire labor vote of America will be cast against us, and that he will see that it is done. He says the Administration will fall in irretrievable ruin the moment it shoots down one insurgent Filipino.

Recalling the harsh suppression of Carnegie steelworkers who went out on strike in 1892, he added: "He does not seem to reflect that the Government is in a somewhat robust condition even after shooting down several citizens in his interest at Homestead." [57]

But Hay and McKinley undoubtedly realized that the excitable Scotsman was only blustering. His Republican loyalties were too strong to permit open disaffection. Richard F. Pettigrew of South Dakota claimed in his sometimes fanciful memoirs that during the Plaza Hotel conference of January 6, 1900, at which a number of anti-imperialists considered organizing a third party for the Presidential election, Carnegie pledged extensive financial backing for the undertaking, only to withdraw his offer and doom the effort some six weeks later at the behest of "the organizers of the steel trust." [58] The claim is unsubstantiated, however, and it seems probable that Pettigrew exaggerated Carnegie's role at the New York meeting. Even at the time of Carnegie's greatest disenchantment with the administration a few months earlier, his complaints had always been registered as those of one "staunch Republican" to another. He cautioned an English friend not to "go out of a party. Stick to it & do your best to keep it straight—Most good comes from this[.] I am a better Republican than the President[.]" [59] By the summer of 1900, in any case, he had formulated a theory that justified voting for McKinley. He explained that the President had always been correct in his original plans and purposes but had been led astray by congressional pressure and outbursts of popular enthusiasm for expansion. If his Republican associates would now give him firm support, McKinley would gain the confidence he needed to follow his own judgment in formulating a just and prudent foreign policy.[60]

Carnegie drew public attention to his plan to vote for McKinley in the October, 1900, issue of the *North American Review*. He denounced the Democratic platform as thoroughly un-American in its assault on property and its "insidious attacks" upon the courts of the land. On balance Carnegie concluded (if he had ever really entertained genuine doubts) that it would be better to go along for a while with the "wrongful effort to force our government upon the Filipinos, in total disregard of Republican ideas, than fail to repel this covert attack upon the reign of law at home." Sound money, a strong Supreme Court, and freedom from "the miserable espionage" of an income tax were more important than peace and independence in the Philippines.[61] Like the mugwump Charles Francis Adams, Carnegie concluded that the greatest threat to America lay within her own borders, and thus it was as a loyal Republican that he went to the polls in 1900.

The war against the Filipino rebels, far more than the Spanish-American War itself, seemed to Carnegie a clear-cut case of imperialism. The United States had forced its authority upon a weak and unwilling people in a conflict marked by the savagery and cruelty characteristic of guerrilla warfare. As a sometime pacifist and consistent nationalist who had long boasted of America's unmatched devotion to the principles of self-government, Carnegie was shocked and embarrassed by his country's conduct in the Philippines. Thus he joined the anti-imperialist movement, and his wealth, fame, and Republican connections were significant contributions to the respectability and solvency of the cause. Yet a certain aura of insincerity clouded his efforts. Compared to the deadly serious Carl Schurz, the outraged and passionate William James, or even the partisan George Hoar, Carnegie was always something of a tinsel anti-imperialist, his gestures against expansionism more show than substance, as ostentatious in their own way as the "united flag" which flapped in the summer breeze over Skibo. The inconsistencies and convenient oversights of Carnegie—this pacifist who had no compunctions about selling armor to the navy, this anti-imperialist who detected nationalist aspirations in the people of the Philippines but not in the people of Cuba, this Republican stalwart who dangled vague promises of political support in front of Bryan in exchange for an emasculation of the latter's reform program —made it difficult to give much credence to his furious pronouncements against empire.

This is not to diminish the significance of Carnegie's stand, however, since the basic distinction he made between those areas into which the United States could expand without committing the sin of "imperialism" and the Philippines was by no means an uncommon one. George Hoar, who in Senate hyperbole offered to undergo decapitation to save the nation from imperialism, nonetheless favored the annexation of Hawaii and accepted American suzerainty over Cuba, maintaining a strictly anti-imperialist position only in the case of the Philippines. E. L. Godkin conceded at one point that the United States might not be able to divest itself of Cuba but was never willing to accept such a compromise with respect to the Philippines.[62] Charles Francis Adams deplored America's conversion to imperialism but considered it inevitable that Cuba would one day be American.[63] Edward Atkinson, even when temporarily reconciled to a general policy of overseas expansion, hoped that either Japan or Great Britain could be induced to take over the Philippines.[64] Thus it was typical of the anti-imperialists to oppose any kind of new territorial acquisition in principle but to worry in practice far more about the Philippines than about any other territory.

The reasons are obvious enough. Many Americans, and not all of them anti-imperialists, boggled at the thought of annexing these faraway islands at the cost of a murderous guerrilla war, while at the same time they accepted the idea of governing apparently passive peoples in lands closer to home. New to the pursuit of empire and by good fortune inexperienced in the subtle ways of tyranny, they failed to see anything amiss in hoisting the flag of the United States above Hawaii and the acquiescent islands of the Caribbean.

If Commodore Dewey had never steamed into Manila and raised hopes of American imperium in Asia, it is extremely doubtful that the anti-imperialist movement would have gained much ground. There would still have been those who protested against the Spanish-American War and the incorporation of Hawaii and Puerto Rico into the American political and economic system. But the protest would have been less strident and there would have been fewer listeners. The Philippines made the difference. They made the debate on imperialism at the end of the nineteenth century one of the major contests in the annals of American politics.

CHAPTER NINE

Old Chiefs and Stalwarts: The Impotent Protest

George Hoar was a prominent United States senator, and Andrew Carnegie was one of the most famous men in the nation. But neither was a power in the inner councils of the Republican Party. Bellwethers of the party like Mark Hanna and Nelson Aldrich had misgivings about territorial expansion but never contemplated a revolt against the McKinley administration. Nor did any of the party's bright young comers join the anti-imperialist opposition, a movement too nostalgic and too enamored of peace and quiet to capture the young and ambitious Theodore Roosevelts and Albert Beveridges of the party. Unlike the old and established or the already retired, these men found foreign adventure attractive. Standing solid with their party was also far more important to them than to men whose careers were already drawing to a close.

Except for Hoar, the few professional Republicans who openly disagreed with the expansionist policies of the administration contributed little to the anti-imperialist movement. The context in which their protests were made robbed them of whatever force they might have had under more favorable circumstances. Former President Benjamin Harrison launched a sharp attack against McKinley's policies but not until after the election of 1900 when it was too late to do the anti-imperialists any good. George Boutwell completely repudiated his Republican ties and furiously criticized the administration, but he had been out of political life for a generation and had left such an unglittering public record that few Americans were interested in what he had to say about imperialism. John Sherman, who was McKinley's Secretary of State until April, 1898, enjoyed both power and reputation, but he was in his dotage and, whether in or out of office, was unable to give much help to the anti-imperialists. Thomas B. Reed was also a man of power, but in 1899 he retired from politics and registered a sarcastic but almost totally private protest against imperialism. Such men clearly could not incite a large-scale rebellion within their party, and they were either unwilling or unable to arouse the nation at large. Forgotten, retired, bitter, senile—they posed little threat to America's emergence as an imperialist power.

The Delayed Reaction

In 1891 Benjamin Harrison wrote his Secretary of State, James G. Blaine: "You know I am not too much of an annexationist; though I do feel that in some directions, as to naval stations and points of influence, we must look forward to a departure from the too conservative opinions which have been held heretofore." [1] Few people were aware of the old Civil War general's reservations about annexing new territories. During his years in the White House (1889–1893), Harrison never actually acquired any colonies for the United States, but his government accepted partial control over Samoa, played host to a major inter-American conference, and, in the wake of the *Baltimore* incident of 1891, threatened violent reprisals against little Chile. More importantly,

the Harrison administration seriously considered the acquisition of Cuba, Puerto Rico, the Danish West Indies, pieces
of Canada, naval bases in Santo Domingo, Haiti, and Peru,
and in its last hours in office sent to the Senate a treaty for
the annexation of Hawaii.[2] In retirement in Indiana the
former President drew further attention to his expansionist tendencies when he condemned his successor Grover
Cleveland for withdrawing the Hawaiian treaty from the
Senate and when he declared during the Venezuela crisis
that he would be willing to fight "the ancient [British]
enemy" side by side with "former rebels."[3]

The record showed Harrison to be a zealous nationalist, a
confirmed twister of the British lion's tail, and a strong advocate of trade expansion. But despite his jingoistic tendencies, he normally acted with considerable caution whenever
the basic traditions of American foreign policy seemed to be
at stake. His saber-rattling against Chile in 1891–1892 reflected the ex-soldier's outrage at an insult against the honor
of the United States, not the designs of an annexationist.[4]
He flatly rejected an opportunity to acquire coaling stations
in Africa and the Indian Ocean from Portugal in exchange
for a promise to protect the latter's interests in these areas;
the proposal, he said, was utterly inconsistent with "the settled and traditional policy" of the United States.[5] Even on
the issue of Hawaii he was never more than a reluctant and
wavering annexationist. Harrison wanted to expand American exports, not acquire colonies, and although his name
would always remain associated with the initial attempt to
make Hawaii an American possession, he had actually been
"overly cautious in pursuing annexation even when the Hawaiian pear was ripe for plucking."[6]

In 1898 the retired President was busily occupied with a
brisk law practice and determined to stay out of current political controversies, even though his dislike of McKinley
often tempted him to public utterance. He turned away reporters without comment in the weeks immediately preced-
ing the outbreak of the war with Spain.[7] After war was de-

clared, he again demonstrated both his militant patriotism and his cautious attitude toward expansionism. On May 3, 1898, he exhorted some departing Indiana artillerymen to help win this "war for humanity" and told them that their duty to the people of Cuba was identical to that of a "brave-hearted man" witnessing a bully beating a woman or a child. He also spoke of the opportunity that the war afforded to obtain "some little unpeopled harbors" in the Philippines and the Caribbean but warned that Americans did not have a sacred commission "to deliver the oppressed the world around" and could not in good conscience deny Cuba to Spain only to seize it for themselves.[8]

In an interview two weeks later Harrison expressed his first tentative disagreement with the policies of the McKinley administration. After applauding the plan to annex Hawaii and reaffirming his interest in the acquisition of naval stations, he went on to disparage recent talk of annexing the Philippines and condemned the idea of a "world policy" alliance with Great Britain. The Monroe Doctrine, he pointed out, had stipulated that the United States should leave Europe and Asia alone.[9] In a letter to editor Richard Watson Gilder he criticized the administration for failing to anticipate that a war over Cuba would lead almost inevitably to annexation of the island, but he claimed that he was insufficiently informed to make such criticisms for publication.[10]

The pattern of Harrison's approach to the issue of imperialism was already set. Although increasingly disenchanted with the McKinley administration, he would publicly air his misgivings only on rare occasions. He gave various excuses for his silence. The plea of insufficient information served well for quite a while. Then, alluding to some exhausting legal work, he pleaded his need for rest.[11] Finally, after McKinley appointed him to the new Hague International Court in 1900, Harrison asserted that it would be improper to "drag the Ermine in the pool of politics."[12] In his personal correspondence, however, he kept up a running critical commentary on the administration's policies, writing

John Hay in 1900 to poke fun at the expansionists' "carrier of civilization" argument and remark that the Boer War in South Africa had come about because "the British wash gold," not because "the Boers do not wash themselves." [13]

Early in 1899 Harrison twice made mild and somewhat enigmatic criticisms of the administration in public.[14] Then, in a July 4 address in Paris, where he was conducting legal business, he indicated his dissatisfaction with events in the Philippines, but he conceded that there was no realistic way for the United States to leave the islands until after the Filipino uprising was beaten down.[15] Eight months passed before he spoke out again; this time, in March, 1900, he emphasized his opposition to the establishing of a tariff against goods from Puerto Rico, which he thought would be "a very grave departure from right principles." There could not be one set of laws for the American people and another for those of Puerto Rico. Both must enjoy the full guarantees of the Constitution.[16]

After this utterance Harrison once more lapsed into silence. By this time, with a Presidential election in the offing, it was clear that his reluctance to speak out against imperialism was based primarily on political considerations. No matter how great his differences with McKinley, he would not say or do anything that could give aid and comfort to William Jennings Bryan and the Democrats. Thus he ruled out discussing "public questions that are at the same time party questions." [17] And since he also wanted to make it clear that he was no friend of the administration's expansionist policies, he flatly refused to aid any Republican candidates, including McKinley. He would neither misrepresent his own attitude by giving blanket endorsements to Republican candidates that implied approval of expansion, nor would he embarrass the party by making declarations that were loaded down with all kinds of anti-imperialist disclaimers and qualifications. As the summer turned to autumn, Republicans with both local and national aspirations repeatedly urged the ex-President to campaign, to speak, to stump for the party. Adamantly, he refused them all. If he did not want to speak, someone suggested, perhaps he could at least grace the platform while others orated. "But it would be noticed," Harrison remarked, "that the chairman did not join in the applause, I fear—or his head might shake at some point in the oratory. It is too risky." [18]

In order to avoid campaign pressures Harrison vacationed in Yellowstone through the early summer of 1900 and then holed up at a favorite lodge deep in the Adirondacks until October. His non-electioneering, however, was in itself highly conspicuous, and newspapers had a field day speculating on his "masterly inactivity . . . in Nominee McKinley's interest." [19] The headlines of a paper from his home state declared:

HARRISON'S SILENCE
MAY LOSE INDIANA

EX-PRESIDENT WILL NOT BUDGE
Leaders Have Urged Him to Declare for McKinley,
but He Is Immovable—Silence Almost as Bad
as if He Favored Bryan
—Hoosier State Democrats Making Use of the Fact [20]

Under terrific pressure to make a statement for McKinley, Harrison finally emerged from the vacation forests and on October 10 in New York City issued a brief political announcement. Republicans sighed with relief at his harsh denunciation of Bryan and emphatic call for the Democrat's defeat. Harrison did not, however, speak one favorable word about McKinley or explicitly state that he would vote for the President.[21] Some Republicans were satisfied with the statement, which its author defended as "the best I could do," but those close to McKinley were furious.[22] One newspaper ran the following headline:

HARRISON'S STATEMENT
Brilliant Flashes of Silence

and "Mr. Dooley," commenting that it was a queer campaign in which "no wan is goin' to vote th' way he believes," remarked:

> Says me friend, Binjamin Harrison: "Th' conduct iv th' administhration has been little short iv hellish. Th' idee that this Gover'mint shud sind out throops to murdher an' pillage an' elope with th' sthrugglin' races iv th' boochoos Ph'lippeens, makes me blood bile almost to th' dew pint. I indorse ivrything Willum J. Bryan says on th' subject, an' though it goes hard f'r me to say it, lifelong Raypublican that I am, I exhort ivry follower iv mine to put inmities aside, f'rget his prejudices an' cast his vote f'r Willum McKinley." [23]

Thus Harrison frittered away the campaign, dodging reporters, refusing requests for help from Republican friends, hiding out in the mountains, maintaining silence on issues that he claimed deeply disturbed him—all in the name of protecting an administration whose chief he disliked and whose expansionist policy he condemned. The McKinley administration never realized what a loyal Republican Harrison really was.

Only after McKinley had been safely returned to office by the American electorate—and, as a consequence, only after the anti-imperialist movement had been started on an irreversible decline—did Harrison come out with an unequivocal repudiation of the administration's imperialist record. With plans already underway for publishing some of his criticisms of imperialism, he proceeded to make an open revelation of his attitude in an address at the University of Michigan on December 14, 1900. His speech put special emphasis on the constitutional argument that the United States government had no right to exercise arbitrary rule over any territory, but it also touched on many other issues. American politics would be disrupted by the incorporation of alien people who would also threaten the prosperity of American workers by their willingness to work for low wages. In addition to such practical considerations, Harrison reviewed the larger issues raised by imperialism. Whether the United States could force itself upon a "hostile" population like that of the Philippines was not really so much a legal question as one of "conscience and historical consistency." [24] Contented that he had finally said his piece, Harrison wrote Andrew Carnegie:

> My whole heart has been aflame with indignation against the monstrous proposition that Congress has absolute power in the territories, and that none of the guaranties of personal liberty and civil rights in the Constitution apply there; and my Ann Arbor address was rather a passionate overflow than a critical analysis or a legal argument.[25]

But Harrison's passionate overflow had come much too late to have any significant impact. If he had seen fit to confront the administration with such criticism in the early months of 1899 when the peace treaty was being considered by the Senate, he might have caused considerable trouble. Admittedly his influence within the Republican Party was not equal to Bryan's in the Democratic Party, but if the latter could persuade a handful of supporters to vote for the treaty, might not Harrison have prevailed upon a few Republicans to join George Hoar and Eugene Hale in voting against the pact? If so, it would have been defeated. But none of this was in the cards. Harrison's sense of loyalty to the Republican Party, though not sufficient to bring him to endorse McKinley's re-election, was sufficient to still his tongue until after that re-election was secured. His belated address to the students of the University of Michigan—a faint echo of a movement already in its decline—caused only a flutter of interest. Harrison had come forward too late with too little.

The Old Stalwart

The president of the Anti-Imperialist League was George S. Boutwell, who celebrated his eightieth birthday in 1898.

The choice was inauspicious for an organization that hoped to make a strong impression on the public mind. Boutwell had been politically active from 1851 to 1877 as governor of Massachusetts, federal internal revenue commissioner, member of the House and Senate, and Secretary of the Treasury under Grant, after which time he devoted himself to his legal practice. By 1898 his active political career was a thing of the past, and people who remembered it at all were likely to recall its mediocrity, the career of a partisan timeserver and stalwart who attempted as late as 1880 to get General Grant and his crowd back into the White House. In the House of Representatives after the Civil War he had helped manage Andrew Johnson's impeachment proceedings, proving himself rather incompetent in the matter and even attempting to connect Johnson with Lincoln's assassination. E. L. Godkin dismissed him as "twenty years of caucus, wires, and stump" at the time of his appointment to the cabinet in 1869.[26] As Henry Adams later wrote, Boutwell's selection as head of the Treasury Department turned out to be "a somewhat lugubrious joke," [27] for he stood in dazed inaction while subordinates frolicked with the Whiskey Ring and Jay Gould and Jim Fisk made their fantastic effort to corner the national gold market. In most quarters his name still conjured up images of the tawdry and irregular era of Grant.[28]

Only during the 1880s when Boutwell served as counsel for the government of Hawaii did he appear to endorse an expansionist position, arguing before congressional committees that commercial reciprocity arrangements between his client and the United States would be essential if the latter wanted to win the contest for "control of the trade of the Pacific" and safeguard its own west coast.[29] But in general he was opposed to overseas involvement; he objected to the annexation of Alaska and Santo Domingo in the 1860s, attacked United States interference in Haitian politics in 1889–1891, and disapproved America's role in the Venezuela affair. When he was no longer an agent of the Hawaiian government, he argued in December of 1897 that annexation of the islands would jeopardize rather than strengthen American security. In a succinct version of Carl Schurz's Law, he declared in a speech to the Boot and Shoe Club of Boston that taking possession of Hawaii would leave the United States with "the alternative of a vassal population within its jurisdiction, or the presence of a Mongolian State in the Union." [30]

Boutwell was disdainful of the Cuban rebels and questioned the necessity of going to war with Spain in their interest,[31] but he felt constitutionally obliged to support the war effort after hostilities began. Even during the war, however, he warned against diverting the conflict to imperialist ends,[32] and after the fighting ceased he promptly condemned the growing sentiment for retention of conquered Spanish territories. With an energy which belied his eighty years, he saturated the Boston area with anti-imperialist speeches from the autumn of 1898 (when he was chosen president of the Anti-Imperialist League) to the closing days of 1900.[33]

Boutwell laid special emphasis on the conflict between democratic principles and imperialist practice, but he also dwelt on the adverse effect a policy of overseas annexations would have on the national interest, prophesying innumerable trials and conflicts in the years ahead if the United States permitted itself to be drawn into the imperialist politics of Asia. He often made concrete proposals for disposing of the booty of 1898, usually urging, as he did in a typical speech delivered in Cambridge on November 4 of that year, that the United States grant Hawaii a liberal territorial government, assist Cuba in setting up an independent regime, and "abandon Porto Rico and the Spanish islands of the Pacific ocean without controversy, debate or negotiations with anyone." [34]

It was over the issue of imperialism that Boutwell broke his ties with the Republican Party. Though acknowledging that Bryan had erred in supporting the Treaty of Paris, he nevertheless considered McKinley the guiltier of the two and, as early as June, 1899, set himself the task of making the latter's administration "odious to the country." [35] He wrote George Hoar that McKinley would somehow have to be blocked in his ambition to "create a Colonial Empire for America," [36] and to accomplish this end he was willing to give unqualified political support to Bryan and the Democrats in 1900. He explained to a meeting of anti-imperialists gathered at the Indianapolis Liberty Congress in August that he was now ready, after nearly half a century as a Republican, to switch his allegiance and throw in his lot with a party that had not "surrendered itself to despotic and tyrannical motives." "I am for Bryan," the old stalwart shouted.[37]

In spite of McKinley's re-election Boutwell continued his work for the anti-imperialists until his death in 1905, pleading the cause, as he expressed it, not of Cuba, Puerto Rico, or the Philippines, but "of America." [38] His political sensitivities were not sharp enough, however, to permit him to discern the real political mood of the day. Only five months after McKinley's overwhelming victory at the polls he remarked rather inexplicably that "the masses" were "losing faith" in the President.[39] Still, he sensed something wrong in a movement that attracted so few youthful supporters: "Where are the young men who ought to be in the lead?" he asked seventy-seven-year-old Thomas Wentworth Higginson on January 30, 1901.[40] Bravely, other anti-imperialists apostrophized his surprising reappearance in public affairs:

> New England glories in thy manhood rare,
> Which, breaking party shackles, stands erect
> And breathing deeply of diviner air,—
> Enrolls thy name among the great elect.
> Thy topmost boughs the richest leafage bear,
> Thy latest fruit compels the world's respect.[41]

Boutwell's campaign against American empire was in fact one of the most appealing acts of his life, but owing to his advanced age and unimpressive past record he was singularly ill-suited to lead the cause of anti-imperialism to a successful conclusion.

The Pathetic End

John Sherman's effort to fight American imperialism was so handicapped by the pitiable circumstances of his own life—his declining health and loss of mental agility—that it was bound to be ineffectual. The anti-imperialists reached out to welcome the old Republican partisan, only to grasp a hand too feeble to aid their cause.

In the years before 1897 John Sherman of Ohio had made an impressive record in politics. While not brilliant or particularly attractive personally, he was a competent and hard-working professional politician, a moderate Republican who "made it a rule always to act with his party; on great matters from principle, and on small matters from policy." [42] He had little to do with either of the major legislative acts of 1890 that bore his name—the Sherman Silver Purchase Act and the Sherman Anti-Trust Act—but he played an important role in the fields of civil service reform, tariffs, and currency, displaying a "singular ability in framing a measure upon which discordant elements of his party could agree." [43] In return for his loyal services, the Republican Party rewarded him generously. Sherman was elected to the House of Representatives in 1854 when he was thirty-one years old, and thenceforward until 1898 he served continuously in the federal government, as congressman for six years, senator for thirty-two years, as Secretary of the Treasury under President Hayes, and finally as Secretary of State in 1897–1898. The highest office of all had seemed within his grasp in 1888 when he led the Republican convention voting for six ballots, but Benjamin Harrison ultimately carried away the party's nomination for President.

Sherman's concern with domestic and party affairs did not prevent him from taking an active interest in foreign policy, an interest heightened when he became chairman of the Senate Foreign Relations Committee in 1886. He welcomed the prospect of a worldwide expansion of American political and economic influence [44] but was usually opposed to the annexation of new territories, as he was in the case of Santo Domingo during the Grant administration.[45] After visiting Cuba in 1887 he predicted that the island would shortly explode in a rebellion led by elements desiring annexation to the United States, and he counseled his countrymen to resist their pressure. The proper way for the United States to "become the ruler of other dominions" was through commercial expansion, "by extending our steamboat lines into South America, by making all the Caribbean Sea one vast American ocean; by planting our influence among the sister republics, by aiding them from time to time . . ." [46] He consistently supported organizations that advocated peace through arbitration treaties and international courts and for the most part urged patience and moderation in the face of such international crises as the 1889 dispute over Samoa and the Venezuela affair of 1895–1896.[47] In the last paragraph of his memoirs, published in 1895, he warned Americans against the "embarrassments" and "complications of foreign acquisitions" and promised that he would do everything in his power "to add to the strength and prosperity of the United States, but nothing to extend its limits . . ." [48] The most glaring exception to this normally moderate outlook in foreign affairs was his attitude toward Hawaii, which he wanted annexed to the Union as a county of the State of California. He was indignant when Cleveland scrapped Harrison's annexation treaty in 1893.[49]

Yet late in the nineties Sherman acquired something of a

jingo's reputation on the Cuban issue. In September, 1895, he had taken the position that the United States should not recognize the belligerency of the Cuban rebels until they actually controlled the island,[50] but five months later he endorsed a resolution that not only accorded belligerent rights to the Cubans but further resolved that President Cleveland should offer his good offices to Spain "for the recognition of the independence of Cuba." If Spain's repressive policies were to continue, he explained, "no earthly power [could] prevent the people of the United States from going over to that island, running all over its length and breadth . . . driving out . . . these barbarous robbers and imitators of the worst men who ever lived in the world." But he still did not favor annexing Cuba. "I do not desire to conquer the Cubans in any sense," he maintained.[51]

E. L. Godkin in the *New York Evening Post* regarded Sherman's switch on Cuba as merely the latest performance of "the most active wobbler in public life." [52] But his fluctuations on the Cuban issue were more than a sign of wobbly convictions. They were actually an early manifestation of fading mental powers. By the fall of 1896 it was being bruited about in public that Sherman had lost his memory, and it therefore came as something of a shock when President-elect McKinley announced in January, 1897, that the seventy-four-year-old Ohioan would be his Secretary of State.[53] Although not all authorities agree on the reasons for the choice, it appears most likely that McKinley wanted to clear a Senate seat for Mark Hanna by kicking Sherman upstairs to the State Department.[54] It was by way of this shabby arrangement—with which Sherman, incidentally, seemed quite content at the time [55]—that the American people were given as Secretary of State a man who was not only old, but who was obviously befuddled by age and given in recent days to making belligerent and unstatesmanlike remarks against the government of Spain. At times unable to recollect what he had said or done the day before or to recognize old friends when he encountered them, Sherman was simply not competent to assume a post of major responsibility.

It was a disastrous appointment, bringing a long career of public service to a pathetic close. After months of urging American intervention in Cuba, Sherman reversed himself shortly before McKinley's inauguration and told the Senate: "I do not believe that the United States Government should interfere in the Cuban trouble. . . . I am opposed to any interference." When McKinley requested help in drafting his inaugural address, he received a confusingly worded memorandum that wandered from position to position, ending (but not necessarily concluding) with the advice that the United States should tender its "friendly offices" in an effort to resolve the dispute in Cuba.[56] Once in office Sherman's memory and hearing both appeared to decline rapidly, leaving him silent and distant during cabinet meetings, and the President and his advisers found it next to impossible to get any intelligible advice from him. At one moment the Secretary of State would be insisting that America's commercial interests should be the sole guide in formulating a Cuban policy and at the next he would be remarking that humanitarian considerations might necessitate an invasion of the island. McKinley, a prudent man, quickly turned over important State Department business to Sherman's subordinates.[57]

But this arrangement raised more problems than it solved. Sherman, often unfamiliar with what was happening in his own office, stumbled into one indiscretion after another. Agents from Hawaii who talked to him could not be sure whether he would support or fight annexation of the islands. When the Japanese minister lodged a protest against the Hawaiian project, the Secretary of State, either unaware or forgetful of the fact that a treaty of annexation was being negotiated at that very moment, assured the minister that nothing of the sort was being contemplated. The Japanese government was understandably offended when Sherman himself signed the completed pact a few days later and brusquely explained that the annexation of Hawaii was "the destined culmination" of "the progressive policies and dependent associations of some seventy years." 58

With even the lowliest clerks in the Department gossiping about his lapses, Sherman wrote a pathetic letter to McKinley, acknowledging that he was "getting old" and promising: "Whenever you think I am too old I will retire with thanks to the Ruler of the Universe for extending my life beyond the allotted three score and ten years." 59 Matters continued to drift while evidence of his condition accumulated. David Starr Jordan, who was advising the government in some fur seal negotiations, spoke with Sherman on numerous occasions only to be asked each time why he was in Washington. Secretary of the Navy John D. Long noted that his fellow cabinet member was "getting a little forgetful and [telling] the same story twice." 60 During the winter of 1897–1898 Sherman granted reporters a series of interviews in which he made indiscreet and hostile remarks about Britain and threatening ones about Spain. Perhaps his worst lapse occurred a few days before the outbreak of the Spanish-American War when he sought out Austrian minister Baron von Hengelmüller in a personal effort to maintain the peace and urged him to prevail upon his emperor to mediate between Spain and the United States. Since it was no secret in the diplomatic community that Sherman's authority in such matters was only nominal, von Hengelmüller lost no time in consulting Assistant Secretary of State William Day who informed him that the administration would not countenance any European interference.61

Sherman had to go. After a little gentle pressure from the President the old man resigned on April 26, 1898, one day after Congress declared war on Spain. *The Nation* remarked that Sherman's appointment, rapid decline in office, and resignation had been "one of the most discreditable [episodes] in our political history, and the sooner it is forgotten, the better." [62]

Sherman emerged from the episode full of bitterness. He began to tell friends that he had gone to the State Department only in order to accommodate McKinley and Hanna and that he had been badly treated while in office. He did not want people to think that he was "a Sore head," however, and he had no intention of discussing the issue in such a manner as "to create divisions in the Republican party." [63] But as time passed he felt increasingly abused and humiliated whenever he surveyed the ruins of his once-proud public career, and in November, 1898, he wrote a fellow Ohioan:

> I hear that both McKinley and Hanna are pitying me for failing memory and physical strength. I do not care for their pity and do not ask them any favors, but wish only to feel independent of them, and conscious that, while they deprived me of the high office of Senator by the temporary appointment as Secretary of State, they have not lessened me in your opinion or in the good-will of the great Republican party of the United States.[64]

Already, in May and June, Sherman had come out publicly against the annexation of "any territory whatever, whether it be Cuba, Puerto Rico, Hawaii, or the Philippines" and had thus tumbled unresistingly into the eager hands of the anti-imperialists who promptly made him an honorary vice-president of the Anti-Imperialist League.[65] Despite the serious illness of his wife, which greatly restricted his activities, he complied with a League request of November, 1898, and wrote a long letter against ratification of the Treaty of Paris, stressing in particular the unfavorable tropical climate of the Philippines, the alien culture of its inhabitants, and the enormous expense that would accompany its pacification and defense. "I sympathize with Aguinaldo," he wrote, "in his ambition to found a Republic in the China Sea, near the equator, and hope he may become the Washington of a new nation, absolutely free from European and American influence." [66]*

After ratification of the treaty Sherman denounced American military action against Aguinaldo's rebellion and wrote McKinley that the United States should withdraw its troops and recognize the islands' independence.[67] But the fatal illness of his wife and his own physical decline so weakened him that he was able to contribute little beyond this to the anti-imperialist movement, and there is no indication that the administration took much notice of his opposition. Fate did not allow him time to reconsider his rule always to act with his party. John Sherman died two weeks before the reelection of William McKinley, the man who, by appointing him Secretary of State, had brought about his political ruin.

"That Fat, Sarcastic Man"

In an age of mediocrities and boodlers, Thomas Brackett Reed stood out as a politician of real stature. After climbing the hard ladder of Maine politics, he served from 1877 to 1899 in the House of Representatives, where he established a reputation as a staunch conservative. A down-the-line Republican, he once proclaimed that "a good party is better than the best man that ever lived." [68] He was elected Speaker of the House in 1889 at the age of fifty and made his most significant mark on American politics shortly thereafter. Ingeniously checking the obstructionist tactics of the minority Democrats and augmenting the powers of his own office, he imposed new rules on the House—"Reed's Rules" —aimed at making it much more responsive to majority will. A young English diplomat described his taming of the obstreperous House in a letter home: "They have passed some

* Sherman may have changed his mind on the treaty later and adopted William Jennings Bryan's view that the main anti-imperialist fight should come after ratification. There is a hint of this possibility in the letter of Edward Atkinson to Erving Winslow, February 10, 1899, Atkinson Papers, MHS.

new rules in the house with the help of our friend, Mr. Reed of Maine, that fat, sarcastic man you remember; the object of them has been, as he tersely put it, to give the minority all the rights which the majority think are good for them." [69] With this maneuver Reed earned his nickname "Czar" and a firm place in the parliamentary history of his country.

"Czar" Reed made an unforgettable visual impression. He stood over six feet three inches tall, weighed 250 to 275 pounds, and possessed an enormous, round, bland, almost babyish face—"a stupendous figure—indeed Brobdingnagian," wrote Champ Clark. William Allen White called him "a huge six-foot, gelatinous walrus of a man." [70] Reed was also conspicuous in intelligence and cultivation, and he exercised a wicked wit that was perhaps his most distinguishing quality. Washington hostesses constantly sought him out as a dinner guest, counting on him to enliven their parties with some of his innumerable *bon mots* about politics and politicians. He once told the bumptious and earnest Theodore Roosevelt: "Theodore, if there is one thing for which I admire you, it is your original discovery of the ten commandments," and he has been credited with defining a statesman as "a successful politician who is dead." In 1900, when William Jennings Bryan insisted upon campaigning once again on a platform of free silver, Reed quipped: "Bryan had rather be wrong than president." [71]

Since he looked upon party loyalty as a matter of deeds, Reed was not reluctant to aim some of his barbed words at his fellow Republicans. An observer commented in 1890 that he did whatever he liked in the House "without consulting the [Harrison] administration, which he detests, or his followers whom he seems to despise." [72] In 1891 he wrote Roosevelt:

> Of course it stirred to renewed enthusiasm my love for the party to find that the question of questions was whether Blaine or Harrison should cover us with the shield of his

majestic name when next we go where glory awaits us. I love Harrison, but I adore Blaine. Harrison has the better manners while Blaine has the sturdier sense of duty. . . . When I think of our army of stags filing and charging by either of these noble lions, the light of battle fills my eye and I can easily see death if not victory ahead.[73]

With his usual disregard for established reputation, Reed described Henry Cabot Lodge as "thin soil highly cultivated." Dubbing Harrison "the ice man" and McKinley the "Emperor of Expediency," he was openly contemptuous of both their administrations.[74]

As a politician Reed was too witty for his own good. He could never resist poking fun at stupidity and pomposity and constantly lost friends and gained foes as a result. One writer, in commenting on his rapierlike tongue, said that Reed "always preferred to make an epigram rather than to make a friend" (proof, incidentally, that Reed inspired as well as made epigrams; Champ Clark once called him "a self-made man who worshiped his Maker") .[75] In 1896, when he made his only serious bid for the Republican Presidential nomination, Henry Adams wrote him off as "too clever, too strong-willed, and too cynical, for a bankers' party." Actually he never stood a chance of winning over McKinley, but having entered the competition with uncharacteristic seriousness, he grew bitter and sarcastic when it became obvious that he would make a poor showing at the convention. He wrote Roosevelt, one of his supporters: "In a word, my dear boy, I am tired of this thing . . . the receding grapes seem to ooze with acid and the whole thing is a farce." [76]

Reed's resentment toward McKinley undoubtedly played some part in his joining the anti-imperialists in 1898, but for years he had shown little enthusiasm for expansionist ventures. He told a reporter during the Chilean fracas that Harrison was wrong in sending such belligerent warnings to "those little Chileans"; since the President was the only one who seemed eager to fight, he should be packed off in a chartered ship ("not too large or too safe") to engage the Chileans in single combat ("He's just about their size"). When Lodge expressed concern that Harrison's chances for re-election might be hurt by the incident, Reed replied: "Why do you try to save him? Let him drive on and break his neck." [77] He was equally critical of Cleveland's bullying of the British four years later, and in the wake of the Venezuela affair, he began to question the wisdom of continuing his long record of support for the construction of a great and modern American navy. When Lodge insisted that the naval buildup was essential as a form of national insurance, Reed countered: "Insurance is a good thing but over insurance creates what the insurance men call Moral Hazard; meaning the hazard . . . that an over insured man will set fire to his house." [78] Anxious about the rising jingoism of the period, he wrote in the *North American Review* of October, 1896, that the United States should resist the new imperialist fever. It had no need for far-off acquisitions as long as it was still an undeveloped nation: "we are but at the beginning of the glories of the Republic, not glories of the conquest of men, but of the conquest of the elemental powers and of resources beyond limit and without stint." [79]

By the end of 1897 Reed had made it clear that he would use all the weapons at his disposal to prevent a war with Spain. Differing from Sherman in his possession of physical and mental strength, from Boutwell in the respect he commanded, and from Harrison in the power he wielded, he was in a peculiarly strong position to throw a wrench into the administration plans. After the explosion of the *Maine* in February, 1898, and the emotional outcry that followed it, he announced that he would no longer support appropriations for battleships. Roosevelt and Lodge were deeply irritated. From the stronghold of his Speaker's chair, Reed berated jingo congressmen, blocked army appropriation bills, obstructed Cuban belligerency resolutions, and in every conceivable way attempted to hold off the eager House expansionists. One congressman complained at the end of March that Reed "has the members of that body bottled up so tight they cannot breathe without his consent." Roosevelt complained bitterly that Reed was "almost crazy in [his] eagerness for peace, and would make almost any sacrifice to get peace." But, finally, Reed's own scruples against blocking the will of a majority prompted him to change course in early April and bow to the obvious wish of the House members to get on with the preparations for war.[80]

Since all his efforts to prevent an armed conflict had proved ineffective, Reed now turned his attention to the probable results of the war. When Dewey destroyed the Spanish fleet at Manila, he expressed the hope that the worthy officer would quickly leave the scene of his victory and avoid getting the United States permanently involved in the Philippines. As the summer wore on it became public knowledge that Reed was in sharp disagreement with administration policy. He would break into "sulphurous language" whenever the question of expansionism came up.[81] His most important public effort to frustrate the expansionists came in the spring of 1898 when he attempted to block House passage of the resolution to annex Hawaii. Businessman George W. Perkins urged Senator Albert J. Beveridge to do what he could to change Reed's mind, but the Senator replied: "I feel that any effort of mine upon the Gibraltar-like mind and will of the Speaker would be absolutely ineffectual." [82] One of Hawaii's agents in Washington informed his government that despite terrific pressure exerted against him, Reed's "opposition to us becomes more and more pronounced, more bitter, more aggressive, and more determined" every day.[83] For three weeks after the resolution was introduced he prevented it from coming to the House floor for a vote. Finally, however, when it became perfectly clear that a majority of the House favored action on the resolution, Reed yielded. He no longer felt able to violate the spirit of his own rules, which had been formulated precisely to prevent a minority from standing in the way of the majority's right to act. On June 15, 1898, the House passed the joint resolution by a vote of 209 to 91. Reed, ill and absent from the chamber, took the extraordinary action of having a colleague announce that he would have voted in opposition had he been present.[84]

Reed's opposition to imperalism was ascribed by some of his contemporaries to his bitterness toward the President. It was "a matter of common knowledge," Champ Clark wrote in his memoirs, "that Reed hated President McKinley intensely." [85] But more than hatred or envy was involved. In a manuscript apparently written in October of 1898 and found among Reed's papers after his death in 1902, he bewailed the great change in America's position that the war had brought about.

> At the beginning of this year we were most admirably situated. We had no standing army which could overrun our people. We were at peace within our own borders and with all the world. . . .
>
> We were then in a condition which secured to us the respect and envy of the civilized world. The quarrels which other nations have we did not have. The sun did set on our dominions and our drum-beat did not encircle the world with our martial airs. Our guns were not likely to be called upon to throw projectiles which cost, each of them, the price of a happy home, nor did any bombardment seem likely to cost us the value of a village.

But 1898 had ended in bloody "degeneracy." America's leaders had found it convenient to dismiss the principles of the Declaration of Independence as "glittering generalities to please the ears of children . . ." They were leading the United States into deep waters, especially in the Philippines, and running "the great risk . . . of forgetting the foundation principles of our government." [86]

Most Americans had scant knowledge of these sober judgments, for Reed kept them pretty much to himself. What the public was more likely to hear were some of his typical witticisms, now more caustic than ever. When the Treaty of Paris was signed he remarked: "We have about 10,000,000 Malays at $2.00 a head unpicked, and nobody knows what it will cost to pick them." With the outbreak of the Filipino rebellion, he amused himself by drawing up a mock petition asking Congress to clear the record of General ("Butcher") Weyler, despised by the American public for his brutal re-concentration camp tactics in Cuba, since these very methods were now being expertly applied by American forces against the stubborn Filipinos.[87] On another occasion, when a friend inquired which route he should take in visiting America's new possessions, the Speaker suggested:

> Well, if you travel westward you'll reach the Philippines by way of Hawaii, and if you travel eastward you'll reach Hawaii by way of the Philippines. The whole question is whether you prefer to take your plague before your leprosy, or take your leprosy before your plague.

In the House he took delight in delaying the passage of private bills involving small appropriations because the money was "needed to pay for the Malays"; when $300,000 was appropriated for the Commercial Museum of Philadelphia, he sighed: "This seems like a great waste of money. We could buy 150,000 naked Sulus with that." [88]

Eventually he grew tired of watching the House as it invariably approved the administration's expansionist measures. It galled him to see McKinley succeed in committing the nation step by step to the path of imperialism. Despite his formidable powers as Speaker, Reed felt hamstrung by his own scruples and rules. Besides, he was bored. There was no longer any satisfaction in public life. At sixty he was feeling his age and wanted to accumulate some money for his family. Disgusted with the national drift toward imperialism, irritated by a House of Representatives he could no longer control, and eager to make some big money, he announced on April 19, 1899, that he would retire from Congress the following September in order to join a law firm in New York. The anti-imperialists were dismayed. George Hoar wrote him that it was "a very bad thing to take off the brake when the wagon is going downhill. I am very much afraid we shall tip over." E. L. Godkin, already sunk in gloom, compared Reed's retirement to "the departure from a ship of the one man on board who understands navigation." [89]

Reed was often mentioned by anti-imperialists as an ideal independent candidate to run against both McKinley and Bryan in 1900, but he never gave them a bit of encouragement. He did not vote in the election.[90] Instead he devoted himself to his law practice and his bitter private jabs at the expansionists. "It's all right," he remarked on one occasion, "to do what we can for the undeveloped races, but I don't believe in making our country a kindergarten for all the rest of the world." [91] He replied to a staff member of the House Committee on Appropriations who had sent him some figures on the cost of the war in the Philippines:

> Thanks for the statistics which I hope to find use for. . . . I have got to hunt all over your figures even to find out how much each yellow man costs us in the bush. As I make it out he has cost $30 per Malay and he is still in the bush.
>
> Why didn't you purchase him of Spain F. O. B., with definite freight-rate, and insurance paid? [92]

But these confidential sallies were no match for a determined administration. Reed's protest against imperialism was no more effective than those of Benjamin Harrison, George Boutwell, and John Sherman.

Anti-imperialists liked to regard the presence of leading Republicans in their ranks as proof of an imminent repudiation by the people of McKinley's entire expansionist program. This was typical anti-imperialist wishful thinking, not an informed estimate of political realities, for, despite their efforts, men like Reed, Harrison, Boutwell, and Sherman had not been able to hurt McKinley or seriously jeopardize public acceptance of his policies. The peculiar circumstances and limitations of these men had much to do with their failure, but so did their place within the Republican Party. None of them was identified with the future of the party. Those who were—younger men of rising prominence—were either ardent expansionists themselves or quite willing to go along with the expansionists in the name of party unity. Even the two Republicans who were most effective and conspicuous as anti-imperialists, George Hoar and Andrew Carnegie, adhered to the party ticket in 1900. Their support helped McKinley blur the expansion issue and convince voters that he was doing everything in his power for the freedom and happiness of the Cubans, Puerto Ricans, Hawaiians, and Filipinos. They managed to keep their places in the orderly ranks of the Republican Party. Those who failed to do so protested in vain.

The Anti-Imperialists and America:
A Conclusion

The Anti-Imperialists
and America:
A Conclusion

The anti-imperialist movement quickly faded after the election of 1900. Under the leadership of a small circle in Boston, a few of the faithful persisted until as late as the 1920s in distributing pamphlets, investigating stories of atrocities in the Philippines, pressing anti-colonial resolutions upon the conventions of both major political parties, and tirelessly advocating independence for the Philippines. But Bryan's defeat and the government's lack of interest in acquiring any more new territories spelled the end of anti-imperialism as a movement of major significance. So did the death of the major anti-imperialists. John Sherman died in 1900, Benjamin Harrison in 1901, Thomas Reed and E. L. Godkin in the following year, George Hoar in 1904, Edward Atkinson and George Boutwell in 1905, Carl Schurz in 1906 (Adams, Carnegie, and five other anti-imperialists officiated at his funeral),[1] Charles Eliot Norton in 1908, William James in 1910, Charles Francis Adams in 1915, and Andrew Carnegie in 1919. Only the retired Scotsman lived long enough to see America enter another war.

The Meaning of the Anti-Imperialist Movement

The anti-imperialists offered a wide range of objections to the acquisition of new territories. They may be summarized as constitutional, economic, diplomatic, moral, racial, political, and historical.

A large number of anti-imperialists believed that imperialism violated the United States Constitution. Some simply contended that the spirit of the Constitution had been contradicted, that it was not right for a government based upon principles of representative rule and the protection of individual liberties to govern other peoples without regard for these principles. Assurances that American colonial rule would be humane did not mollify them, since they believed that benevolence arbitrarily offered could be just as arbitrarily withdrawn. Those who were convinced that imperialism violated not only the spirit but the letter of the Constitution averred that neither Congress nor the President possessed the legal authority to pass laws or set rules for the governing of colonial peoples which were not in strict accord with those established for the people of the United States themselves. Thus Benjamin Harrison, protesting that there could not be one law for the citizen and another for the subject, held that it was unconstitutional for Congress to impose a tariff on goods entering the continental United States from the territory of Puerto Rico; his position was summarized in the popular phrase, "the Constitution follows the flag." The Supreme Court, however, somewhat ambiguously affirmed Congress' extra-constitutional powers in the colonies in the "Insular Cases" of 1901, a verdict that reportedly prompted Elihu Root, the urbane Secretary of War, to comment: "Ye-es, as near as I can make out the Constitution follows the flag—but doesn't quite catch up with it." [2]

In making an economic case against imperialism, critics

denied the truth of another contemporary aphorism, to wit, that "trade follows the flag." Men like Carl Schurz and Andrew Carnegie felt that it was unnecessary to plant the flag in the spongy soil of the tropics in order to capture the area's trade. The laws of commerce would determine how successful the Americans were in selling their surplus abroad. If they found profitable markets it would be because the products of their mills, mines, factories, and farms were cheap and attractive enough to compete with those of other nations and not because they had seized and roped off markets for their exclusive use. Occasionally an anti-imperialist would add that a reduced tariff schedule which allowed foreigners a better opportunity to sell their wares in the United States would enhance their ability to purchase American goods in return and thus promote a greater increase in American exports than McKinley's policy of imperialism.

Businessmen Andrew Carnegie and Edward Atkinson suggested additional economic reasons for rejecting an annexationist policy. According to the former, any effort to regularize commercial relations within an American empire would be accompanied by hopeless economic and political difficulties. Free trade between the United States and the Philippines would bankrupt American farmers and certain groups of raw material producers, yet a tariff on the colony's goods would violate the Constitution and destroy the islands' economy. To open the market of the Philippines on equal terms to the United States and other nations would fulfill the principle of the open door but would ruin American exporters who had to pay heavier transportation charges than those incurred by their German, British, and Australian competitors. If, on the other hand, the Philippines market were kept exclusively for the United States the resulting anger of European powers interested in Far Eastern trade would produce a dangerous diplomatic crisis.

Edward Atkinson took another tack. For years he had been an eager advocate of increased economic activity in

Latin America and the Far East, but in 1899 he concluded that the prize of Oriental trade (and, to a certain extent, of Latin American trade) was not worth the cost of acquiring it. There would be time enough to bid for those markets when China and other undeveloped nations had industrialized and generated enough purchasing power to buy in quantity the kind of sophisticated goods that the United States produced. In the meantime more significant profits could be made from trade with America's traditional partners, the industrial nations of Europe and Canada.

Anti-imperialists also objected to a policy of colonialism because it threatened to involve America more deeply in international politics, especially in Asia. They abhorred this prospect on three counts. First, it was a contradiction of their conception of American diplomatic traditions, a departure from the path of non-entanglement laid down by the founders of the nation and a negation of the Monroe Doctrine, which they interpreted as meaning "Europe for the Europeans" and "Asia for the Asians" as well as "America for the Americans." Secondly, involvement in Asian imperial politics would endanger the security of the United States. Anti-imperialists charged that by extending American responsibility to Hawaii and the Philippines, the McKinley administration had broken the nation's ocean belt of security and placed the flag in outlying regions where it was vulnerable to intimidation or attack by other powers. With its security no longer ensured by geography, the United States would have to build an enormous navy and an army of respectable strength to protect its new possessions against any action that seemed to threaten them, however remotely. Thirdly, the domestic repercussions of a leading role in world politics would prove costly. Future wars and the permanent maintenance of forces strong enough to wage them would require a vast amount of money, discourage industry, impose heavy tax burdens on the American people, and distract attention from the solution of domestic problems that had a far greater bearing on the future than any foreign policy issues could have—problems of race and radicalism, currency and the cities, trusts and the tariff.

The moral critique of the anti-imperialists requires few words to summarize although it was just as important as their constitutional, economic, or strategic objections to imperialism. They believed—simply, genuinely, and emphatically—that it was *wrong* for the United States forcibly to impose its will on other peoples. No economic or diplomatic reasoning could justify slaughtering Filipinos who wanted their independence. No standard of justice or morality would sustain the transformation of a war that had begun as a crusade to liberate Cuba from Spanish tyranny into a campaign of imperialist conquest.

As genuine if not as high-minded were the racial attitudes that contributed to the anti-imperialist stand. With a few rare exceptions like George Hoar, the opponents of imperialism shared entirely the expansionists' belief in the inferiority and incapacity of the world's colored races (and of some that were not colored). But while those in the imperialist camp usually proceeded from these racist assumptions to a belief in the duty of Americans to uplift and care for the backward and benighted savages of Puerto Rico and the Philippines, the anti-imperialists appealed to these same assumptions to justify excluding such peoples from a place in the American political system. They believed that the United States should belong to its own kind, the Anglo-Saxons (or "Germanic" races as Carl Schurz would have it). The blood of tropical peoples would taint the stream of American political and social life and further complicate the nation's already festering racial problems. As the *New York World* asked on June 19, 1898, did the United States, which already had a "black elephant" in the South, "really need a white elephant in the Philippines, a leper elephant in Hawaii, a brown elephant in Porto Rico and perhaps a yellow elephant in Cuba?"[3]

In their political objections to expansionism the anti-imperialists were guided by abstract principles. For the most part they were political fundamentalists—they believed in the literal truth and universal applicability of the ideas of liberty and republican government. Free of the skepticism and self-consciousness of later generations, they asserted that a republican government could not also be an imperial government; that the rule of self-government did not permit exceptions in faraway territories; that freedom was a value of universal appeal, in the Philippines and Puerto Rico as well as in the United States; and that all men, whatever their attainments and wherever they lived, possessed the right to enjoy the blessings of freedom. The United States could not preserve its own democracy if it denied the right of self-rule to others.

Finally, anti-imperialists had what might be called historical motives for opposing imperialism. Most of them were traditionalists who believed imperialism to be in sharp conflict with established ideals and practices. Acquiring overseas colonies and joining the worldwide struggle for power and empire were inconsistent with American diplomatic traditions, with America's historic identification with the ideal of liberty, and with the lofty notion that America should serve the world not through force but through the force of her example. Imperialism destroyed the unquestioned belief in American innocence and uniqueness.

The anti-imperialists were primarily and overwhelmingly concerned with their own country—its security, prosperity, constitutional integrity, and moral and political health—and not with the fate of Filipinos, Cubans, Hawaiians, or Puerto Ricans. Although they could and did defend the rights of these peoples, their fundamental purpose was to defend the interests of the United States.

On other points the anti-imperialists did not always agree among themselves, nor did they react to the events of 1898–1900 in a uniform manner. Bleak pessimism about the future of the nation was a common sentiment, yet Edward Atkinson remained optimistic and adaptable to the end. Some anti-imperialists were content to enunciate general principles while refusing to address themselves to day-to-day problems, but Charles Francis Adams, Jr., never one just to gnash his teeth and write despairing letters, tried to channel the energies of the anti-imperialist movement in a direction that would yield tangible results in public policy. Many leading anti-imperialists had been fearful of American expansionism long before the war with Spain, but others became concerned only during the war itself and still others refrained from criticism until as late as 1901, by which time the issue was for all practical purposes dead. Anti-imperialists to a man were opposed to the annexation of the Philippines, but on other issues they were often badly divided. Many were against going to war with Spain from the outset, but others were not. The Hawaiian issue caused considerable disunity and confusion. In principle many opposed the annexation of Puerto Rico, but little was made of the issue, so great was the preoccupation with the Philippines. Some anti-imperialists who were dead set against annexing new territories were not averse to dominating them by means of American economic power, but most anti-imperialists were no more inclined to this informal brand of imperialism than they were to more formal varieties. While many anti-imperialists joined the ranks of the various leagues established in 1898 and 1899, others took a more independent route and shied away from organizational activity. And although a clear majority of anti-imperialists regarded imperialism as a most serious threat to American institutions and values and thus the most important issue facing voters in 1900, Adams, Carnegie, and others judged internal questions to be of greater moment—a situation that gave rise to some of the disunity among anti-imperialists during the campaign.

What the anti-imperialists had in common, however, was more important than what separated them. Their consensus on constitutional, moral, and other questions was but part of a broader unity. To them imperialism was both an example and a product of a large number of unfortunate and dangerous developments that had taken place since the Civil War. Their criticisms therefore took the form of a commentary on the forces transforming America in the last third of the nineteenth century, a critique of American society in general.

The anti-imperialists viewed the world from a conservative framework. They preferred a stable society and almost always reacted to what was novel and unprecedented with suspicion and disapproval. Men as dissimilar as Charles Eliot Norton and Andrew Carnegie did not, of course, have identical images of the kind of America they wished to protect from change. But in general they all shared the same biases and for the most part cherished the same conservative vision of an ideal American society. As elitists they were not so much interested in conserving a system of economic privilege for themselves as in defending a style of life and a social tone against the leveling influences of *arriviste* businessmen and the democratic masses. They preferred—even if they did not like to admit it to themselves—a nation led by the educated and well-born. Possessing genuine doubts about the desirability of a mass democracy, they feared the effect of equality upon literature and the fine arts, the makeup and tone of society, and the practice of politics and diplomacy. Lovers of gentility and stability, they were happiest in a nation of neat and picturesque farms and clean, attractive, manageable cities where all classes lived together in harmony. The wealth of the nation would flow from the steady and contented labor of yeoman farmers and native workers. This essentially pre-industrial and Anglo-Saxon America would fulfill its ideals by remaining aloof from the wars and alliances of the outside world. In the years 1898–1900 the anti-imperialists believed they were defending this conception of America by resisting the new order of expansionism.

Elitists can be idealists, too, and the anti-imperialists were among those who believed their nation worth saving only as long as it remained true to the social and political ideals that had made it "American." The mission of America was to establish liberty and justice for all men (as interpreted by these sturdy defenders of rank and order) and to create a society that safeguarded the property and rights of everyone. Above all the national mission dictated that these marvels could be brought into being only if America remained unburdened by standing armies and uninvolved in the endless quarrels and wars of Europe, the world's old Adam.

The belief in American uniqueness provided the capstone of anti-imperialist idealism. The United States was alone among nations in being able to fulfill the social and political goals required by its peculiar mission. There could be no purposeful life for America apart from these goals. "We have it in our power to begin the world over again. . . . The birthday of a new world is at hand." The words are those of an eighteenth-century radical, Thomas Paine, but they could well have been those of the conservatives who led the anti-imperialist movement.

It was according to such rigorous, perfectionist standards that these men measured the progress of their nation. Any sign of backsliding looked to them like a major defeat of national ideals. This is why anti-imperialists were so anguished. They did not go to the trouble of protesting with such vehemence merely because they disagreed with a particular venture in foreign affairs but because they were certain that imperialism reflected the final failure of the American mission. Traditionalists, idealists, perfectionists, they had been appalled by the hammer blows of industrialization, the floodtide of immigration, and the expansion of American economic and diplomatic interests. Everywhere they turned they saw their vision of America mocked. The filthy and burgeoning cities rang with an alien and Babelic clamor. There seemed to be more ignorant rabblerousers than virtuous yeomen on the countryside. Bloody strikes and killings punctuated the fast-vanishing calm of industrial relations. In the national capital crude politicians and officeholders had seized the seats of power and were now elbowing their way into the international scene with increasing abandon. Whirl and change were king, worshiped and spurred on by a people heedless and ignorant of the great principles and lessons of their own nation's past.

Except for the crudeness of the politicians, all this seemed ominously similar to the anti-imperialists' picture of European life. America, founded in reaction to the ways of Europe, was now succumbing to them. Imperialism proved the fact that America was not immune to evil or indifferent to the lure of wealth and power. She had abandoned her peculiar mission and stripped off her garb of uniqueness to reveal a disappointing commonness with the rest of the world. The poet William Vaughn Moody, in "An Ode in Time of Hesitation," asked:

> Are we the eagle nation Milton saw
> Mewing its mighty youth,
> Soon to possess the mountain winds of truth,
> And be a swift familiar of the sun
> Where aye before God's face his trumpets run?
> Or have we but the talons and the maw,
> And for the abject likeness of our heart
> Shall some less lordly bird be set apart?—
> Some gross-billed wader where the swamps are fat?
> Some gorger in the sun? Some prowler with the bat? [4]

The revelation of sameness in place of uniqueness came as a shock. Daniel Boorstin has described the mood of twentieth-century Americans in words that could just as well characterize the feelings of the anti-imperialists: "It [was] as if the Athenians had suddenly begun to doubt whether they were unlike the Spartans, or the Romans to suspect that they were really barbarians at heart." [5]

The anti-imperialists were not, of course, the only ones

who thought that America had a special mission. But the manner in which they interpreted her unique role explains why they believed that imperialism spelled, in Charles Eliot Norton's words, the doom of "the America exceptionally blessed among the nations." This was the meaning of the anti-imperialist movement—a protest against the abandonment of the American mission.

The Impact of the Anti-Imperialists

The Treaty of Paris was nearly defeated in the Senate in February, 1899. Anti-imperialists had succeeded in stirring up a major public discussion in the country. Anti-imperialist leagues sprang up in Boston and Springfield, Massachusetts, in New York, Philadelphia, Baltimore, Washington, Cincinnati, Cleveland, Detroit, St. Louis, Los Angeles, and Portland, Oregon. In the years 1898 to 1900 the parent Anti-Imperialist League distributed well over half a million pamphlets and other items in an effort to influence public opinion. In 1899 the League claimed to have 30,000 members and over half a million "contributors." [6]

The precise public effect of all this activity has not been a subject of this book, but it is possible to assess it in a general way. It appears true, for instance, that the anti-imperialists succeeded in putting the expansionists a bit on the defensive. Drawing upon traditional American ideals, attitudes, and prejudices, they were able to check the annexationist mania of the moment and arouse the normal sentiment against colonialism. This helped in forcing the more zealous expansionists to trim their sails. Under a steady barrage of anti-imperialist speeches, pamphlets, and articles, they adopted more temperate and even defensive justifications for McKinley's policies, dwelling less on the ennobling virtues of war, the white man's burden, and America's Asian destiny and more on potential profits and the difficulty of withdrawing from the new possessions. The colonialist surge, subject to anti-imperialist attack and other weakening influences, faded after 1900 as quickly as the anti-imperialist movement itself. By 1902 a close associate of Theodore Roosevelt, Charles J. Bonaparte, could tell a Danish friend that no one but a few "Jingoes" wanted any more colonies. The Philippines had "cost us a great deal of money; and any benefits which have resulted from it to this country, are, as yet, imperceptible to the naked eye." [7]

The fact remains that the anti-imperialists failed to achieve the goals they set for themselves, either in an immediate or long-range sense. New territories were officially annexed. The insurrection in the Philippines was mercilessly stamped out. McKinley, whose defeat in the election of 1900 was sought by a large number of anti-imperialists, won re-election easily and after his assassination was succeeded by the arch-expansionist Roosevelt. The American empire was established as a fact over the protests of the anti-imperialists.

The failure of the anti-imperialists to prevent the expansionists' victory of 1898–1900 had several causes. The most obvious was simply their inability to persuade their countrymen of the truth of their dire forecasts.

Hitches, flaws, inconsistencies, and compromises in their own activities and arguments weakened the anti-imperialist position. Those who listened to Carl Schurz must have been confused by the fact that he alternated between an insistence upon immediate and full independence for the new possessions and schemes for setting up protectorates until the inhabitants were "ready" for independence. No matter how honest his motives or practical his objectives, Charles Francis Adams' attack on his fellow anti-imperialists in the spring of 1899 certainly did the movement no good in the eyes of the general public. Nor did the strained logic revealed by Andrew Carnegie and many others when they declared imperialism wrong as a matter of principle but stood firm only against the annexation of the Philippines. Or George Hoar's willingness to accept an expansionist victory by default in Hawaii prior to putting up a real fight against the annexation of the Philippines and Puerto Rico. How impressive could the anti-imperialists be when Benjamin Harrison waited until the dust had settled from the 1900 campaign before entraining for Ann Arbor to make his tardy declaration against imperialism? Or when "Czar" Reed, at the very moment when his voice and influence were badly needed by other anti-imperialists, quit Congress for moneymaking and the scribbling of ironical anti-imperialist memos that never left the privacy of his study?

President McKinley's own actions made it difficult for the anti-imperialists to translate their moral and idealistic fervor into a political force strong enough to block his program. Understanding a President's tremendous power to take the political initiative, McKinley committed the United States to a series of *faits accomplis* before any effective protest could be made: ordering Dewey to Manila Bay, sending American troops to the Philippines to secure the results of the Commodore's triumph, and dispatching a compliant peace commission to Paris to negotiate the treaty. These events occurred within the space of a few months, and it would have taken an extraordinarily strong, united, and determined lot of anti-imperialists to check the President during this period.

But anti-imperialists were in no such position of strength and unity. The Democrats were at a disadvantage because they had bellowed for war in 1898 as loudly as anyone, because Bryan had intervened in behalf of the peace treaty, and because their party had no other leader of national importance who could take charge of a bi-partisan anti-imperialist coalition aimed at defeating the treaty. The impact of the mugwumps was limited by their disunity on objectives and their position as independent critics standing completely aloof from the national party system. Suspicious of the wiles of professional politicians and hostile to compromise, they spent valuable time reciting the past errors of both Republicans and Democrats, thus courting trouble in broadening the base of their support. The Republican anti-imperialists, on the other hand, were hamstrung by partisanship. It prevented either Hoar or Harrison from making full-fledged commitments to the movement. Hoar, who refused to consider taking the lead of any but a pure Republican protest, spent an inordinate amount of time fending off and quarreling with mugwumps and justifying McKinley to other anti-imperialists. Harrison, though full of venom against the President, delayed attacking his administration until December, 1900, precisely because he wished to do nothing that would cause it political damage.

Another handicap facing the anti-imperialists in their attempts to influence public opinion was the matter of age. Had the twelve men discussed in this book all celebrated their birthdays on the same day in 1900, their collective cake would have groaned under the weight of 835 candles: Schurz was seventy-one, James fifty-eight, Godkin sixty-nine, Norton seventy-three, Atkinson seventy-three, Adams sixty-five, Hoar seventy-four, Carnegie sixty-five, Harrison sixty-seven, Boutwell eighty-two, Sherman seventy-seven, and Reed sixty-one —their average age was over sixty-nine years. Men born in the 1820s and 1830s were unlikely to have great powers of persuasion over a nation just entering a brave new century.

Finally, the anti-imperialists labored under the disadvantage of having the negative side of the debate. They had to say no, to ask a people aroused by American armed triumphs to surrender the fruits of victory. They had "to blow cold upon the hot excitement," as William James put it. Failure came in part because it was not possible to make Americans ashamed of themselves and afraid of the future at a time when they were enjoying fresh breezes of prosperity, glory, and optimism after more than a decade of depression and social strife. The anti-imperialists had run headlong into the fact that nothing succeeds like success.

Thus they were unable to prevent the acquisition of an empire. The record of later years shows that their long-run impact was comparably slight. Anti-imperialist sentiment was of secondary importance in the decision of the 1930s to set the Philippines on the road to full independence.[8] The fact that Puerto Rico has to date been denied statehood cannot be regarded as a vindication of the anti-imperialists because they wanted no colonies at all, and most of them believed that, if new territories were annexed, America's constitutional traditions required that they be made states. It is interesting to note that as late as 1963 one of the nation's most prominent political columnists, Walter Lippmann, remarked that the chances for Puerto Rican statehood were "virtually nil" because Congress would never grant full political status in the Union to "what is in fact a foreign people speaking a foreign language and living under quite different social institutions."[9] Carl Schurz would have applauded Congress' reasoning but deplored its keeping the Caribbean island in a dependent and unequal state.

The anti-imperialists may have helped discourage the eruption of another campaign to annex foreign territories, but they did not prevent the wholesale intervention in the Caribbean and Central America that characterized the hemispheric policy of the United States until the 1930s. More importantly, they failed to stop the international clock. Despite temptations, the United States never retreated into the isolationism of the nineteenth century but remained on the scene as a major participant in world affairs. At this writing the United States is involved politically and economically everywhere in the world, a veteran of four major wars in this century, and the greatest military and naval power in the world. Perhaps a few of the anti-imperialists would have taken pride in these facts, but most of them would have been dismayed. They would not have called this the "American Century." More likely they would have taken their cue from William Graham Sumner, who branded American imperialism as "The Conquest of the United States by Spain," and would have called the twentieth-century story of involvement, war, and power "The Final Victory of Europe."

An Appraisal of the Anti-Imperialists

The historian has the duty to judge as well as analyze and describe. Besides appraising their impact on America it is necessary to appraise the anti-imperialists themselves and weigh both their errors and their achievements.

As political tacticians they are vulnerable to criticism, not only because they failed to maintain a united front (the result of honest disagreements) but also because they took a perverse delight in airing their differences in public. This open squabbling spoke well for their irrepressible individualism and their faith in free debate but not so well for their political judgment. They made another tactical error by reacting to all their opponents as if they were headstrong and romantic belligerents like Theodore Roosevelt and Albert Beveridge. The more cautious and influential, like McKinley and Hay, saw no way to escape from the Philippines, and perhaps did not even want to, but they had no interest in studying the map for new lands to conquer. In fact, when McKinley sent civilian commissions to the Philippines to study the problems of governing the islands, he twice appointed as chairmen men who had originally opposed annexing them, Jacob G. Schurman and William Howard Taft. Anti-imperialists certainly had grounds for disagreement with the administration, but few of them understood how narrow the grounds of opposition were on certain issues.[10]

The anti-imperialists may be criticized as diplomatic strategists and as advocates of alternative policies that were notably impracticable. It is the virtually unanimous judgment of diplomatic historians that there was no politic way to get out of the Philippines after Dewey's naval victory of May 1, 1898. The American people would have rejected returning the islands to Spain as a perfidious betrayal of those Filipinos who had cooperated in the American victory at Manila. A protectorate, a favorite scheme of some of the more prominent anti-imperialists, would have committed the United States to involvement in the Far East without providing it with the power necessary to exercise its responsibilities. Ceding the Philippines to a foreign power other than Spain would have sparked fierce resentment among other nations and endangered the peace of the area. It is highly unlikely that it would have been possible to create any kind of international consortium to guarantee the neutrality and protect the security of the Philippines, or to make it work if it could have been created. Giving the Philippines immediate independence and then leaving them to their own devices might have touched off a general Asian war among the great powers with interests in the Far East, a war into which the United States would almost surely have been drawn. One can only speculate on these matters, of course, but there is little assurance that Aguinaldo and his followers could have united the Filipinos behind them and established a workable system of self-government and even less that they could have resisted falling prey to the aggression of another country. As George F. Kennan has written:

> The alternative to the establishment of American power in the Philippines . . . was not a nice, free, progressive Philippine Republic: it was Spanish, German, or Japanese domination. Abstention on our part from the taking of the Philippines could have been argued, and was, from the standpoint of *our* interests; it could scarcely have been argued from the interests of the Filipinos themselves.[11]

As prophets the anti-imperialists also fell into error. Three of their most important prophecies were proved wrong by the passage of time. Undemocratic modes of colonial rule did not produce a tyrannical backlash in the United States. The annexation of the Philippines, Hawaii, and Puerto Rico, although foreshadowing a long-term extension of American interests in Asia and three decades of interventionist diplomacy in Central America and the Caribbean, did not lead to a continuing orgy of territorial expansion. And American colonial rule, however imperfect, was not characterized by incompetence, corruption, brutality, or injustice. Perhaps because the United States had no vital need to exploit the resources of its colonies it made a record as imperial master which, compared with traditional European examples, was notably intelligent, restrained, and humane.[12]

There is also the question of whether the anti-imperialists failed as moralists. Christopher Lasch, noting that many anti-imperialists believed the Filipinos unfit for self-government by American standards, charges that they were "un-Christian" in wanting to abandon the natives to their own fate.[13] This criticism fails to reckon with what most anti-imperialists thought the consequences of independence would be. Despite their prevailing assumption that Filipinos were not as competent in political matters as their American masters, the anti-imperialists did not believe that independence would be followed by anarchy, misery, and resumed foreign domination. Impressed by Aguinaldo's talent in setting up his own insurrectionary "republic" and leading the fight against American forces, the advocates of independence were convinced that their policy would lead, not to disaster, but to the founding of an independent Philippine republic. Had the Filipinos tried and failed in their attempt to govern themselves and fend off foreign pressures, the anti-imperialists would have been proved wrong as prophets, not as moralists.

They can be condemned as racists. Whether they used words like "superior" and "inferior" or "civilized" and "uncivilized," they thought of peoples in the categories of racism. George Hoar was generally an exception, but even he gave himself over to this kind of thinking on occasion. The unhappy fact is that few Americans were immune to the prevailing racism of the late nineteenth century. The anti-imperialists were no better or worse than their countrymen.

The anti-imperialists also left much to be desired in their role as guardians of and spokesmen for the nation's ideals. Their idealism and selflessness were too often offset by a narrow conservatism and meanness of spirit. Their motives were both noble and ignoble, their declarations both grand and picayune. At times they seemed to be men with little faith in the resiliency of their own nation. Although they claimed to regard it as the most wonderful on earth, they made it sound like one of the most fragile. How much faith could Carl Schurz have had in the strength and viability of America's vaunted democratic principles and institutions if he believed that colonial rule in the Philippines would rapidly erode the principles or that Puerto Rican statehood would inexorably poison the institutions?

Finally, the anti-imperialists failed to offer an alternative vision of the nation's future. Criticizing the new expansionist conception of America's place in international affairs, they prescribed nothing more enticing than a return to the past. They knew that the annexation of faraway territories and alien peoples was inconsistent with America's past traditions, but it did not occur to them to question the continued worth and relevance of the traditions themselves. Making no effort to remold the American heritage in new patterns and adapt it to the twentieth century, they served notice that an imperial career would signal the end of the America that had been. They did not offer a vision of what America could become.

There is also much to praise in the anti-imperialist record. Later events vindicated their prediction that the possession of Pacific colonies would weaken rather than strengthen the diplomatic and military position of the United States. As early as 1907 President Theodore Roosevelt acknowledged that the distant and poorly defended Philippines were the "heel of Achilles" of American policy in the Far East and considered announcing to the world that they would soon be given their independence. Nothing of the sort was done, however, and for forty years the islands remained a hostage to American strategy in Asia, complicating and inhibiting policy *vis-à-vis* Japan from the time of Theodore Roosevelt to Franklin Roosevelt. When Japanese-American relations finally degenerated into open hostility, war commenced with a Japanese strike at the two exposed flanks of American power—Hawaii and the Philippines, the gains of 1898.

A judgment on the anti-imperialists' contention that colonies would not add important strength to the American economy depends upon one's definition of the word "important." Individual firms and industries obviously profited from the colonies while many others were quite unaffected by the new order. What is clear, however, is that Edward Atkinson and others were correct in their belief that imperial possessions would not measurably enhance the health and vigor of the American economy. Exports to Latin America and the Far East have increased significantly in the course of the twentieth century, as have capital investments, but the increase has been a general one, not restricted to or explainable by America's presence in her new colonies.[14]

Although the anti-imperialists were wrong in their dark predictions of what would happen in the United States as a direct result of colonialism abroad, their political logic on this point was irrefutable. There *is* no answer to their charge that a nation that believes in representative government has no business ruling other peoples against their consent, no matter how gentle the rule or how little it impinges on the lives of the people in the mother country. "Kings can have subjects; it is a question whether a republic can," George Kennan has remarked, adding:

> If it is true that our society is really capable of knowing only the quantity which we call "citizen," that it debauches its own innermost nature when it tries to deal with the quantity called "subject," then the potential scope of our

system is limited; then it can extend only to people of our own kind—people who have grown up in the same peculiar spirit of independence and self-reliance, people who can accept, and enjoy, and content themselves with our institutions. In this case, the ruling of distant peoples is not our dish.[15]

One could have hoped that men as intelligent, as broad in their vision, as socially established as the leading anti-imperialists might have succeeded in transcending the racist thinking of their times. Yet even their racism was more realistic than the patronizing policies of uplift offered by the expansionists because it took into account the difficulty Americans would have in dealing with "inferior" races. Charles Francis Adams was scornful of prattle about the "white man's burden" and "lifting up inferior races." Considering the "unchristian, brutal, exterminating" treatment the Indian had been subjected to by American settlers and the nation's "long, shameful record" with Negroes and Chinese, it was ridiculous to think of the United States as in any way specially fitted to govern less familiar peoples.[16] Adams was right. The bloody streak of racial tension evident throughout the history of the United States, the all-too-evident fact that the streak is nowhere near its end, the inability of Americans abroad (soldiers and civilians) to resist stereotyping colored peoples as "little brown brothers," "chinks," "Japs," "gooks," or whatever—all this points to the conclusion that the "Anglo-Saxon" majority of the United States has found it unusually difficult to deal with people of other races and cultures. America's relatively good record as colonial ruler was not the result of an abandonment of racism but the product of ideals and circumstances that operated in spite of racist thinking. Racism, in fact, caused some of the worst blots on that colonial record.

There was a great need in 1899 and 1900 for someone to challenge the self-congratulatory paternalism of expansionists in the Philippines, who explained that the bloody spanking they were administering to the childish but devious natives was for the latters' own good. The anti-imperialists provided the moral challenge to this arrogant and expedient explanation. William James, remarking the ease with which imperialists justified killing in the name of political abstractions, launched devastating attacks against the amorality and pointlessness of Theodore Roosevelt's love of violence and struggle. Even earlier Charles Eliot Norton had warned that the United States could not escape guilt by punishing Spanish murder in Cuba with still more death. The moral dilemmas and ironies of imperialism were perhaps never dissected more expertly than by Finley Peter Dunne's "Mr. Dooley," who declaimed:

> We say to thim: "Naygurs," we say, "poor, dissolute, uncovered wretches," says we, "whin th' crool hand iv Spain forged man'cles f'r ye'er limbs, as Hogan says, who was it crossed th' say an' sthruck off th' comealongs? We did,—by dad, we did. An' now, ye mis'rable, childish-minded apes, we propose f'r to larn ye th' uses iv liberty. In ivry city in this unfair land we will erect schoolhouses an' packin' houses an' houses iv correction; an' we'll larn ye our langauge, because 'tis aisier to larn ye ours than to larn oursilves yours. An' we'll give ye clothes, if ye pay f'r thim; an', if ye don't, ye can go without." [17]

The anti-imperialists displayed admirable spirit in making their protest in the face of hostile public opinion. They constantly encountered bitter criticism, including the accusation that they were encouraging the Filipino rebels in their resistance to American authority and thus indirectly causing the deaths of American soldiers. The *New York Times* declared: "The Anti-Imperialist League might go one step further. It might send rifles, Maxim guns, and stores of ammunition to the Filipinos . . . it would be more openly and frankly treasonable." [18] The commander of the New York chapter of the Grand Army of the Republic proclaimed in 1899 that anti-imperialists were unworthy of "the protection of the flag they dishonor and . . . the name of American citizens." [19] After his June 7, 1898, address on "True Patriotism," Charles Eliot Norton was the target of abusive letters and public scoldings, even from George Hoar, a fellow anti-imperialist. One correspondent informed him that "there are stray bullets somewhere that are liable to hit our country's enemies," and another simply warned: "You had better pull out[.] Yours with contempt—A white man." The *Chicago Tribune,* not passing up a chance to criticize an eastern professor, accused Norton of trying "to kill the generous impulses of patriotism and to besmirch the noble cause of humanity upon which the war against Spain is based." [20] Vice-President Roosevelt in 1901 described the anti-imperialists in a letter as "simply unhung traitors, and . . . liars, slanderers and scandalmongers to boot." [21] Dissent in the face of such condemnation was an act of considerable moral courage.

Above all the anti-imperialists served their countrymen well by reminding them of their own identity and purpose in the world. Knowing that it was a departure from traditional American practice to acquire distant, heavily populated colonies for which statehood was not intended, they also understood the deeper significance of this change—that it denoted America's intention to take a place among the great powers of the world in active international politics. The anti-imperialists deserve credit for drawing attention to the magnitude of this new departure, for pointing out the political and moral problems that would follow in its wake, and for refusing to concede that America's new status must necessarily mean the abandonment of her traditional practices. Great powers are not expected to conduct themselves like YMCA counselors. This the anti-imperialists did not fully appreciate, but they did hold out the hope that great power could yield, not greed and amorality, but a sense of national security and a record of justice and magnanimity.

The Heritage of the Anti-Imperialists

The anti-imperialists' concern was always more with the morality and justice of American policy than with the diplomatic decisions and judgments that influenced it. It was partly for this reason that they were unable to propose feasible alternative policies. But this is not a fatal shortcoming in movements of this sort. Their primary accomplishment was to lodge a protest, to demand answers to moral questions that were hard and perhaps impossible to answer, to reassert traditional American ideals. The anti-imperialists are still a reminder of the value of conservative dissent; with their concern for America's traditional values and their own ideological heritage, they were better able than the less historically minded to compare present performance with past principle and then ask: Do they match? Can they be reconciled?

Their answers did not always satisfy a people nurtured on optimism and faith in progress. Their conservatism often prevented them from appreciating the beneficial effects change could have on their nation. Even so, they did comprehend the need for a changing society to remain aware of its founding principles. They understood that a nation that violated its own declared purposes could be wrenched from its moral and spiritual moorings. The anti-imperialists knew that a democratic people were ill-suited to a career as colonialists. They knew that war and imperialism could have unfortunate and unpredictable effects on their own nation and that a preoccupation with problems halfway around the world might divert important national resources to unworthy ends, lower standards of government and political conduct, cause the neglect of pressing domestic problems, and even alter the moral foundations of society itself.

When Charles Francis Adams expressed his misgivings during the Spanish-American War, he was told, "Oh, no!

—such ideas are 'pessimistic'; you should have more faith in the American people!" These reassurances came from a people who believed they were beyond the reach of history—that they could live forever and that nothing could ever happen to their liberties and privileges. The anti-imperialists found it difficult to see far into the future, but at least they knew that it could bring decay, deterioration, and the perversion of principle just as easily as endless progress. It was their office, their purpose, and their achievement to warn a nation of optimists that America could not escape the consequences of its own conduct.

Note on Sources

By far the most important sources for this book are the letters and diaries of the anti-imperialists themselves. In the Manuscript Division of the Library of Congress are the papers of Carl Schurz, Andrew Carnegie, Benjamin Harrison, and John Sherman. Schurz's papers are especially valuable, for they include many letters written by other anti-imperialists as well as Schurz's own correspondence. The Moorfield Storey Papers in the Library of Congress are extremely useful for the same reason, as are the W. A. Croffut Papers in the same location. Occasional letters of interest also appear in the Library's collections of the papers of Grover Cleveland, William Jennings Bryan, William McKinley, and Justin Morrill. At the Houghton Library of Harvard University are four collections of special importance, the papers of William James, E. L. Godkin, Charles Eliot Norton, and Thomas Wentworth Higginson. The other manuscript repository of particular interest to the student of anti-imperialism is the Massachusetts Historical Society in Boston, where one may consult the papers of Edward Atkinson, Charles Francis Adams, Jr., and George F. Hoar.

In addition to the manuscript collections, the following sources have been helpful in the preparation of this book. For Carl Schurz, important primary materials are to be found in Frederic Bancroft (ed.), *Speeches, Correspondence and Political Papers of Carl Schurz*, 6 vols., G. P. Putnam's Sons, New York, 1913; Carl Schurz, *The Reminiscences of Carl Schurz*, 3 vols., Doubleday, Page & Company, Garden City, N.Y., 1907–1917; Joseph Schafer (trans. and ed.), *Intimate Letters of Carl Schurz, 1841–1869*, "Publications of the State Historical Society of Wisconsin, Collections," vol. XXX, State Historical Society of Wisconsin, Madison, Wis., 1928; and Robert I. Fulton and Thomas C. Trueblood (compilers), *Patriotic Eloquence Relating to the Spanish-American War and Its Issues*, Charles Scribner's Sons, New York, 1900 (a collection of speeches in which the utterances of other anti-imperialists also appear). The best biographical studies of Schurz are Chester Verne Easum,

The Americanization of Carl Schurz, University of Chicago Press, Chicago, 1929; Claude M. Fuess, *Carl Schurz, Reformer (1829–1906)*, Dodd, Mead & Company, New York, 1932; and Joseph Schafer, *Carl Schurz: Militant Liberal*, The Antes Press, Evansville, Wis., 1930.

For William James, letters are by far the most important sources. In addition to the James Papers at the Houghton Library, the most useful collections are in Henry James (ed.), *The Letters of William James*, 2 vols., The Atlantic Monthly Press, Boston, 1920; and Ralph Barton Perry, *The Thought and Character of William James, As Revealed in Unpublished Correspondence and Notes, Together with His Published Writings*, 2 vols., Little, Brown, and Company, Boston, 1935 (which is also a good biography). Thoughtful remarks about James appear in George Santayana's autobiographical volumes, *Persons and Places: The Background of My Life*, Charles Scribner's Sons, New York, 1944, and *The Middle Span*, Charles Scribner's Sons, New York, 1945.

The student of E. L. Godkin should begin with Godkin's own writings. For his day-to-day reaction to newsworthy events *The Nation* is essential, as is a guide to its contents prepared by Daniel C. Haskell, *The Nation: Volumes 1–105, New York, 1865–1917. Indexes of Titles and Contributors*, 2 vols., The New York Public Library, New York, 1951. For comments on particular issues see Godkin's "Diplomacy and the Newspaper," *North American Review*, CLX (May, 1895), 570–79; and "The Condition of Good Colonial Government," *The Forum*, XXVII (April, 1899), 190–203. Indispensable to an understanding of his role as social critic are the collections of his essays: *Problems of Modern Democracy: Political and Economic Essays*, Charles Scribner's Sons, New York, 1896; *Reflections and Comments, 1865–1895*, Charles Scribner's Sons, New York, 1896; and *Unforeseen Tendencies of Democracy*, Houghton, Mifflin and Company, Boston, 1898. For an outline of his life and some of his letters see Rollo Ogden (ed.), *Life and Letters of Edwin Lawrence Godkin*, 2 vols., The Macmillan Company, New York, 1907. The better secondary studies of Godkin include William M. Armstrong, *E. L. Godkin and American Foreign Policy, 1865–1900*, Bookman Associates, New York, 1957; Allan Nevins, *The Evening Post: A Century of Journalism*, Boni and Liveright, New York, 1922; Gustav Pollak, *Fifty Years of American Idealism: The New York Nation, 1865–1915*, Houghton Mifflin Company, Boston, 1915; and Mary V. MacLachlin, "Edwin Lawrence Godkin: Utilitarian Editor," unpublished Ph.D. dissertation, University of Minnesota, 1948.

For the early political and social views of Charles Eliot Norton, see his *Considerations on Some Recent Social Theories*, Little, Brown, and Co., Boston, 1853. The indispensable work on Norton is that of Sara Norton and M. A. DeWolfe Howe (eds.), *Letters of Charles Eliot Norton with Biographical Comment*, 2 vols., Houghton Mifflin Company, Boston, 1913. A more recent and quite helpful account is to be found in Kermit Vanderbilt, *Charles Eliot Norton: Apostle of Culture in a Democracy*, The Belknap Press of Harvard University Press, Cambridge, Mass., 1959. Two interesting essays are Edward H. Madden, "Charles Eliot Norton on Art and Morals," *Journal of the History of Ideas*, XVIII (July, 1957), 430–38; and Malcolm M. Marsden, "Discriminating Sympathy: Charles Eliot Norton's Unique Gift," *New England Quarterly*, XXXI (December, 1958), 463–83.

For Edward Atkinson see in particular his polemical bulletin, *The Anti-Imperialist*; the pamphlet *The Cost of War and Warfare, from 1898 to 1902, inclusive, Seven Hundred Million Dollars, $700,000,000*, 6th ed., no publisher or city listed, 1902; and several important articles, including "Jingoes and Silverites," *North American Review*, CLXI (November, 1895), 554–60; and "Eastern Commerce: What Is It Worth?" *North American Review*, CLXX (February, 1900), 295–304. A good biography is Harold F. Williamson, *Edward Atkinson: The Biography of an American Liberal, 1827–1905*, Old Corner Book Store, Inc., Boston, 1934.

More for a guide to his ideas than a narrative of his life, see Charles Francis Adams' *Charles Francis Adams, 1835–1915: An Autobiography; With a Memorial Address Delivered November 17, 1915, by Henry Cabot Lodge*, Houghton Mifflin Company, Boston, 1916; and his major historical work *Three Episodes of Massachusetts History: The Settlement of Boston Bay, The Antinomian Controversy, A Study of Church and Town Government*, 2 vols., rev. ed., Houghton Mifflin and Company, Boston, 1903. His most revealing anti-imperialist speech is *"Imperialism" and "The Tracks of our Forefathers," A Paper Read by Charles Francis Adams Before the Lexington, Massachusetts, Historical Society, Tuesday, December 20, 1898*, Dana Estes & Company, Boston, 1899. His salvo at the anti-imperialist movement is printed in the *Springfield Daily Republican* (Springfield, Mass.), May 18, 1899. Edward C. Kirkland has written an excellent and amusing biography, *Charles Francis Adams, Jr., 1835–1915: The Patrician at Bay*, Harvard University Press, Cambridge, Mass., 1965.

George F. Hoar of Massachusetts is best studied through the collection of his letters at the Massachusetts Historical Society; the *Congressional Record*; his *Autobiography of Seventy Years*, 2 vols., Charles Scribner's Sons, New York, 1903; and the biography by Frederick H. Gillett, *George Frisbie Hoar*, Houghton Mifflin Company, Boston, 1934. For an understanding of his attitude toward politics and mugwumps, see Hoar's "Popular Discontent with Representative Government," *Annual Report of the American Historical Association for The Year 1895*, Government Printing Office, Washington, 1896, pp. 19–43; "Has the Senate Degenerated?" *The Forum*, XXIII (April, 1897), 129–44; and "Party Government in the United States: The Importance of Government by the Republican Party," *The International Monthly*, II (October, 1900), 418–36. On the imperialism issue see his "Our Duty to the Philippines," *The Independent*, November 9, 1899, pp. 2995–3000. A perceptive contemporary appraisal of Hoar's career is to be found in Thomas Wentworth Higginson, "George Frisbie Hoar," *Proceedings of the American Academy of Arts and Sciences*, XL (July, 1905), 761–69. Two recent essays by Richard E. Welch, Jr., are "Senator George Frisbie Hoar and the Defeat of Anti-Imperialism, 1898–1900," *The Historian*, XXVI (May, 1964), 362–80; and "Opponents and Colleagues: George Frisbie Hoar and Henry Cabot Lodge, 1898–1904," *New England Quarterly*, XXXIX (June, 1966), 182–209.

The most important published work on Carnegie is still Burton J. Hendrick's *The Life of Andrew Carnegie*, 2 vols., Doubleday, Doran & Company, Inc., Garden City, N.Y., 1932, which also includes many letters. Carnegie's own books, both those published before the period of the Spanish-American War and his memoirs published years later, are quite interesting: *An American Four-in-Hand in Britain*, Charles Scribner's Sons, New York, 1884; *Round the World*, Charles Scribner's Sons, New York, 1884; *Triumphant Democracy or Fifty Years' March of The Republic*, Doubleday, Doran & Company, Inc., Garden City, N.Y., 1933 (originally published in 1885); and *Autobiography*, Doubleday, Doran & Company, Inc., Garden City, N.Y., 1933 (originally published in 1920). On the issue of expansion, one should see Carnegie's "The Venezuelan Question," *North American Review*, CLXII (February, 1896), 129–44; "Distant Possessions—The Parting of the Ways," *North American Review*, CLXXVII (August, 1898), 239–48; "Americanism *Versus* Imperialism," *North American Review*, CLXVIII (January, 1899), 1–13; and "Americanism *Versus* Imperialism—II," *North American Review*, CLXVIII (March, 1899), 362–72.

For Benjamin Harrison see his *Views of an Ex-President: Being his Addresses and Writings on Subjects of Public Interest since the Close of his Administration as President of the United States*, The Bowen-Merrill Company, Indianapolis, 1901; A. T. Volwiler, "Harrison, Blaine, and American Foreign Policy, 1889–1893," *Proceedings of the American Philosophical Society*, LXXIX (November, 1938), 637–48; and George W. Baker, Jr., "Benjamin Harrison and Hawaiian Annexation: A Reinterpretation," *Pacific Historical Review*, XXXIII (August, 1964), 295–309.

George S. Boutwell's literary remains make rather drab reading today, but the student of anti-imperialism should see his *Reminiscences of Sixty Years in Public Affairs*, 2 vols., McClure, Phillips & Co., New York, 1902; *The Crisis of the Republic*, Dana Estes & Company, Boston, 1900; *Hawaiian Annexation. Hon. Geo. S. Boutwell's Address before the Boot and Shoe Club of Boston, December 22, 1897*, J. E. Farwell & Co., Printers, Boston, 1898; and *The War of Despotism in the Philippine Islands. Address of the Hon.*

George S. Boutwell, at Springfield, Mass., Sept. 5, 1899, Anti-Imperialist League, no city or date mentioned (probably Boston, 1899 or 1900).

Aside from his papers and an occasional reference that turns up in other scattered works, one has little to go on in an attempt to study the career of John Sherman. Of some help are his *Recollections of Forty Years in the House, Senate and Cabinet: an Autobiography,* 2 vols., The Werner Company, Chicago, 1895; and Theodore E. Burton, *John Sherman,* Houghton Mifflin Company, Boston, 1907. Winfield S. Kerr, *John Sherman: His Life and Public Services,* 2 vols., Sherman, French & Company, Boston, 1908, is heavy going.

The sources for Reed are similarly meager. The material on Reed in this book comes in little bits and pieces from various works. Most helpful is William A. Robinson, *Thomas B. Reed, Parliamentarian,* Dodd, Mead & Company, New York, 1930; less so is Samuel W. McCall's *The Life of Thomas Brackett Reed,* Houghton Mifflin Company, Boston, 1914. See also Reed's "The Safe Pathway of Experience," *North American Review,* CLXIII (October, 1896), 385–94. An essay by Barbara W. Tuchman adds nothing distinctly new but is good reading, "Czar of the House," *American Heritage,* XIV (December, 1962), 32–35, 92–102; Mrs. Tuchman's evaluation of Reed, and the anti-imperialist movement, also appears in Chapter 3 of *The Proud Tower: A Portrait of the World before the War, 1890–1914,* The Macmillan Company, New York, 1966.

A number of interpretations of the anti-imperialist movement deserve careful consideration. The standard work is Fred H. Harrington, "The Anti-Imperialist Movement in the United States, 1898–1900," *Mississippi Valley Historical Review,* XXII (September, 1935), 211–30. One should also see his "Literary Aspects of American Anti-Imperialism, 1898–1902," *New England Quarterly,* X (December, 1937), 650–67. A slow-moving but informative discussion of "The Anti-Imperialist League" by Maria C. Lanzar is to be found in the *Philippine Social Science Review,* III (August, November, 1930), 7–41, 118–32; IV (July, October, 1932), 189–98, 239–54, and V (July, October, 1933), 222–30, 248–79. See Harold Baron on "Anti-Imperialism and the Democrats," *Science & Society,* XXI (Summer, 1958), 222–39. On the problem of racist attitudes in the anti-imperialist movement see Christopher Lasch, "The Anti-Imperialists, the Philippines, and the Inequality of Man," *Journal of Southern History,* XXIV (August, 1958), 319–31. On earlier anti-imperialist manifestations, see Donald Marquand Dozer, "Anti-Expansionism during the Johnson Administration," *Pacific Historical Review,* XII (September, 1943), 253–75; and Dozer's "Anti-Imperialism in the United States, 1865–1895: Opposition to Annexation of Overseas Territories," unpublished Ph.D. dissertation, Department of History, Harvard University, [1936].

The view of the anti-imperialists as advocates of an informal empire is developed in William Appleman Williams, *The Contours of American History*, The World Publishing Company, Cleveland, 1961; Williams, *The Tragedy of American Diplomacy*, rev. ed., A Delta Book, New York, 1962; Walter LaFeber, *The New Empire: An Interpretation of American Expansion, 1860–1898*, Cornell University Press, Ithaca, N.Y., 1963; and John W. Rollins, "The Anti-Imperialists and Twentieth Century American Foreign Policy," *Studies on the Left*, III (1962), 9–24.

Sharp contemporary attacks against the anti-imperialists may be found in Elting E. Morison et al. (eds.), *The Letters of Theodore Roosevelt*, 8 vols., Harvard University Press, Cambridge, Mass., 1951–1954; and Fred C. Chamberlin, *The Blow from Behind*, Lee and Shepard, Boston, 1903.

On the election of 1900 see "Bryan or McKinley? The Present Duty of American Citizens," *North American Review*, CLXXI (October, 1900), 433–516, a symposium by Adlai E. Stevenson, Ben Tillman, Richard Croker, George F. Hoar, Andrew Carnegie, and others; and Thomas A. Bailey, "Was the Presidential Election of 1900 a Mandate on Imperialism?" *Mississippi Valley Historical Review*, XXIV (June, 1937), 43–52.

Two recent and excellent works on America's colonies and how they were governed are Whitney T. Perkins, *Denial of Empire: The United States and Its Dependencies*, A. W. Sythoff, Leyden, Netherlands, 1962; and Theodore Friend, *Between Two Empires: The Ordeal of the Philippines, 1929–1946*, Yale University Press, New Haven, 1965. Earlier works of interest on the subject are Garel A. Grunder and William E. Livezey, *The Philippines and the United States*, University of Oklahoma Press, Norman, Okla., 1951; and Julius W. Pratt, *America's Colonial Experiment: How the United States Gained, Governed, and In Part Gave Away a Colonial Empire*, Prentice-Hall, Inc., New York, 1950.

On the issue of mugwumpery see Geoffrey Blodgett, *The Gentle Reformers: Massachusetts Democrats in the Cleveland Era*, Harvard University Press, Cambridge, Mass., 1966; Blodgett, "The Mind of the Boston Mugwump," *Mississippi Valley Historical Review*, XLVIII (March, 1962), 614–34; Gordon S. Wood, "The Massachusetts Mugwumps," *New England Quarterly*, XXXIII (December, 1960), 435–51; and Gerald W. McFarland, "The New York Mugwumps of 1884: A Profile," *Political Science Quarterly*, LXXVIII (March, 1963), 40–58.

Other works of particular interest include Richard Hofstadter's essay, "Manifest Destiny and the Philippines," in *America in Crisis: Fourteen Crucial Episodes in American History*, edited by Daniel Aaron, Alfred A. Knopf, New York, 1952; William E. Leuchtenburg, "Progressivism and Imperialism: The Progressive Movement and American Foreign Policy, 1898–1916," *Mississippi Valley Historical Review*, XXXIX (December, 1952), 483–

504; Matthew Josephson, *The Politicos, 1865–1896*, Harcourt, Brace and Company, New York, 1938, still a fund of fascinating political information; Edward C. Kirkland's two works on the thought of businessmen and conservatives, including interesting discussions of Carnegie, Adams, Godkin, and Atkinson, *Business in the Gilded Age: The Conservatives' Balance Sheet*, University of Wisconsin Press, Madison, Wis., 1952, and *Dream and Thought in the Business Community, 1860–1900*, Quadrangle Books, Chicago, 1964; H. Wayne Morgan, *William McKinley and His America*, Syracuse University Press, Syracuse, N.Y., 1963; Margaret Leech, *In the Days of McKinley*, Harper & Brothers, New York, 1959; William A. Russ, Jr.'s two works on Hawaii, *The Hawaiian Revolution (1893–94)* and *The Hawaiian Republic (1894–98) and Its Struggle To Win Annexation*, published in 1959 and 1961, respectively, by Susquehanna University Press in Selinsgrove, Pennsylvania; Leon Wolff, *Little Brown Brother: America's Forgotten Bid for Empire which Cost 250,000 Lives*, Longmans, Green and Co., Ltd., London, 1961; and two articles by Paolo E. Coletta, "Bryan, Anti-Imperialism and Missionary Diplomacy," *Nebraska History*, XLIV (September, 1963), 167–87, and "Bryan, McKinley, and the Treaty of Paris," *Pacific Historical Review*, XXVI (May, 1957), 131–46.

Addendum, 1985

The most important new works on American anti-imperialism in 1898–1900 published since the original appearance of this book are cited in the new preface (see pp. vii–xx). Other books and articles of significance appear in this addendum.

Among general assessments of the anti-imperialist movement, one of the most stimulating is Frank Freidel, "Dissent in the Spanish-American War and the Philippine Insurrection," in Samuel Eliot Morison, Frederick Merk, and Frank Freidel, *Dissent in Three American Wars*, Harvard University Press, Cambridge, 1970, which relies substantially on Fred H. Harrington's pioneering essays, and on *Twelve Against Empire*. An able summary from a European perspective is available in Göran Rystad, "Ambiguous Anti-Imperialism: American Expansionism and Its Critics at the Turn of the Century," in Marc Chénetier and Rob Kroes, eds., *Impressions of a Gilded Age: The American Fin De Siècle*, Amerika Instituut, Universiteit van Amsterdam, Amsterdam, 1983, pp. 242–67. Another competent summary, generally uncritical of the anti-imperialists' outlooks and actions, is E. Berkeley Tompkins, "Anti-Imperialism," in Alexander DeConde, ed., *Encyclopedia of American Foreign Policy: Studies of the Principal Movements and Ideas*, 3 vols., Charles Scribner's Sons, New York, 1978, vol. I, pp. 25–32.

Several books covering subjects of greater scope embody able summaries and assessments of anti-imperialism. These include two in which the authors see the anti-imperialist movement in light of the historic "peace movement." Especially interesting for its analysis of why anti-imperialists and those in the peace movement sometimes agreed and often did not is David S. Patterson, *Toward a Warless World: The Travail of the American Peace Movement, 1887–1914,* Indiana University Press, Bloomington, 1976; noting the failure of peace societies to contribute significantly to anti-imperialism is Charles DeBenedetti, *The Peace Reform in American History,* Indiana University Press, Bloomington, 1980. Ernest R. May, *American Imperialism: A Speculative Essay,* Atheneum, New York, 1968, emphasizes the transatlantic connections of anti-imperialists, relating this to the wave of anti-colonialism in Britain and on the Continent. Attempting obliquely to relate anti-imperialism to contemporary social concerns in the United States is Gerald F. Linderman, *The Mirror of War: American Society and the Spanish-American War,* University of Michigan Press, Ann Arbor, 1974. An uncontroversial summary can be found in Charles S. Campbell, *The Transformation of American Foreign Relations, 1865–1900,* Harper & Row, New York, 1976.

A brief but convenient essay that places Andrew Carnegie's anti-imperialism in the context of his interest in peace movements is David S. Patterson, "Andrew Carnegie's Quest for World Peace," *Proceedings of the American Philosophical Society,* CXIV (October, 1970), 371–83. Stressing the limitations of William James's commitment to social causes generally is George R. Garrison and Edward H. Madden, "William James—Warts and All," *American Quarterly,* XXIX (Summer, 1977), 207–21. Two able works on Moorfield Storey, a prominent anti-imperialist not discussed in this book, are William B. Hixson, Jr., *Moorfield Storey and the Abolitionist Tradition,* Oxford University Press, New York, 1972; and Richard E. Welch, Jr., "The Law, Right Conduct, and Moorfield Storey," *Historian,* XLI (February, 1979), 225–40.

Willard B. Gatewood, Jr., emphasizes the vacillating and ambivalent response of American blacks to American imperialism in *Black Americans and the White Man's Burden, 1898–1903,* University of Illinois Press, Urbana, 1975. More about the mugwump background of many anti-imperialists, and about how historians have treated mugwumpery, is available in Geoffrey Blodgett, "The Mugwump Reputation, 1870 to the Present," *Journal of American History,* LXVI (March, 1980), 867–87; John G. Sproat, *"The Best Men": Liberal Reformers in the Gilded Age,* Oxford University Press, New York, 1968; and Dale Baum, " 'Noisy but not Numerous': The Revolt of the Massachusetts Mugwumps," *Historian,* XLI (February, 1979), 241–56, who believes mugwumps are overrated historically and "overstudied."

Though incorporated in his book on anti-imperialism, E. Berkeley Tompkins's intriguing account of the anti-imperialist scramble to find the right issues and candidates in the election of 1900 is also available in the article, "Scylla and Charybdis: The Anti-Imperialist Dilemma in the Election of 1900," *Pacific Historical Review,* XXXVI (May, 1967), 143–61. John M. Gates contends but does not prove that Aguinaldo's guerrillas increased their military activities in proportion to anti-imperialist rhetoric during the 1900 campaign in "Philippine Guerrillas, American Anti-Imperialists, and the Election of 1900," *Pacific Historical Review*, XLVI (February, 1977), 51–64.

More on the issue of racism is in Walter L. Williams, "United States Indian Policy and the Debate over Philippine Annexation: Implications for the Origins of American Imperialism," *Journal of American History*, LXVI (March, 1980), 810–31; Williams argues the similarity between "colonial" treatment of Indians and of Filipinos, noting that all but a few anti-imperialists, such as Charles Francis Adams, Jr., rejected the analogy.

An earlier instance of anti-imperialism may be examined in Thomas J. Osborne, *"Empire Can Wait": American Opposition to Hawaiian Annexation, 1893–1898*, Kent State University Press, Kent, Ohio, 1981, a full if immodestly written account of anti-imperialists' efforts to block annexation of the Hawaiian islands.

Philip S. Foner and Richard C. Winchester, eds., *The Anti-Imperialist Reader: A Documentary History of Anti-Imperialism in the United States. Volume I: From the Mexican War to the Election of 1900,* Holmes & Meier Publishers, New York, 1984, is a rich and excellent collection of primary sources documenting the views and actions of American anti-imperialists. The documents in the otherwise-naïve Roger J. Bresnahan, *In Time of Hesitation: American Anti-Imperialists and the Philippine-American War,* New Day Publishers, Quezon City, Philippines, 1981, are valuable.

Reference Notes

INTRODUCTION

1. On the Democrats and imperialism, see John A. Garraty, *Henry Cabot Lodge: A Biography*, Alfred A. Knopf, New York, 1953, p. 201; Richard Hofstadter, "Manifest Destiny and the Philippines," in *America in Crisis: Fourteen Crucial Episodes in American History*, ed. Daniel Aaron, Alfred A. Knopf, New York, 1952, p. 189; William E. Leuchtenburg, "Progressivism and Imperialism: The Progressive Movement and American Foreign Policy, 1898–1916," *Mississippi Valley Historical Review*, XXXIX (December, 1952), 486; H. Wayne Morgan, *William McKinley and His America*, Syracuse University Press, Syracuse, N.Y., 1963, p. 419; Harold Baron, "Anti-Imperialism and the Democrats," *Science & Society*, XXI (Summer, 1958), 222–39; and Christopher Lasch, "The Anti-Imperialists, the Philippines, and the Inequality of Man," *Journal of Southern History*, XXIV (August, 1958), 319–31.

   For Bryan, see Merle Curti, *Bryan and World Peace*, "Smith College Studies in History," vol. XVI, nos. 3–4, Department of History of Smith College, Northampton, Mass., 1931, pp. 120–26; Paolo E. Coletta, "Bryan, McKinley, and the Treaty of Paris," *Pacific Historical Review*, XXVI (May, 1957), 131–46, and "Bryan, Anti-Imperialism and Missionary Diplomacy," *Nebraska History*, XLIV (September, 1963), 168–70.

2. Quoted in Geoffrey Blodgett, *The Gentle Reformers: Massachusetts Democrats in the Cleveland Era*, Harvard University Press, Cambridge, Mass., 1966, p. 267.

CHAPTER 1/*The American Mugwump*

1. Diary of Thomas Wentworth Higginson, February 10, 1899, Thomas Wentworth Higginson Papers, Houghton Library, Harvard University, Cambridge, Massachusetts. Cited hereafter as Higginson Papers.

2. Clipping, *Boston Evening Transcript*, June 13, 1884, Moorfield Storey Papers, Library of Congress, Washington, D.C. Cited hereafter as Storey Papers.

3. Diary entry, April 21, 1898, David A. Shannon (ed.), *Beatrice Webb's American Diary, 1898*, The University of Wisconsin Press, Madison, Wis., 1963, p. 41.

4. Everett P. Wheeler, *Sixty Years of American Life: Taylor to Roosevelt, 1850 to 1910*, E. P. Dutton & Company, New York, 1917, p. 173; Edward Atkinson to George F. Hoar, August 12, 1898, Edward Atkinson Papers, Massachusetts Historical Society, Boston, Massachusetts. Cited hereafter as Atkinson Papers, MHS.

5. Clipping attached to Diary of Thomas Wentworth Higginson, November 30, 1873, Higginson Papers.

6. Edward Atkinson to G. F. Hoar, August 12, 1898, Atkinson Papers, MHS.

7. William James to F. B. Bromberg, June 30, 1884, in Ralph Barton Perry, *The Thought and Character of William James, As Revealed in Unpublished Correspondence and Notes, Together with his Published Writings*, Little, Brown, and Company, Boston, 1935, vol. II, p. 297.

8. E. L. Godkin to Carl Schurz, June 28, 1872 (draft), quoted in Edwin Lawrence Godkin, *Problems of Modern Democracy: Political and Economic Essays*, ed. Morton Keller, The Belknap Press of Harvard University Press, Cambridge, Mass., 1966, p. xxx.

9. E. L. Godkin to Moorfield Storey, May 23, 1891, E. L. Godkin Papers, Houghton Library, Harvard University, Cambridge, Massachusetts. Cited hereafter as Godkin Papers.

10. Mark Twain to William Dean Howells, September 17, 1884, Henry Nash Smith and William M. Gibson (eds.), *Mark Twain—Howells Letters: The Correspondence of Samuel L. Clemens and William D. Howells, 1872–1910*, The Belknap Press, Cambridge, Mass., 1960, vol. II, pp. 508–09.

11. See his analysis of this culture and the "mugwump mind" in *Anti-Intellectualism in American Life*, Alfred A. Knopf, New York, 1963, pp. 400–403.

12. E. L. Godkin to Moorfield Storey, May 23, 1891, Godkin Papers; statement of Erving Winslow, *Boston Evening Transcript*, November 24, 1900.

13. Gerald W. McFarland, "The New York Mugwumps of 1884: A Profile," *Political Science Quarterly*, LXXVIII (March, 1963), 47, 49. McFarland makes the important point that "the Mugwumps were a minority within a minority; most of the members of their class did not support the Mugwump movement. . . . The point is not that all men of a certain class were Mugwumps—such class solidarity not being characteristic of American political life—but that nearly all the Mugwumps were members of one class." p. 44.

14. Van Wyck Brooks, *New England: Indian Summer, 1865–1915*, E. P. Dutton & Co., Inc., New York, 1940, p. 98.

15. William James to Henry James, May 9, 1886, in Henry James (ed.), *The Letters of William James*, The Atlantic Monthly Press, Boston, 1920, vol. I, p. 252.

16. C. E. Norton to Dewitt Miller, July 6, 1894, quoted in Kermit Vanderbilt, *Charles Eliot Norton: Apostle of Culture in a Democracy*, The Belknap Press of Harvard University Press, Cambridge, Mass., 1959, p. 198.

17. Arthur Mann, *Yankee Reformers in the Urban Age*, The Belknap Press of Harvard University Press, Cambridge, Mass., 1954, pp. 2–3.

18. Quoted in Vernon Louis Parrington, *Main Currents in American Thought: An Interpretation of American Literature from the Beginnings to 1920*, Vol. III: *The Beginnings of Critical Realism in America, 1860–1920*, Harcourt, Brace and Company, New York, 1930, p. 58.

19. Quoted in Leonard D. White (with assistance of Jean Schneider), *The Republican Era: 1869–1901: A Study in Administrative History*, The Macmillan Company, New York, 1958, p. 8.

20. Charles Francis Adams, *Charles Francis Adams, 1835–1915: An Autobiography; With a Memorial Address delivered November 17, 1915, by Henry Cabot Lodge*, Houghton Mifflin Company, Boston, 1916, p. 190.

21. For some examples of Norton's complaints, see C. E. Norton to Thomas Carlyle, November 16, 1873, to Edward Lee-Childe, September 24, 1876, in Sara Norton and M. A. DeWolfe Howe (eds.), *Letters of Charles Eliot Norton with Biographical Comment*, Houghton Mifflin Company, Boston, 1913, vol. II, pp. 18, 64–65; and C. E. Norton to E. L. Godkin, March 13, 1867, Godkin Papers. The quotation from Godkin is in Samuel P. Hays, *The Response to Industrialism, 1885–1914*, The University of Chicago Press, Chicago, 1957, p. 25.

22. *The Nation*, October 14, 1869, p. 308; Herbert Agar, *The Price of Union*, Houghton Mifflin Company, Boston, 1950, p. 545; Edwin L. Godkin, *Unforeseen Tendencies of Democracy*, Houghton Mifflin and Company, Boston, 1898, pp. 72–74, 79, 90–91; Edwin Lawrence Godkin, *Problems of Modern Democracy: Political and Economic Essays*, Charles Scribner's Sons, New York, 1896, pp. 201, 212.

23. Charles Francis Adams, Jr., *Three Episodes of Massachusetts History: The Settlement of Boston Bay, The Antinomian Controversy, A Study of Church and Town Government*, rev. ed., Houghton, Mifflin and Company, Boston, 1903, vol. II, pp. 965–66, 973ff., 1008–09.

24. George Ticknor, quoted in James Ford Rhodes, *Historical Essays*, The Macmillan Company, New York, 1909, pp. 288–89.

25. Quoted in David Starr Jordan, *The Question of the Philippines. An Address Delivered before the Graduate Club of Leland Stanford Junior*

University on February 14, 1899, John J. Valentine, Palo Alto, Calif., 1899, p. 42.

26. Theodore Roosevelt to H. C. Lodge, April 16, 1886, in Elting E. Morison et al. (eds.), *The Letters of Theodore Roosevelt,* Harvard University Press, Cambridge, Mass., 1951–1954, vol. I, p. 97; James G. Blaine to James A. Garfield, 1880, quoted in Harry Thurston Peck, *Twenty Years of the Republic, 1885–1905,* Dodd, Mead & Company, New York, 1932, p. 32.

27. Richard Hofstadter, *The American Political Tradition and the Men Who Made It,* Vintage Books, New York, 1955, p. 177.

28. Gordon Milne, *George William Curtis & the Genteel Tradition,* Indiana University Press, Bloomington, Ind., 1956, p. 180.

29. Horace N. Fisher to John D. Long, June 16, 1898, in Gardner W. Allen (ed.), *Papers of John Davis Long, 1897–1904,* "Massachusetts Historical Society Collections," Vol. LXXVIII, Massachusetts Historical Society, Boston, 1939, p. 139.

30. Quoted in Paul W. Glad, *The Trumpet Soundeth: William Jennings Bryan and His Democracy, 1896–1912,* University of Nebraska Press, Lincoln, 1960, p. 191.

31. Henry Steele Commager, *The American Mind: An Interpretation of American Thought and Character Since the 1880s,* Yale University Press, New Haven, 1959, pp. 318–19.

32. William Allen White, *Masks in a Pageant,* The Macmillan Company, New York, 1929, p. 81.

33. For other discussions of the mugwumps, see Geoffrey T. Blodgett, "The Mind of the Boston Mugwump," *Mississippi Valley Historical Review,* XLVIII (March, 1962), 614–34; Geoffrey Blodgett, *The Gentle Reformers: Massachusetts Democrats in the Cleveland Era,* Harvard University Press, Cambridge, Mass., 1966; and Frederic Cople Jaher, *Doubters and Dissenters: Cataclysmic Thought in America, 1885–1918,* The Free Press of Glencoe, London, 1964.

CHAPTER 2/*Carl Schurz: The Law and the Prophet*

1. Chester Verne Easum, *The Americanization of Carl Schurz,* University of Chicago Press, Chicago, 1929, p. 42.

2. Carl Schurz to Adolf Meyer, April 19, 1852, and to Henry Meyer, November 20, 1856, in Joseph Schafer (trans. and ed.), *Intimate Letters of Carl Schurz, 1841–1869,* "Publications of the State Historical Society of Wisconsin, Collections," Vol. XXX, State Historical Society of Wisconsin, Madison, Wis., 1928, pp. 109, 173–74.

3. Easum, pp. 332–33.

4. Schafer, pp. 191, 224; Claude M. Fuess, *Carl Schurz, Reformer (1829–1906)*, Dodd, Mead & Company, New York, 1932, p. 213; and Frederic Bancroft (ed.), *Speeches, Correspondence and Political Papers of Carl Schurz*, G. P. Putnam's Sons, New York, 1913, vol. IV, p. 475.

5. Fuess, pp. 2, 158, 235, 282, 322–23; Bancroft, vol. III, p. 98; [Oswald Garrison Villard], "Carl Schurz," *Dictionary of American Biography*, ed. Allan Johnson and Dumas Malone, Charles Scribner's Sons, New York, 1928–1936, vol. XVI, p. 469; and Herbert Agar, *The Price of Union*, Houghton Mifflin Company, Boston, 1950, pp. 519–20.

6. Easum, pp. 222–23, 228–29, 231, 278; Bancroft, vol. I, p. 36.

7. Carl Schurz to G. W. M. Pittman, June 15, 1884, and anti-Blaine campaign speech, August 5, 1898, Bancroft, vol. IV, pp. 204–05, 245–46. Schurz campaigned so vigorously against Blaine that the latter sued him for libel, based on remarks made by Schurz in a Brooklyn campaign speech. The suit was not pushed and never came to a decision. Allan Nevins, *Grover Cleveland: A Study in Courage*, Dodd, Mead & Company, New York, 1933, p. 162.

8. Fuess, p. 387.

9. This was precisely the case in 1896, when Schurz, after a twelve-year stay with the Democrats, switched sides in order to campaign against William Jennings Bryan, whose platform Schurz called "the triumph of sectionalism and communism." Just four years later Schurz switched again and accepted a Democratic platform quite similar to the one of 1896 and this time backed Bryan against William McKinley, whom he opposed as the candidate of imperialism. See below, Chapter 6.

10. James G. Blaine, *Twenty Years of Congress: from Lincoln to Garfield. With a Review of the Events which Led to the Political Revolution of 1860*, The Henry Bill Publishing Company, Norwich, Conn., 1884, vol. II, pp. 152, 439–40.

11. Bancroft, vol. II, pp. 75, 84, 95.

12. *Ibid.*, pp. 77–78, 83–84, 93, 98–99.

13. *Ibid.*, vol. VI, pp. 270–71.

14. *Ibid.*, pp. 271–73.

15. Carl Schurz to William McKinley, April 1 and 12, 1898, Carl Schurz Papers, Library of Congress, Washington, D.C., cited hereafter as Schurz Papers; Carl Schurz to William McKinley, April 8, 1898, Bancroft, vol. V, pp. 457–58; and Schurz, "National Honor," *Harper's Weekly* (March 19, 1898), in Bancroft, vol. V, pp. 456–57.

16. Bancroft, vol. V, pp. 462–63, 471; Carl Schurz to Thomas F. Bayard, April 24, 1898, and draft of letter to [Franklin Smith?], April 25, 1898, Schurz Papers.

17. Carl Schurz to William McKinley, May 9, 1898, Bancroft, vol. V, pp. 465–66.

18. *Ibid.*, vol. V, pp. 480–87, 497–98, vol. VI, p. 76.

19. "Thoughts on American Imperialism," *Century Magazine* (September, 1898), in Bancroft, vol. V, pp. 503–06. After Schurz held a private conversation with Charles Francis Adams in October, 1898, the latter observed that Schurz was "very despondent over the political situation. . . . The phantom of 'Imperialism' weighed upon him. He addressed himself to it like a statesman, and also like a German. If, he argued, we were going to annex Porto Rico, it meant, as a logical sequence, Cuba and Hayti; if we were going to build a Nicaraguan Canal, it meant the ultimate annexation of every thing intervening to it. We were then going to try to absorb some twenty millions of Spanish and African descent with a system of Asiatic and colonial dependencies behind it. This we could not successfully do,—the assimilation attempted was too large." Adams, "Memorabilia," October 27, 1898, Adams Papers, Massachusetts Historical Society, Boston, Massachusetts. Cited hereafter as Adams Papers.

20. Address by Schurz, entitled "The Policy of Imperialism," delivered at the Anti-Imperialistic Conference in Chicago, October 17, 1899, Bancroft, vol. VI, p. 87, and Robert I. Fulton and Thomas C. Trueblood (comps.), *Patriotic Eloquence Relating to the Spanish-American War and Its Issues,* Charles Scribner's Sons, New York, 1900, p. 288; address delivered at the Philadelphia Anti-Imperialistic Conference, February 22, 1900, Bancroft, vol. VI, p. 172.

21. Fulton and Trueblood, p. 271.

22. Bancroft, vol. VI, pp. 101–02. For a discussion of the censorship that did exist, see Margaret Leech, *In the Days of McKinley,* Harper & Brothers, New York, 1959, pp. 364, 400.

23. Bancroft, vol. VI, pp. 182–83, 187, 236–37, 239, 242.

24. *Ibid.*, vol. V, p. 213.

25. Carl Schurz to William McKinley, June 1, 1898, *ibid.*, pp. 472–73.

26. Carl Schurz to William McKinley, September 22, 1898, *ibid.*, p. 519.

27. Fulton and Trueblood, pp. 282–83; Carl Schurz to C. F. Adams, January 16, 1899, Bancroft, vol. VI, pp. 37–38; "The Policy of Imperialism," anti-imperialist address at Chicago, October 17, 1899, Bancroft, vol. VI, pp. 102, 105–06.

28. John Hay to Dr. Waldstein, October 21, 1899, [Henry Adams] (ed.), *Letters of John Hay and Extracts from Diary,* By the author, Washington, D.C., 1908, vol. III, pp. 100–101; the date of the letter is incorrectly given as 1897. After Schurz's Chicago speech, Theodore Roosevelt wrote Henry Cabot Lodge: "I didn't read what Schurz said: I don't care what

that prattling foreigner shrieks or prattles in this crisis." Elting E. Morison et al. (eds.), *The Letters of Theodore Roosevelt*, Harvard University Press, Cambridge, Mass., 1951–1954, vol. II, p. 1086.

29. Richard E. Welch, Jr., "Opponents and Colleagues: George Frisbie Hoar and Henry Cabot Lodge, 1898–1904," *New England Quarterly*, XXXIX (June, 1966), 196.

30. A historian who takes the scheme for a Philippines protectorate more seriously is Richard E. Welch, Jr., "Senator George Frisbie Hoar and the Defeat of Anti-Imperialism, 1898–1900," *The Historian*, XXVI (May, 1964), 362–80.

31. Below, Chapter 5.

32. Carl Schurz to J. G. Schurman, May 8, 1902, Bancroft, vol. VI, pp. 289–90.

CHAPTER 3/*William James: Paradise Lost*

1. James further exhorted Godkin: "Don't curse God and die, dear old fellow. Live and be patient and fight for us a long time yet in this new war." See William James to E. L. Godkin, April 15, 1889, and Christmas Eve, 1895, Henry James (ed.), *The Letters of William James*, The Atlantic Monthly Press, Boston, 1920, vol. I, p. 284, vol. II, pp. 28–30.

2. Ralph Barton Perry, *The Thought and Character of William James, As Revealed in Unpublished Correspondence and Notes, Together with his Published Writings*, Little, Brown, and Company, Boston, 1935, vol. II, p. 208.

3. William James to Carl Schurz, March 16, 1900, Schurz Papers; William James to F. G. Bromberg, June 30, 1884, Perry, vol. II, pp. 296–97; William James to Havelock Ellis, December 4, 1900, William James Papers, Houghton Library, Harvard University, Cambridge, Massachusetts, cited hereafter as James Papers.

4. William James to Henry James, January 22, 1876, Perry, vol. I, p. 365.

5. William James to Henry James, May 9, 1886, to Dickinson S. Miller, August 30, 1896, and to Theodore Flournoy, December 7, 1896, Henry James, vol. I, p. 252, vol. II, pp. 50, 55; William James to Hugo Munsterberg, September 2, 1896, Perry, vol. II, p. 146.

6. William James to Charles Renouvier, May 14, 1878, Perry, vol. I, p. 668.

7. William James to Mrs. E. L. Godkin, March 14, 1902, *ibid.*, vol. II, pp. 294, 298–99.

8. *Ibid.*, p. 702.

9. William James to C. E. Norton, June 26, 1901, and to E. L. Godkin, August 29, 1901, Henry James, vol. II, pp. 152, 161.

10. William James to Mrs. A. V. G. Allen, June 26, 1901, James Papers.

11. Wallace E. Davies, *Patriotism on Parade: The Story of Veterans' and Hereditary Organizations in America, 1783–1900,* Harvard University Press, Cambridge, Mass., 1955, p. 335.

12. William James to William M. Salter, September 11, 1899, Henry James, vol. II, p. 100.

13. William James to Frances R. Morse, September 17, 1899, to Mrs. Henry Whitman, October 5, 1899, to C. E. Norton, June 26, 1901, and to E. L. Godkin, August 29, 1901, *ibid.*, pp. 102–03, 105, 106, 152–53, 161; William James to Carl Stumpf, November 24–28, 1896, Perry, vol. II, p. 191. To Godkin he playfully remarked: "Notwithstanding its 'humble'ness, its fatigues, and its complications, there's no place like home."

14. William James to Frederic Myers, January 1, 1896, Perry, vol. II, p. 305; William James to E. L. Godkin, Christmas Eve, 1895, Henry James, vol. II, pp. 23–29.

15. William James to Theodore Flournoy, June 17, 1898, Perry, vol. II, pp. 307–08; William James to François Pillon, June 15, 1898, Henry James, vol. II, pp. 73–74. On April 22, 1898, James wrote: "Now let baseball and prizefights hang their heads. For really exciting sport there is nothing like such a naval battle as now seems to be imminent." William James to J. Mark Baldwin, James Papers.

16. William James to William M. Salter, November 18, 1898, Perry, vol. II, pp. 309–10.

17. William James to Theodore Flournoy, May 30, 1899, James Papers.

18. William James to Andrew Seth (A. S. Pringle-Pattison), December 26, 1895, and January 26, 1896, *ibid.*

19. William James to William M. Salter, November 18, 1898, Perry, vol. II, p. 309.

20. William James, *Memories and Studies,* Longmans, Green, and Co., New York, 1917, pp. 56–58.

21. *Boston Evening Transcript,* April 15, 1899.

22. Perry, vol. II, pp. 298–99. James's most ambitious personal effort to blunt the power of the war instinct was presented some years later in "The Moral Equivalent of War," a provocative essay first published in 1910. See *Memories and Studies,* pp. 269, 272, 275–77, 283–92.

23. William James to Carl Schurz, March 16, 1900, Schurz Papers.

24. William James to F. C. S. Schiller, August 6, 1902, James Papers.

25. William James to C. F. Adams, December 29, 1898, Adams Papers; William James to Henry Rutgers Marshall, February 8, 1899, Henry James, vol. II, p. 88; and William James to G. Stanley Hall, May 14, 1900, James Papers.

26. George Santayana, *Character and Opinion in the United States, with Reminiscences of William James and Josiah Royce and Academic Life in*

America, Charles Scribner's Sons, New York, 1921, p. 82. See also Henry Steele Commager, *The American Mind: An Interpretation of American Thought and Character Since the 1880's*, Yale University Press, New Haven, 1959, p. 99; Perry, vol. II, pp. 281, 300–303, 318; and George Santayana, *Persons and Places: The Background of My Life*, Charles Scribner's Sons, New York, 1944, p. 241.

27. William James to William M. Salter, [early?] 1896, Perry, vol. II, p. 306; William James to Andrew Seth, January 26, 1896, James Papers.

28. *Boston Evening Transcript*, April 15, 1899.

29. *Ibid.*, March 4, 1899.

30. *Ibid.*, March 1, 1899; *Springfield Republican* (Springfield, Mass.), June 4, 1900.

31. William James to Mrs. Henry Whitman, June 7, 1899, Henry James, vol. II, p. 90.

32. *Boston Evening Transcript*, March 1, 1899.

33. William James to Theodore Flournoy, May 30, 1899, James Papers; William James to Theodore Flournoy, June 17, 1898, Perry, vol. II, pp. 307–08 (also p. 316); *Springfield Daily Republican*, June 4, 1900; William James to François Pillon, June 15, 1898, and to Frances R. Morse, September 17, 1899, Henry James, vol. II, pp. 73–74, 102–03; and Mary E. Raymond, "Memories of William James," *New England Quarterly*, X (September, 1937), 426.

34. William James to Carl Schurz, March 16, 1900, Schurz Papers.

35. William James to François Pillon, June 15, 1898, Henry James, vol. II, pp. 73–74; William James to Henry Lee Higginson, September 18, 1900, James Papers.

36. William James to W. Cameron Forbes, June 11, 1907, Henry James, vol. II, p. 289.

37. See William James to Carl Schurz, March 16, 1900, Schurz Papers; William James to Carl Stumpf, August 6, 1901, Perry, vol. II, pp. 199–200; *Boston Evening Transcript*, March 1, 1899; William James to Henry S. Mackintosh, April 9, 1899, and to Theodore Flournoy, May 30, 1899, James Papers; William James to James Sully, March 3, 1901, and to C. E. Norton, June 26, 1901, Henry James, vol. II, pp. 140–41, 152–53; and Elizabeth G. Evans, "William James and His Wife," *Atlantic*, CXLIV (September, 1929), 378–79.

38. William James to Henry James, April 10, 1898, and to Theodore Flournoy, June 17, 1898, Perry, vol. II, pp. 307–08.

39. William James to François Pillon, June 15, 1898, Henry James, vol. II, p. 74.

40. William James to James Sully, March 3, 1901, *ibid.*, p. 141.

41. Perry, vol. II, pp. 306–07.

42. The quotations in the remainder of this chapter, except when other-
    wise indicated, are from George Santayana, *The Middle Span,* Charles
    Scribner's Sons, New York, 1945, pp. 167–70.

43. Quoted in Henry Hallam Saunderson, *Charles W. Eliot: Puritan Liberal,*
    Harper & Brothers, New York, 1928, p. 246.

CHAPTER 4/*E. L. Godkin and Charles Eliot Norton:
The Last Straw*

1. Allan Nevins, *The Evening Post: A Century of Journalism,* Boni and
   Liveright, New York, 1922, p. 543; C. E. Norton to E. L. Godkin, July 3,
   1897, Godkin Papers.

2. Nevins, *The Evening Post,* p. 543.

3. "The 'Nation's' Jubilee," *The Nation,* July 8, 1915, p. 33.

4. Oswald Garrison Villard, *Some Newspapers and Newspaper-Men,* Alfred
   A. Knopf, New York, 1933, pp. 292–93.

5. C. E. Norton to Leslie Stephen, June 3, 1902, in Sara Norton and M. A.
   DeWolfe Howe (eds.), *Letters of Charles Eliot Norton with Biographical
   Comment,* Houghton Mifflin Company, Boston, 1913, vol. II, p. 323.

6. Theodore Roosevelt to H. C. Lodge, July 28, 1884, and December 27,
   1888, Elting E. Morison et al. (eds.), *The Letters of Theodore Roosevelt,*
   Harvard University Press, Cambridge, Mass., 1951–1954, vol. I, pp. 75,
   151.

7. Lincoln Steffens, *The Autobiography of Lincoln Steffens, Complete in
   One Volume,* Harcourt, Brace and Company, New York, 1931, p. 180;
   Henry L. Higginson to William James, February 7, 1903, in Ralph Barton
   Perry, *The Thought and Character of William James, As Revealed in
   Unpublished Correspondence and Notes, Together with his Published
   Writings,* Little, Brown, and Company, Boston, 1935, vol. II, p. 295.

8. The best sources of biographical information for Norton are Norton and
   Howe, *Letters of Charles Eliot Norton,* and Kermit Vanderbilt, *Charles
   Eliot Norton: Apostle of Culture in a Democracy,* The Belknap Press of
   Harvard University Press, Cambridge, Mass., 1959.

9. C. E. Norton to Thomas Carlyle, July 26, 1880, Norton and Howe, vol.
   II, p. 112; see also *ibid.,* p. 8.

10. Vanderbilt, pp. 134, 136; Rollo Walter Brown, *Harvard Yard in the
    Golden Age,* Current Books, Inc., New York, 1948, p. 153; Helen Howe,
    The Gentle Americans, 1864–1960: Biography of a Breed, Harper and
    Row, New York, 1965, p. 199.

11. Van Wyck Brooks, *New England: Indian Summer, 1865–1915,* E. P. Dut-
    ton & Co., Inc., New York, 1940, pp. 253–54; Malcolm M. Marsden, "Dis-
    criminating Sympathy: Charles Eliot Norton's Unique Gift," *New Eng-
    land Quarterly,* XXXI (December, 1958) , 464.

Reference Notes

12. E. L. Godkin to Carl Schurz, May 19, 1872, in Frederic Bancroft (ed.), *Speeches, Correspondence and Political Papers of Carl Schurz*, G. P. Putnam's Sons, New York, 1913, vol. II, p. 376.

13. C. E. Norton to James Russell Lowell, June 27, 1880, Norton and Howe, vol. II, p. 111.

14. Godkin in the *London Daily News*, February 23, 1859, quoted in Mary V. MacLachlin, "Edwin Lawrence Godkin: Utilitarian Editor," unpublished Ph.D. dissertation, University of Minnesota, 1948, p. 65.

15. The quotation may be found in Edwin Lawrence Godkin, *Reflections and Comments, 1865–1895*, Charles Scribner's Sons, New York, 1896, p. 50. See also his *Unforeseen Tendencies of Democracy*, Houghton, Mifflin and Company, Boston, 1898, and *Problems of Modern Democracy: Political and Economic Essays*, Charles Scribner's Sons, New York, 1896.

16. Godkin, "Commercial Immorality and Political Corruption," *North American Review* (1868), quoted in Leonard D. White (with assistance of Jean Schneider), *The Republican Era: 1869–19 1: A Study in Administrative History*, The Macmillan Company, New York, 1958, p. 8; Edward C. Kirkland, *Business in the Gilded Age: The Conservatives' Balance Sheet*, University of Wisconsin Press, Madison, Wis., 1952, pp. 36–37.

17. Norton and Howe, vol. II, pp. 8–9.

18. C. E. Norton to J. R. Lowell, November 24, 1873, September 20, 1875, and February 10, 1884, *ibid.*, pp. 23, 57, 158; C. E. Norton to E. L. Godkin, November 3, 1871, Godkin Papers; Austin Warren, *New England Saints*, The University of Michigan Press, Ann Arbor, 1956, p. 131.

19. Christina Hopkinson Baker (ed.), *Diary and Letters of Josephine Preston Peabody*, Houghton Mifflin Company, Boston, 1925, p. 73.

20. Godkin, "Aristocratic Opinions of Democracy," originally published in the *North American Review* (January, 1865), reprinted in Godkin, *Problems of Modern Democracy* (see pp. 9–13, 16, 25–26, 38–42, 49–53). This essay anticipated some of the general lines of Frederick Jackson Turner's thesis regarding the influence of the frontier in American history.

21. Matthew Josephson, *The Politicos, 1865–1896*, Harcourt, Brace and Company, New York, 1938, p. 480.

22. Henry Holt, "A Young Man's Oracle," *The Nation*, July 8, 1915, p. 47.

23. Godkin, *Reflections and Comments*, p. 279.

24. Godkin, *Unforeseen Tendencies*, pp. 30, 46.

25. Vanderbilt, p. 109.

26. *Ibid.*, p. 95.

27. *Ibid.*, p. 131; Charles Eliot Norton, *Historical Studies of Church-Building in the Middle Ages: Venice, Siena, Florence*, Harper & Brothers, New York, 1880, p. 164.

28. [Charles Eliot Norton], *Considerations on Some Recent Social Theories*, Little, Brown, and Co., Boston, 1853, pp. 130–31.

29. C. E. Norton to Chauncey Wright, December 5, 1869, and to Sir Mountstuart E. Grant-Duff, September 10, 1889, Norton and Howe, vol. I, p. 370, vol. II, p. 193.

30. Vanderbilt, p. xvi.

31. *Ibid.*, p. 75; C. E. Norton to E. L. Godkin, March 13, 1867, Godkin Papers; C. E. Norton to Edward Lee-Childe, September 29, 1883, to J. R. Lowell, November 16, 1884, to Leslie Stephen, March 1, 1893, to Sir Mountstuart E. Grant-Duff, November 8, 1895, and April 19, 1896, and to Edward Lee-Childe, April 20, 1896, Norton and Howe, vol. II, pp. 156–57, 166, 216, 235, 242–43.

32. C. E. Norton to Edward Lee-Childe, September 29, 1883, to J. R. Lowell, November 16, 1884, and to S. G. Ward, April 26, 1896, Norton and Howe, vol. II, pp. 156, 166, 243–44.

33. William M. Armstrong, *E. L. Godkin and American Foreign Policy, 1865–1900*, Bookman Associates, New York, 1957, pp. 122, 151; *The Nation*, January 19, 1893, p. 43.

34. C. E. Norton to Arthur H. Clough, October 16, 1854, and January 13, 1856, and to S. G. Ward, July 14, 1897, Norton and Howe, vol. I, pp. 116–17, 144, vol. II, p. 254; Vanderbilt, p. 219.

35. Edward C. Kirkland, *Industry Comes of Age: Business, Labor, and Public Policy, 1860–1897*, Holt, Rinehart and Winston, New York, 1961, p. 248; Kirkland, *Business in the Gilded Age*, p. 27; Alan Pendleton Grimes, *The Political Liberalism of the New York Nation, 1865–1932*, "The James Sprunt Studies in History and Political Science," Vol. XXXIV, The University of North Carolina Press, Chapel Hill, 1953, pp. 24–25.

36. C. E. Norton to J. R. Lowell, July 24, 1877, and May 19, 1878, Norton and Howe, vol. II, pp. 69, 80–81; Josephson, *The Politicos*, p. 570.

37. Grimes, p. 33.

38. Vanderbilt, pp. 31, 43, 47, 133, 188, 192; Norton and Howe, vol. II, pp. 89–90, 94, 97, 99, 456; Brooks, pp. 340–41.

39. Kermit Vanderbilt, "Howells and Norton: Some Frustrations of the Biographer," *New England Quarterly*, XXXVII (March, 1964), 86–87.

40. C. E. Norton to J. B. Harrison, March 13, 1894, Norton and Howe, vol. II, p. 220.

41. C. E. Norton to E. L. Godkin, April 7, 1871, and January 3, 1897, Godkin Papers; C. E. Norton to Edward Lee-Childe, November 29, 1884, Norton and Howe, vol. II, pp. 167–68; C. E. Norton to S. G. Ward, July 3, 1897, Charles Eliot Norton Papers, Houghton Library, Harvard University, Cambridge, Massachusetts, cited hereafter as Norton Papers; and C. E.

Norton to E. L. Godkin, November 27, 1896, quoted in Vanderbilt, *Charles Eliot Norton*, p. 212.

42. E. L. Godkin to C. E. Norton, January 12, 1895, Rollo Ogden (ed.), *Life and Letters of Edwin Lawrence Godkin*, The Macmillan Company, New York, 1907, vol. II, p. 199; C. E. Norton to Leslie Stephen, March 20, 1896, Norton and Howe, vol. II, p. 241.

43. C. E. Norton to Arthur H. Clough, October 25, 1857, Norton and Howe, vol. I, p. 185.

44. [Norton], *Considerations*, pp. 130–32.

45. C. E. Norton to George W. Curtis, December 25, 28, 1870, Norton Papers; C. E. Norton to E. L. Godkin, February 8, 1872, and April 4, 1872, Godkin Papers.

46. *The Nation*, July 20, 1865, p. 36; August 3, 1865, p. 132; November 30, 1865, p. 678; November 15, 1866, p. 381; November 29, 1866, p. 432; and July 18, 1867, p. 52.

47. Armstrong, p. 104.

48. *The Nation*, January 2, 1868, p. 5; December 29, 1870, p. 432; January 23, 1873, p. 52.

49. Matthew Josephson, *The President Makers: The Culture of Politics and Leadership in an Age of Enlightenment, 1896–1919*, Harcourt, Brace and Company, New York, 1940, p. 10.

50. Gustav Pollak, *Fifty Years of American Idealism: The New York Nation, 1865–1915*, Houghton Mifflin Company, Boston, 1915, pp. 148–49; Armstrong, pp. 126–27, 133, 146–47.

51. Armstrong, pp. 127, 142; Pollak, p. 135; David M. Pletcher, *The Awkward Years: American Foreign Relations Under Garfield and Arthur*, University of Missouri Press, Columbia, Mo., 1962, p. 281.

52. Armstrong, p. 54.

53. Foster Rhea Dulles, *America in the Pacific: A Century of Expansion*, 2d ed., Houghton Mifflin Company, Boston, 1938, p. 119; *The Nation*, February 4, 1892, pp. 82–83; Julius W. Pratt, "The Hawaiian Revolution: a Re-Interpretation," *Pacific Historical Review*, I (September, 1932), 274.

54. Godkin, *Reflections and Comments*, pp. 4–8.

55. Nevins, *The Evening Post*, p. 472.

56. E. L. Godkin, "Diplomacy and the Newspaper," *North American Review*, CLX (May, 1895), 571–72, 576–79.

57. E. L. Godkin to C. E. Norton, December 29, 1895, Ogden, vol. II, pp. 202–03; Armstrong, p. 182.

58. C. E. Norton to Leslie Stephen, January 3, 1896, Norton and Howe, vol. II, pp. 236–37; C. E. Norton to E. L. Godkin, December 22, 1895, Godkin Papers.

59. Joseph E. Wisan, *The Cuban Crisis as Reflected in the New York Press (1895–1898)*, Columbia University Press, New York, 1934, pp. 53–54, 96, 209, 293; Nevins, *The Evening Post*, p. 512. During the Spanish-American War he called the Cuban revolutionaries "brigands and half-breeds." *The Nation*, April 28, 1898, p. 316.

60. *The Nation*, April 21, 1898, p. 296.

61. *Ibid.*, January 13, 1898, p. 23.

62. *Ibid.*, October 6, 1898, p. 254.

63. *Ibid.*, May 19, 1898, p. 377.

64. *Ibid.*, May 19, 1898, pp. 376–77; January 26, 1899, p. 60; E. L. Godkin to Emily Tuckerman, February 4, 1899, Ogden, vol. II, p. 218; and E. L. Godkin, "The Conditions of Good Colonial Government," *The Forum*, XXVII (April, 1899), 190, 196, 203.

65. *The Nation*, April 20, 1899, p. 288; March 2, 1899, pp. 158–59.

66. Armstrong, p. 194; *The Nation*, March 9, 1899, p. 174.

67. E. L. Godkin to F. Sheldon, July 5, 1898, Godkin Papers.

68. *The Nation*, December 1, 1898, p. 404.

69. E. L. Godkin to C. E. Norton, November 29, 1898, Norton Papers; E. L. Godkin to James Bryce, April 23, 1899, Godkin Papers; E. L. Godkin to E. B. Smith, *ca.* May, 1899, to F. E. Leupp, late 1899, and to W. R. Huntington, November 13, 1899, Ogden, vol. II, pp. 219, 237, 245.

70. Ogden, *Life and Letters*, vol. II, pp. 243, 250, 255; [Rollo Ogden], "Edwin Lawrence Godkin," *Dictionary of American Biography*, ed. Allan Johnson and Dumas Malone, Charles Scribner's Sons, New York, 1928–1936, vol. VII, p. 350.

71. Pollak, p. 63.

72. "True Patriotism," June 7, 1898, address to the Men's Club of the Prospect Street Congregational Church, Cambridge, Massachusetts, Norton and Howe, vol. II, pp. 261–69.

73. C. E. Norton to Leslie Stephen, June 24, 1898, and to Charles Waldstein, November 18, 1899, Norton and Howe, vol. II, pp. 270, 290; C. E. Norton to William Roscoe Thayer, August 16, 1898, quoted in William Roscoe Thayer, "The Sage of Shady Hill," *The Unpartizan Review*, XV (January–March, 1921), 84.

74. Thayer, *The Unpartizan Review*, XV, 84.

75. C. E. Norton to Leslie Stephen, June 24, 1898, and to S. G. Ward, March 13, 1901, Norton and Howe, vol. II, pp. 270, 303–04; C. E. Norton to Goldwin Smith, February 20, 1900, Norton Papers. Godkin's reaction was similar. Writing to Norton on November 29, 1898, he exclaimed: "We all expected too much of the human race. What stuff we used to talk!" Norton Papers.

76. *The Nation*, December 1, 1898, p. 404.

77. C. E. Norton to William James, September 1, 1902, James Papers; C. E. Norton to W. A. Croffut, September 5, 1902, William A. Croffut Papers, Library of Congress, Washington, D.C., cited hereafter as Croffut Papers.

CHAPTER 5/*Edward Atkinson: The Informal Empire*

1. Adam Smith, *An Enquiry into the Nature and Causes of The Wealth of Nations*, The Modern Library, New York, 1937, p. 592.

2. For a detailed and provocative study of this aspect of American expansionism in the nineteenth century, see Walter LaFeber, *The New Empire: An Interpretation of American Expansion, 1860–1898*, Cornell University Press, Ithaca, N.Y., 1963. Kasson's remarks are in David M. Pletcher, *The Awkward Years: American Foreign Relations Under Garfield and Arthur*, University of Missouri Press, Columbia, Mo., 1962, pp. 102–03.

3. William Appleman Williams, *The Contours of American History*, The World Publishing Company, Cleveland, 1961, pp. 367–68.

4. John W. Rollins, "The Anti-Imperialists and Twentieth Century American Foreign Policy," *Studies on the Left*, III (1962), 18.

5. "Comment," *Yale Review*, VII (August, 1898), 123–24.

6. Harold Baron, "Comment," *Studies on the Left*, III (1962), 26.

7. For Adams and Hoar, see Chapters 6 and 7.

8. For Carnegie, see Chapter 8.

9. Thomas Wentworth Higginson, *Carlyle's Laugh and other Surprises*, Houghton Mifflin Company, Boston, 1909, p. 216.

10. William A. Williams, who uses these words to describe Schurz's position, recognizes that Schurz's anti-imperialism was not totally dictated by economic considerations, but he clearly regards them as by far the most significant factor in determining his viewpoint.

11. Quoted in *Boston Evening Transcript*, May 3, 1899.

12. Edward Chase Kirkland, *Charles Francis Adams, Jr., 1835–1915: The Patrician at Bay*, Harvard University Press, Cambridge, Mass., 1965, p. 184; Harold F. Williamson, *Edward Atkinson: The Biography of an American Liberal, 1827–1905*, Old Corner Book Store, Inc., Boston, 1934, pp. v–ix, 1–3, 50, 257; [Roswell C. McCrea], "Edward Atkinson," *Dictionary of American Biography*, ed. Allan Johnson and Dumas Malone, Charles Scribner's Sons, New York, 1928–1936, vol. I, pp. 406–07; and Higginson, p. 215.

13. Edward Atkinson to the editor of the "New York Sunday Herald," August 1, 1900, Atkinson Papers, MHS; *Dictionary of American Biography*, vol. I, p. 407; Geoffrey T. Blodgett, "The Mind of the Boston Mugwump," *Mississippi Valley Historical Review*, XLVIII (March, 1962), 627; and

Sidney Fine, *Laissez Faire and the General-Welfare State: A Study of Conflict in American Thought, 1865–1901,* The University of Michigan Press, Ann Arbor, 1956, p. 64.

14. Fine, p. 61; Williamson, pp. 82, 137–38, 208; Blodgett, *Mississippi Valley Historical Review,* XLVIII, 626; Joseph Dorfman, *The Economic Mind in American Civilization,* The Viking Press, New York, 1946–1949, vol. III, p. 29.

    Atkinson strongly backed continued free immigration, believing the immigrant no danger to American institutions, an essential source of labor, and an important consumer of American produce and manufactures. See Edward Atkinson to Arthur J. Scott, March 13, 1890, quoted in Blodgett, *Mississippi Valley Historical Review,* XLVIII, 624; Barbara Miller Solomon, *Ancestors and Immigrants: A Changing New England Tradition,* Harvard University Press, Cambridge, Mass., 1956, pp. 176–78; and Williamson, p. 38.

15. Edward Atkinson to Senator J. R. McPherson, February 20, 1894, quoted in Williamson, p. 189; see also pp. 3–5, 8–9, 89, 91, 98, 134, 161, 210–11.

16. Memo of Edward Atkinson, sent to Grover Cleveland, February 15, 1895, Grover Cleveland Papers, Library of Congress, Washington, D.C., cited hereafter as Cleveland Papers.

17. Edward Atkinson, "Jingoes and Silverites," *North American Review,* CLXI (November, 1895) , 559–60.

18. Edward Atkinson to Grover Cleveland, November 12, 1895, Cleveland Papers.

19. *Boston Morning Journal,* December 18, 1895.

20. Edward Atkinson to Grover Cleveland, December 20, 1895, Atkinson Papers, MHS; Allan Nevins, *Grover Cleveland: A Study in Courage,* Dodd, Mead & Company, New York, 1933, p. 645.

21. Edward Atkinson to J. Sterling Morton, December 19, 1895, Atkinson Papers, MHS.

22. Edward Atkinson to Joseph R. Hawley, December 30, 1895, and January 2, 1896, *ibid.*

23. Edson L. Whitney, *The American Peace Society: A Centennial History,* 3d ed., rev., The American Peace Society, Washington, 1929, p. 322; Edward Atkinson to William McKinley, March 25, 1898, Atkinson Papers, MHS.

24. Edward Atkinson to William E. Dodge, February 15, 1898, and to Charles W. Eliot and C. F. Adams, February 23, 1898, Atkinson Papers, MHS; Edward Atkinson to L. T. Chamberlain, March 3, 1898, Adams Papers.

25. Edward Atkinson, *The Development of the Resources of the Southern States. An Address to the Atlanta Chamber of Commerce. By Edward*

Atkinson, LL.D., Ph.D., of Boston, Mass. *April Fourteenth, 1898*, n.n., n.p., 1898, pp. 11–13.

26. Edward Atkinson to Charles Nordhoff, June 27, 1898, Atkinson Papers, MHS.

27. Edward Atkinson to William Fowler, April 29, May 10, and May 20, 1898, to David A. Wells, May 5, May 12, and July 8, 1898, to Lord Farrer, June 20, 1898, to Charles Nordhoff, June 27, 1898, to George B. Cowlam, July 27, 1898, to R. S. Ashton, August 26, 1898, and "Memorandum on Present Status," June 2, 1898, *ibid.*

28. Edward Atkinson to editor of the *Textile Excelsior* (Charlotte, N.C.), May 26, 1898, *ibid.*

29. Edward Atkinson to William McKinley, August 25, 1898, *ibid.*

30. Edward Atkinson to R. S. Ashton, August 26, 1898, *ibid.*

31. Edward Atkinson, "Addenda to 'The Hell of War and Its Penalties,'" printed in *The Anti-Imperialist*, I (May 27, 1899), 23.

32. Edward Atkinson to William McKinley, January 26, 1899, Atkinson Papers, MHS.

33. Atkinson, "Memorandum," February 1, 1899, *ibid.*

34. Edward Atkinson to William McKinley (copy), November 14, 1898, Andrew Carnegie Papers, Library of Congress, Washington, D.C., cited hereafter as Carnegie Papers.

35. Maria C. Lanzar, "The Anti-Imperialist League," *Philippine Social Science Review*, III (August, 1930), 15–16; Edward Atkinson to Andrew Carnegie, November 28, 1898, Carnegie Papers; Edward Atkinson to Carl Schurz, February 2, 1899, Schurz Papers.

36. *The Anti-Imperialist*, I (May 27, 1899), inside front cover and pp. 25, 34; Leon Wolff, *Little Brown Brother: America's Forgotten Bid for Empire which Cost 250,000 Lives*, Longmans, Green and Co., Ltd., London, 1961, p. 274.

37. Edward Atkinson to the Secretary of War, April 22, 1899, Atkinson Papers, MHS.

38. *The Anti-Imperialist*, I (May 27, 1899), inside front cover; Erving Winslow (Secretary of the Anti-Imperialist League) to Andrew Carnegie, April 12, 1899, Carnegie Papers; Wolff, pp. 274–75.

39. Edward Atkinson to Erving Winslow, April 26, 1899, Atkinson Papers, MHS.

40. Fred H. Harrington, "The Anti-Imperialist Movement in the United States, 1898–1900," *Mississippi Valley Historical Review*, XXII (September, 1935), 224–25; Lanzar, *Philippine Social Science Review*, III, 31–32; Edward Atkinson to Andrew Carnegie, May 22, 1899, Atkinson Papers, MHS.

41. Edward Atkinson to Charles Nordhoff, June 23, 1899, Atkinson Papers, MHS.

42. Edward Atkinson to William Fowler, October 18, 1900, *ibid.*; *The Anti-Imperialist,* I (September 15, 1899) , 9; Wolff, p. 299; Lanzar, *Philippine Social Science Review,* III, 128.

43. *The Anti-Imperialist,* I (May 27, 1899) , 46.

44. Rollins, *Studies on the Left,* III, 17.

45. Atkinson Papers, MHS.

46. Edward Atkinson to H. Strong, August 30, 1899, *ibid.* See also letters to George A. Parker, June 20, 1899, to Emory R. Johnson, October 30, 1899, to the editor of "The Advertiser" (Boston?) , November 10, 1899, and to J. H. Slayden, December 19, 1899, *ibid.*; and *The Anti-Imperialist,* I (May 27, 1899) , 16.

47. Edward Atkinson, "Eastern Commerce: What Is It Worth?" *North American Review,* CLXX (February, 1900) , 295–304.

48. Quoted in Rollins, *Studies on the Left,* III, 17. For other, including later, expressions of the same line of thought, see Edward Atkinson to the editor of the (New York?) *Journal of Commerce and Daily Commercial Bulletin,* February 5, 1900, and February 12, 1900, and letters to C. E. Littlefield, February 26, 1900, to William P. Frye, August 23 and August 27, 1900, and to George F. Hoar, August 28, 1900, Atkinson Papers, MHS.

49. Atkinson Papers, MHS, summer, 1900, *passim.*

50. Edward Atkinson, *The Cost of War and Warfare, from 1898 to 1902, inclusive, Seven Hundred Million Dollars, $700,000,000,* 6th ed., n.n., n.p., 1902, p. 3; Edward Atkinson to Charles Nordhoff, December 14, 1900, quoted in Williamson, p. 238.

51. See Frederic Bancroft (ed.) , *Speeches, Correspondence and Political Papers of Carl Schurz,* G. P. Putnam's Sons, New York, 1913, vol. V, pp. 213, 435–39, 473–74, 476, 488–92, vol. VI, pp. 180–81; Robert I. Fulton and Thomas C. Trueblood (comps.) , *Patriotic Eloquence Relating to the Spanish-American War and Its Issues,* Charles Scribner's Sons, New York, 1900, pp. 274–75, 282–84.

52. David Starr Jordan, "The Control of the Tropics," *Gunton's Magazine,* XVIII (May, 1900) , 408–10.

53. Albert G. Keller and Maurice R. Davie (eds.) , *Essays of William Graham Sumner,* Yale University Press, New Haven, 1934, vol. I, pp. 189ff., vol. II, pp. 290–91, 303; Albert G. Keller (ed.) , *War and Other Essays by William Graham Sumner,* Yale University Press, New Haven, 1911, p. 289.

54. See Julius W. Pratt, *America's Colonial Experiment: How the United States Gained, Governed, and In Part Gave Away a Colonial Empire,* Prentice-Hall, New York, 1950, pp. 242–44, 296; Ethel B. Dietrich, *Far*

Eastern Trade of the United States, International Secretariat, Institute of Pacific Relations, New York, 1940, pp. 10, 54, 106; *Trends in the Foreign Trade of the United States,* National Industrial Conference Board, Inc., New York, 1930, pp. 29–30, 40; Norman S. Buchanan and Friedrich A. Lutz, *Rebuilding the World Economy: America's Role in Foreign Trade and Investment,* The Twentieth Century Fund, New York, 1947, p. 328; A. Whitney Griswold, *The Far Eastern Policy of the United States,* Harcourt, Brace and Company, New York, 1938, pp. 468–69; Tang Tsou, *America's Failure in China, 1941–50,* The University of Chicago Press, Chicago, 1963, p. 6.

55. Griswold, pp. 451–52; Grayson L. Kirk, *Philippine Independence: Motives, Problems, and Prospects,* Farrar & Rinehart, Inc., New York, 1936, pp. 58–59, 73–124, 127–35, 212; Whitney T. Perkins, *Denial of Empire: The United States and Its Dependencies,* A. W. Sythoff, Leyden, Netherlands, 1962, pp. 243–44; Garel A. Grunder and William E. Livezey, *The Philippines and the United States,* University of Oklahoma Press, Norman, Okla., 1951, pp. 195–219; Theodore Friend, *Between Two Empires: The Ordeal of the Philippines, 1929–1946,* Yale University Press, New Haven, 1965, pp. 81, 107–08.

CHAPTER 6/*Charles Francis Adams and the Election of 1900*

1. The quotation in the above paragraph ·is from Edward C. Kirkland's excellent *Charles Francis Adams, Jr., 1835–1915: The Patrician at Bay,* Harvard University Press, Cambridge, Mass., 1965, p. 80.
2. Before the word was coined. See Charles F. Adams, Jr., and Henry Adams, *Chapters of Erie and Other Essays,* Henry Holt, New York, 1886.
3. Charles Francis Adams, *Charles Francis Adams, 1835–1915: An Autobiography; With a Memorial Address delivered November 17, 1915, by Henry Cabot Lodge,* Houghton Mifflin Company, Boston, 1916, pp. 13, 170, 180, 195. Adams also invested heavily in mines, stockyards, and city lots. See Kirkland, *Charles Francis Adams, Jr.,* for biographical detail.
4. Charles Francis Adams, *Three Episodes of Massachusetts History: The Settlement of Boston Bay, The Antinomian Controversy, A Study of Church and Town Government,* rev. ed., Houghton, Mifflin and Company, Boston, 1903, vol. II, p. 957; Kirkland, *Charles Francis Adams, Jr.,* p. 160. Adams served as treasurer of the Social Science Association, president of the Massachusetts Tariff Reform League, and vice-president of the New England Free Trade League, the National Civil-Service Reform League, and the Massachusetts Reform Club.
5. Adams, *An Autobiography,* pp. 15–16.

6. *Ibid.*, p. liii.

7. Henry Adams to C. F. Adams, May 21, 1869, in Worthington C. Ford (ed.), *Letters of Henry Adams*, Houghton Mifflin Company, Boston, 1930–1938, vol. I, p. 160.

8. C. F. Adams to C. É. Norton, November 30, 1883, quoted in Kermit Vanderbilt, *Charles Eliot Norton: Apostle of Culture in a Democracy*, The Belknap Press of Harvard University Press, Cambridge, Mass., 1959, p. 137.

9. Robert L. Beisner, "Brooks Adams and Charles Francis Adams, Jr.: Historians of Massachusetts," *New England Quarterly*, XXXV (March, 1962), 63–65; Adams, *An Autobiography*, pp. xlviii, 208.

10. Adams, *Three Episodes of Massachusetts History*, vol. II, pp. 801–02.

11. John A. Abbott, "The Day of Mr. Charles Francis Adams," *Proceedings of the Massachusetts Historical Society*, LXXII (1957–1960), 228–29.

12. C. F. Adams to Carl Schurz, November 13, 1873, quoted in Ari Hoogenboom, *Outlawing the Spoils: A History of the Civil Service Reform Movement, 1865–1883*, University of Illinois Press, Urbana, Ill., 1961, p. 127.

13. Adams, "Memorabilia," April 4, 1898, May 8, 1898, Adams Papers.

14. *Ibid.*, April 4, 1898; Geoffrey Blodgett, *The Gentle Reformers: Massachusetts Democrats in the Cleveland Era*, Harvard University Press, Cambridge, Mass., 1966, p. 266.

15. Charles Francis Adams, *"Imperialism" and "The Tracks of our Forefathers," A Paper Read by Charles Francis Adams Before the Lexington, Massachusetts, Historical Society, Tuesday, December 20, 1898*, Dana Estes & Company, Boston, 1899, p. 9.

16. Adams, "Memorabilia," December 21, 1898, and May 5, 1900, Adams Papers.

17. *Ibid.*, September 19, 26, 1898.

18. *Ibid.*, October 27, 1898.

19. *Ibid.*, December 4, 1898.

20. *Ibid.*

21. Adams, *"Imperialism" and "The Tracks of our Forefathers," passim.* The Burke quotation is from his "Speech on Conciliation with America" (1775).

22. Adams, "Memorabilia," December 21, 1898, Adams Papers.

23. C. F. Adams to Carl Schurz, November 24, 1898, and January 17, 1899, Schurz Papers; C. F. Adams to Carl Schurz, December 21, 1898, printed in Adams, *"Imperialism" and "The Tracks of our Forefathers,"* p. 31.

24. In addition Adams recommended that it be explicitly understood that the colonies would in no way become an integral part of the American federal system, and to this end he proposed a constitutional amendment stipulating the right of the United States government to govern "extra-

territorial" areas and establish for them "a wholly different system of imposts, taxes, and trade regulations" than those observed in the continental United States. C. F. Adams to Carl Schurz, January 17, 1899, Schurz Papers.

25. *Springfield Daily Republican,* May 18, 1899, clipping attached to May 20, 1899, entry of Adams, "Memorabilia," Adams Papers.

26. Moorfield Storey to C. F. Adams, May 19, 1899, Charles Codman to C. F. Adams, May 19, 1899, Winslow Warren to C. F. Adams, May 19, 1899, and Thomas Wentworth Higginson to C. F. Adams, May 20, 1899, Adams Papers; *Springfield Daily Republican,* May 18, 1899, and May 19, 1899, which includes the quotation from the *Hartford Times.*

27. Adams, "Memorabilia," May 20, 1899, Adams Papers.

28. *Ibid.*

29. Thomas A. Bailey, "Was the Presidential Election of 1900 a Mandate on Imperialism?" *Mississippi Valley Historical Review,* XXIV (June, 1937), 43–52.

30. Quoted in Richard W. Leopold, *The Growth of American Foreign Policy: A History,* Alfred A. Knopf, New York, 1962, p. 194.

31. For the Democratic platform see Maria C. Lanzar, "The Anti-Imperialist League," *Philippine Social Science Review,* III (August, 1930), 38.

32. Joseph Rogers Hollingsworth, "A Study in Party Division: The Democratic Party, 1893–1900," unpublished Ph.D. dissertation, Department of History, University of Chicago, 1960, p. 244. This work has been published as *The Whirligig of Politics: The Democracy of Cleveland and Bryan,* University of Chicago Press, Chicago, 1963.

33. Grover Cleveland to Judson Harmon, July 17, 1900, in Allan Nevins (ed.), *Letters of Grover Cleveland, 1850–1908,* Houghton Mifflin Company, Boston, 1933, p. 533.

34. C. F. Adams to Carl Schurz, March 15, 1899, Schurz Papers.

35. C. F. Adams to Carl Schurz, November 3, 1899, November 6, 1899, and March 30, 1900, *ibid.*

36. Adams, "Memorabilia," June 22 and September 16, 1900, Adams Papers.

37. *Ibid.,* June 22, 1900.

38. C. F. Adams to Carl Schurz, March 25, 1900, Schurz Papers.

39. C. F. Adams to Carl Schurz, November 6, 1899, *ibid.*

40. Adams, "Memorabilia," June 22, 1900, Adams Papers.

41. *Ibid.,* August 10 and September 16, 1900.

42. *Ibid.,* May 15 and June 22, 1900.

43. *Ibid.,* July 11 and October 14, 1900.

44. Italics mine. *Ibid.,* June 22, 1900. As it happened, the election of 1900 changed the Republican-Democratic ratio in the House of Representatives from 201–150 to 208–172 (the total membership of the House in-

creasing) , with the membership (6) from minor parties remaining constant. DeAlva Stanwood Alexander, *History and Procedure of the House of Representatives*, Houghton Mifflin Company, Boston, 1916, p. 412.

45. Carl Schurz to editor of the *New York Evening Post*, October 21, 1898, in Frederic Bancroft (ed.) , *Speeches, Correspondence and Political Papers of Carl Schurz*, G. P. Putnam's Sons, New York, 1913, vol. V, pp. 524–25.

46. Carl Schurz to C. F. Adams, March 11, 1899, *ibid.,* vol. VI, pp. 46–47.

47. Carl Schurz to Erving Winslow, August 29, 1899, and to Moorfield Storey, March 20, 1900, Schurz Papers; R. F. Pettigrew, *Imperial Washington: The Story of American Public Life from 1870 to 1920*, Charles H. Kerr & Company, Co-operative, Chicago, 1922, pp. 321–22; Fred H. Harrington, "The Anti-Imperialist Movement in the United States, 1898–1900," *Mississippi Valley Historical Review*, XXII (September, 1935) , 226; Carl Schurz to C. F. Adams, April 3, 1900, Adams Papers; Carl Schurz to E. B. Smith, August 7, 1900, and to Moorfield Storey, August 11, 1900, in Bancroft, vol. VI, pp. 201–03.

48. Carl Schurz to E. B. Smith, March 11 and March 19, 1900, Schurz Papers.

49. Carl Schurz to E. B. Smith, August 7, 1900, and to Moorfield Storey, August 11, 1900, Bancroft, vol. VI, pp. 201–03; Lanzar, *Philippine Social Science Review*, III, 37.

50. Carl Schurz to Lyman J. Gage, September 10, 1900, Bancroft, vol. VI, pp. 208–09.

51. C. F. Adams to Carl Schurz, October 20, 1900, and Carl Schurz to C. F. Adams, October 25, 1900, Adams Papers; John Hay to Henry Adams, October 31, 1900, [Henry Adams], (ed.) , *Letters of John Hay and Extracts from Diary*, By the author, Washington, D.C., 1908, vol. III, p. 200. Henry Adams, in editing these volumes, often deleted proper names for reasons of discretion, but they are usually identifiable in the context.

    Two days before the election Schurz wrote that he had anticipated Bryan's defeat for many months but had nonetheless felt it as necessary to support him as it had been to back Horace Greeley in 1872. Carl Schurz to C. F. Adams, November 5, 1900, Adams Papers. Two months later Schurz wrote a friend: "Whatever good qualities Bryan may possess, I have always considered him the evil genius of the anti-imperialistic cause. To vote for him was the most distasteful thing I ever did." Carl Schurz to E. B. Smith, January 17, 1901, Bancroft, vol. VI, p. 276.

52. For Codman, Garrison, Godkin, Higginson, Norton, Storey, Smith, and Welsh, see clipping from unidentified and undated (probably early October, 1900) newspaper which lists those signing a "call" in support of Bryan on the basis of his anti-imperialist stance. Storey Papers.

    For Atkinson, see Edward Atkinson to George F. Washburn, October

18, 1900, Atkinson Papers, MHS; Edward Atkinson to Andrew Carnegie, November 19, 1900, Carnegie Papers. For James, see William James to Carl Schurz, March 16, 1900, Schurz Papers; William James to Francis Boott, 1900, in Ralph Barton Perry, *The Thought and Character of William James, As Revealed in Unpublished Correspondence and Notes, Together with his Published Writings*, Little, Brown, and Company, Boston, 1935, vol. II, p. 312. For Storey, see clipping from the *Boston Herald*, September 19, 1900, Storey Papers; Moorfield Storey to Carl Schurz, March 14, 1900, Schurz Papers. For Jordan, see David Starr Jordan to William Jennings Bryan, February 7, March 7, and April 13, 1900, William Jennings Bryan Papers, Library of Congress, Washington, D.C., cited hereafter as Bryan Papers; David Starr Jordan, *The Days of a Man: Being Memoirs of a Naturalist, Teacher and Minor Prophet of Democracy*, World Book Company, New York, 1922, vol. I, p. 135.

For Sumner, see Bailey, *Mississippi Valley Historical Review*, XXIV, 48. For Bradford, see Pettigrew, pp. 321–22; Gamaliel Bradford to George F. Hoar, April 21, 1900, George F. Hoar Papers, Massachusetts Historical Society, Boston, Massachusetts, cited hereafter as Hoar Papers. For Higginson, see T. W. Higginson, "Reasons for Voting for Bryan," *Springfield Daily Republican*, September 1, 1900. For Eliot, see C. W. Eliot to William James, January 24, 1901, Perry, vol. I, p. 434. For Mark Twain, see William Merriam Gibson, "Mark Twain and William Dean Howells: Anti-Imperialists," unpublished Ph.D. dissertation, Department of English, University of Chicago, 1940, pp. 72, 84. For Croffut, see W. A. Croffut to W. J. Bryan, July 7, 1900, Croffut Papers. For Smith, see E. B. Smith to Elwood S. Corser, February 26, 1900, Bryan Papers. For Bacon, see Theodore W. Bacon to Chairman, Executive Committee, National Association of Anti-Imperialist Clubs, September 10, 1900, *The Anti-Imperialist*, I (October 1, 1900), 67–68. For Bowles, see Samuel Bowles to Carl Schurz, March 27, 1900, Schurz Papers. For Cuyler, see Theodore Cuyler to Edward Ordway, June 1, 1900, Edward Ordway Papers, New York City Public Library, New York. For Haskins, see David G. Haskins to Erving Winslow, March 29, 1900, Schurz Papers. For White, see *The Evening Post Hundredth Anniversary, November 16, 1801–1901*, The Evening Post Publishing Co., New York, 1902, pp. 82–83; Horace White to Carl Schurz, July 21, 1899, and March 23, 1900, Schurz Papers. For Winslow, see Erving Winslow to Carl Schurz, March 21, 1900, Schurz Papers.

53. Benjamin Harrison to W. H. H. Miller, September 18, 1900, Benjamin Harrison Papers, Library of Congress, Washington, D.C., cited hereafter as Harrison Papers.

54. Frederick H. Gillett, *George Frisbie Hoar*, Houghton Mifflin Company, Boston, 1934, p. 292.

PART TWO/*Republicans Out of Step*

1. Lawrence S. Mayo (ed.) , *America of Yesterday as Reflected in the Journal of John Davis Long*, The Atlantic Monthly Press, Boston, 1923, p. 214.

2. H. Wayne Morgan, *William McKinley and His America*, Syracuse University Press, Syracuse, N.Y., 1963, p. 388.

3. John Hay to Andrew Carnegie, August 22, 1898, quoted in Andrew Carnegie, *Autobiography*, Doubleday, Doran & Company, Inc., Garden City, N.Y., 1933, p. 347.

4. Alfred T. Mahan to H. C. Lodge, July 27, 1898, in William E. Livezey, *Mahan on Sea Power*, University of Oklahoma Press, Norman, Okla., 1947, p. 183.

5. Shelby Cullom to Richard J. Oglesby, December 10, 1898, Oglesby Papers, Illinois State Historical Library, Springfield, Illinois. I am indebted to Professor Joel Tarr for calling this letter to my attention.

6. Quoted in Howard K. Beale, *Theodore Roosevelt and the Rise of America to World Power*, Collier Books, New York, 1962, p. 33.

7. Mayo, p. 213.

CHAPTER 7/*George F. Hoar: The Trials of Dissent*

1. A. Whitney Griswold, *The Far Eastern Policy of the United States*, Harcourt, Brace and Company, New York, 1938, p. 32.

2. Edward Atkinson to Samuel C. Parks, January 24, 1901, Atkinson Papers, MHS.

3. For biographical material see George F. Hoar, *Autobiography of Seventy Years*, 2 vols., Charles Scribner's Sons, New York, 1903, subsequently referred to in this chapter simply as *Autobiography;* Frederick H. Gillett, *George Frisbie Hoar*, Houghton Mifflin Company, Boston, 1934; [George H. Haynes], "George Frisbie Hoar," *Dictionary of American Biography*, ed. Allan Johnson and Dumas Malone (1928–1936) , vol. IX; and Edward E. Hale, "George F. Hoar," *Proceedings of the American Antiquarian Society*, New Series, XVII (April, 1905–April, 1906) , 150–66.

4. Lawrence S. Mayo (ed.) , *America of Yesterday as Reflected in the Journal of John Davis Long*, The Atlantic Monthly Press, Boston, 1923, pp.

148–49; Edward O. Wolcott to Moreton Frewen, May 4, 1896, Moreton Frewen Papers, Library of Congress, Washington, D.C.

5. Frances Carpenter (ed.), *Carp's Washington*, McGraw-Hill Book Company, Inc., New York, 1960, p. 20.

6. Charles Francis Adams, Jr., "Memorabilia," March 11, 1899, Adams Papers.

7. Quoted in Bliss Perry's essay on Hoar in M. A. DeWolfe Howe (ed.), *Later Years of the Saturday Club, 1870–1920,* Houghton Mifflin Company, Boston, 1927, p. 136.

8. George F. Hoar, "Has the Senate Degenerated?" *The Forum*, XXIII (April, 1897), 130.

9. Quoted in David S. Muzzey, *James G. Blaine: A Political Idol of Other Days,* Dodd, Mead & Company, New York, 1934, p. 301.

10. George F. Hoar, "Popular Discontent with Representative Government," *Annual Report of the American Historical Association for The Year 1895,* Government Printing Office, Washington, 1896, p. 24; Hoar, *The Forum*, XXIII, 144.

11. *Autobiography,* vol. I, p. 132.

12. U.S., *Congressional Record,* 55th Cong., 2d Sess., 1898, p. 6663 (July 5).

13. Quoted in Theodore H. White, *The Making of the President 1960,* Pocket Books, Inc., New York, 1961, p. 429.

14. Hoar, "Popular Discontent . . . ," pp. 31, 35.

15. *Autobiography,* vol. I, p. 313.

16. Howe, *Later Years of the Saturday Club*, p. 52.

17. Matthew Josephson, *The Politicos, 1865–1896,* Harcourt, Brace and Company, New York, 1938, p. 164; *Autobiography,* vol. I, pp. 380, 385, 406, 410.

18. Thomas Wentworth Higginson, "George Frisbie Hoar," *Proceedings of the American Academy of Arts and Sciences*, XL (July, 1905), 768.

19. Hoar, "Popular Discontent . . . ," pp. 34–35.

20. U.S., *Congressional Record,* 54th Cong., 1st Sess., 1896, p. 2679 (March 11).

21. Hoar, *The Forum*, XXIII, 130.

22. Carl Schurz (quoting Hoar) to George F. Hoar, August 22, 1884, Frederic Bancroft (ed.), *Speeches, Correspondence and Political Papers of Carl Schurz,* G. P. Putnam's Sons, New York, 1913, vol. IV, p. 277.

23. *Autobiography,* vol. I, p. 196.

24. He later apologized for the last phrase, declaring that Queen Liliuokalani was "an excellent Christian woman." *Ibid.,* vol. II, pp. 263–65; George F. Hoar to C. F. Adams, January 14 and January 20, 1896, Adams Papers.

25. U.S., *Congressional Record,* 54th Cong., 1st Sess., 1895, p. 36 (December 4); Gillett, p. 270.

26. Donald Marquand Dozer, "Anti-Imperialism in the United States, 1865–1895: Opposition to Annexation of Overseas Territories," unpublished Ph.D. dissertation, Department of History, Harvard University, [1936], pp. 64–65; *Autobiography*, vol. II, p. 123.

27. See U.S., *Congressional Record*, 54th Cong., 1st Sess., 1896, pp. 815, 2682 (January 21 and March 11); Joseph E. Wisan, *The Cuban Crisis as Reflected in the New York Press (1895–1898)*, Columbia University Press, New York, 1934, pp. 292–93; Gillett, pp. 196–97; and Hoar, *The Forum*, XXIII, 134.

28. Gillett, p. 201.

29. James D. Richardson (ed.), *Messages and Papers of the Presidents*, Bureau of National Literature, Inc., New York, 1896–1922, vol. XII, p. 6292.

30. U.S., *Congressional Record*, 55th Cong., 2d Sess., 1898, p. 3835 (April 14). See also George F. Hoar to William Claflin, April 12, 1898, quoted in Gillett, pp. 203–04.

31. U.S., *Congressional Record*, 55th Cong., 2d Sess., 1898, pp. 4040–41.

32. *Ibid.*, pp. 4242, 4244. After the armistice with Spain was concluded, however, Hoar spoke of the war as just in its origins and referred to the war resolutions as "inevitable and righteous" statements that had met with his approval. See George F. Hoar to Edward Atkinson, September 2, 1898, and to William H. Ryder, November 3, 1898, Hoar Papers.

33. *Autobiography*, vol. II, p. 307.

34. Merze Tate, *The United States and the Hawaiian Kingdom: A Political History*, Yale University Press, New Haven, 1965, p. 284.

35. Theodore Roosevelt to Alfred T. Mahan, December 9, 11, 13, 1897, Elting E. Morison et al. (eds.), *The Letters of Theodore Roosevelt*, Harvard University Press, Cambridge, Mass., 1951–1954, vol. I, pp. 725, 741; William E. Livezey, *Mahan on Sea Power*, University of Oklahoma Press, Norman, Okla., 1947, p. 170; *Autobiography*, vol. II, pp. 307–08; Margaret Leech, *In the Days of McKinley*, Harper & Brothers, New York, 1959, p. 213. William A. Russ, Jr., in *The Hawaiian Republic (1894–98) and Its Struggle To Win Annexation*, Susquehanna University Press, Selinsgrove, Penna., 1961, pp. 126, 129–77, disparages the seriousness of any threat from Japan and argues that the Hawaiian government used the Japanese bogey "as a lever to win support for annexation in the United States." Walter LaFeber believes that an actual threat of Japanese intervention did exist, *The New Empire: An Interpretation of American Expansion, 1860–1898*, Cornell University Press, Ithaca, N.Y., 1963, pp. 363–64, but Russ's evidence to the contrary seems more convincing.

36. Albert S. Parsons to George F. Hoar, June 25, 1898, and George F. Hoar

to Albert S. Parsons, June 28, 1898, Hoar Papers; *Autobiography*, vol. II, p. 310.

37. U.S., *Congressional Record*, 55th Cong., 2d Sess., 1898, p. 6143 (June 20). This was Morrill's last major anti-imperialist speech; he died six months later.

38. *Ibid.*, pp. 6660–65 (July 5); *Autobiography*, vol. II, p. 306.

39. U.S., *Congressional Record*, 55th Cong., 2d Sess., 1898, p. 6666 (July 5); R. F. Pettigrew, *The Course of Empire: An Official Record*, Boni & Liveright, New York, 1920, p. 195.

40. *Autobiography*, vol. II, p. 311.

41. *The Nation*, July 7, 1898, p. 2.

42. For examples of these letters see George F. Hoar to Justin Morrill, September 26, 1898, Justin Morrill Papers, Library of Congress, Washington, D.C., cited hereafter as Morrill Papers; George F. Hoar to William H. Ryder, November 3, 1898, to George S. Boutwell, November 5, 1898, to O. K. Lapham, December 2, 1898, and to A. P. Putnam, January 9, 1899, Hoar Papers; George F. Hoar to Edward Atkinson, December 16, 1898, Edward Atkinson Papers, New York Public Library, New York; and George F. Hoar to C. F. Adams, February 11, 1899, Adams Papers.

43. Sara Norton and M. A. DeWolfe Howe (eds.), *Letters of Charles Eliot Norton with Biographical Comment*, Houghton Mifflin Company, Boston, 1913, vol. II, pp. 457–59. Hoar repeated his attack later in the month. See *The Nation*, August 4, 1898, p. 81.

44. Edward Everett Hale to George F. Hoar, July 30, 1898, Hoar Papers. Hale's son, Edward Everett Hale, Jr., was in total disagreement with his father. Edward E. Hale [Jr.] to C. E. Norton [July, 1898], and C. E. Norton to Edward E. Hale [Jr.], July 22, 1898, Norton Papers.

45. David G. Haskins, Jr., to George F. Hoar, July 19, 1898, Hoar Papers; *The Nation*, August 4, 1898, p. 81.

46. Remarks on imperialism made by Hoar in Worcester, Massachusetts, November 1, 1898, clipping attached to letter of C. F. Adams to George F. Hoar, November 2, 1898, Hoar Papers.

47. *Autobiography*, vol. II, p. 315.

48. George F. Hoar to editor of the *Worcester Gazette*, November 30, 1898, quoted in Gillett, p. 225; George F. Hoar to William D. Sohier, December 10, 1898, Hoar Papers.

49. George F. Hoar to Beverly K. Moore, Secretary, Boston Merchants' Association, copy-draft, December 29, 1898, Hoar Papers.

50. George F. Hoar to George S. Boutwell, November 12, 1898, and to Carl Schurz, January 12, 1899, quoted in Gillett, pp. 222–23, 225–26; George F. Hoar to George S. Boutwell, November 5, 1898, Hoar Papers; George F.

Hoar to Carl Schurz, December 5, 1898, Schurz Papers; *The Nation*, November 10, 1898, p. 342.

51. William McKinley to George F. Hoar, September 13, 1898, *Autobiography*, vol. II, p. 295; George F. Hoar to William F. McKinley, telegram, September 14, 1898, William McKinley Papers, Library of Congress, Washington, D.C., hereafter cited as McKinley Papers. Hoar was also considered for appointment to the Peace Commission. Bascom N. Timmons (ed.), *A Journal of The McKinley Years by Charles G. Dawes*, The Lakeside Press, Chicago, 1950, p. 167.

52. George F. Hoar to Carl Schurz, December 5, 1898, and January 28, 1899, and Carl Schurz to C. F. Adams, January 19, 1899, Schurz Papers.

53. George F. Hoar to C. F. Adams, November 29, 1898, Adams Papers. St. Thomas is one of the Virgin Islands, then in the possession of Denmark.

54. *Ibid.*

55. U.S., *Congressional Record*, 55th Cong., 3d Sess., 1899, pp. 493–503 (January 9) .

56. George F. Hoar to Carl Schurz, January 12, 1899, quoted in Gillett, pp. 225–26; George F. Hoar to Carl Schurz, January 28, 1899, Schurz Papers.

57. As reported by Henry Adams. Upon hearing of Hoar's fervent declaration from Henry Cabot Lodge, Adams commented: "I would gladly see the execution, on the same condition, if I could see how under the scaffold of this sainted man I could find an escape from the Philippines." Worthington C. Ford (ed.) , *Letters of Henry Adams*, Houghton Mifflin Company, Boston, 1930–1938, vol. II, p. 209.

58. George F. Hoar to William C. Lovering, February 3, 1899, quoted in Gillett, pp. 226–27.

59. U.S., Congress, Senate, *Treaty of Paris between the United States and Spain, Signed at the City of Paris December 10, 1898, with Senate Joint Resolution No. 240, Fifty-Fifth Congress, Third Session, and the Votes upon Said Treaty and Joint Resolution and the Amendments in the Senate*, 57th Cong., 1st Sess., 1902, Senate Document No. 182, U.S. Government Printing Office, Washington, 1902, pp. 12–16.

60. For analyses of the votes on the Treaty, resolutions, and amendments, see Julius W. Pratt, *Expansionists of 1898: The Acquisition of Hawaii and the Spanish Islands*, The Johns Hopkins Press, Baltimore, 1936, p. 358; Richard W. Leopold, *The Growth of American Foreign Policy: A History*, Alfred A. Knopf, New York, 1962, p. 191; Merle Curti, *Bryan and World Peace*, "Smith College Studies in History," vol. XVI, nos. 3–4, Department of History of Smith College, Northampton, Mass., 1931, p. 122; and Thomas A. Bailey, *A Diplomatic History of the American People*, 4th ed., Appleton-Century-Crofts, Inc., New York, 1950, p. 524. Lodge's letter to Roosevelt was written February 9, 1899, Henry Cabot

Lodge (ed.), *Selections from the Correspondence of Theodore Roosevelt and Henry Cabot Lodge, 1884–1918*, Charles Scribner's Sons, New York, 1925, vol. I, p. 391.

61. Henry Adams to Elizabeth Cameron, February 12, 1899, Ford, vol. II, p. 217.

62. George S. Boutwell to George F. Hoar, December 27, 1899, and George F. Hoar to George S. Boutwell, October 11, December 23, and December 29, 1899, Hoar Papers. Hoar was unwilling to confront Bryan directly with this charge, writing to him on May 15, 1900: "I cannot help thinking that, *next to* President McKinley, you are the person in the country most responsible for the adoption of the treaty . . . " (Italics mine.) Bryan Papers.

63. George F. Hoar to George S. Boutwell, March 2, 1899, Hoar Papers; George F. Hoar to W. A. Croffut, January 13, 1900, Croffut Papers.

64. George F. Hoar to Moorfield Storey, March 6, 1899, Storey Papers. For an excellent discussion of Hoar's determination to separate himself from mugwump anti-imperialists and to maintain his Republican associations, see Richard E. Welch, Jr., "Opponents and Colleagues: George Frisbie Hoar and Henry Cabot Lodge, 1898–1904," *New England Quarterly*, XXXIX (June, 1966), 182–209.

65. George F. Hoar to George F. Edmunds, December 13, 1899, Croffut Papers; U.S., *Congressional Record*, 56th Cong., 1st Sess., 1900, p. 4303 (April 17).

66. *The Anti-Imperialist*, I (May 27, 1899), 53; U.S., *Congressional Record*, 56th Cong., 1st Sess., 1900, p. 714 (January 9).

67. *Autobiography*, vol. I, p. 259.

68. U.S., *Congressional Record*, 56th Cong., 1st Sess., 1900, p. 4285 (April 17).

69. On this issue see George F. Hoar to Henry A. Marsh, December 30, 1899, Hoar Papers; W. A. Croffut to George F. Hoar, January 15, 1900, Croffut Papers; Maximo M. Kalaw, *The Development of Philippine Politics (1872–1920): an Account of the Part Played by the Filipino Leaders and Parties in the Political Development of the Philippines*, Oriental Commercial Company, Inc., Manila, n.d., pp. 250, 252; Leon Wolff, *Little Brown Brother: America's Forgotten Bid for Empire which Cost 250,000 Lives*, Longmans, Green and Co., Ltd., London, 1961, pp. 275–76; Dean C. Worcester and Ralston Hayden, *The Philippines Past and Present*, The Macmillan Company, New York, 1930, pp. 248–52; and Fred C. Chamberlin, *The Blow from Behind*, Lee and Shepard, Boston, 1903, pp. 95–99, 108–10.

70. George F. Hoar to John D. Long, October 6, 1898, Gardner W. Allen (ed.), *Papers of John Davis Long, 1897–1904*, "Massachusetts Historical Society Collections," vol. LXXVIII, Massachusetts Historical Society, Bos-

ton, 1939, p. 196; George F. Hoar to Carl Schurz, October 26, 1898, Bancroft, vol. V, pp. 527–28; and George F. Hoar to H. C. Lodge, November 4, 1898, Hoar Papers.

71. George F. Hoar, "Party Government in the United States: The Importance of Government by the Republican Party," *The International Monthly,* II (October, 1900) , 433.

72. Thomas A. Bailey, "Was the Presidential Election of 1900 a Mandate on Imperialism?" *Mississippi Valley Historical Review,* XXIV (June, 1937) , 45–46; George F. Hoar to George S. Boutwell, April 23 and October 26, 1900, Hoar Papers; George F. Hoar to W. J. Bryan, May 15, 1900, Bryan Papers; Leech, p. 552; Charles S. Olcott, *The Life of William McKinley,* Houghton Mifflin Company, Boston, 1916, vol. II, p. 288; "Bryan or McKinley? The Present Duty of American Citizens," *North American Review,* CLXXI (October, 1900) , 477–80, 485; and *Autobiography,* vol. II, p. 319.

73. David F. Healy, *The United States in Cuba, 1898–1902: Generals, Politicians, and the Search for Policy,* The University of Wisconsin Press, Madison, Wis., 1963, pp. 165–66. McKinley tactfully declined the invitation to the 1901 Harvard commencement (personal attendance was required of all recipients of honorary degrees) , thereby stilling the controversy. The Overseers had voted 20 to 3 to award the degree, but much ill feeling had been aroused. Those opposed were all anti-imperialists: Charles Eliot Norton, Moorfield Storey, and Charles Joseph Bonaparte. Four of those in favor were also anti-imperialists: Hoar, Charles W. Eliot (whose anti-imperialism was tepid) , Charles Francis Adams, and Winslow Warren. For the controversy, see clipping on the vote in the Storey Papers; M. A. DeWolfe Howe, *Portrait of an Independent: Moorfield Storey, 1845–1929,* Houghton Mifflin Company, Boston, 1932, p. 177; Gillett, pp. 272–75; and George F. Hoar to John D. Long, May 13 and June 20, 1901, Gardner W. Allen, pp. 363–64, 372–73.

74. *Autobiography,* vol. II, pp. 316–17.

75. Leech, p. 570; *Autobiography,* vol. I, p. 161; Everett Walters, *Joseph Benson Foraker: An Uncompromising Republican,* The Ohio History Press, Columbus, Ohio, 1948, p. 193.

76. Gillett, p. 265.

77. *Autobiography,* vol. II, pp. 304, 324.

78. Higginson, *Proceedings of the American Academy of Arts and Sciences,* XL, 767–68.

79. The reader should also see Richard E. Welch, Jr., "Senator George Frisbie Hoar and the Defeat of Anti-Imperialism, 1898–1900," *The Historian,* XXVI (May, 1964) , 362–80, which, though different in emphasis from this chapter, does stress the role played by partisanship in Hoar's

anti-imperialist efforts. This article also discusses in detail Hoar's interest in a protectorate scheme for the Philippines.

CHAPTER 8/*Andrew Carnegie: The Primacy of the Philippines*

1. Clipping enclosed in letter of John Beatty to Andrew Carnegie, December 8, 1898, Carnegie Papers; Carl Schurz to Andrew Carnegie, July 2, 1902, in Frederic Bancroft (ed.), *Speeches, Correspondence and Political Papers of Carl Schurz*, G. P. Putnam's Sons, New York, 1913, vol. VI, p. 292.

2. Burton J. Hendrick, *The Life of Andrew Carnegie*, Doubleday, Doran & Company, Garden City, N.Y., 1932, vol. I, p. ix.

3. For interesting discussions of Carnegie's writings, see Edward C. Kirkland, *Dream and Thought in the Business Community, 1860–1900*, Quadrangle Books, Chicago, 1964, and Robert Green McCloskey, *American Conservatism in the Age of Enterprise: A Study of William Graham Sumner, Stephen J. Field and Andrew Carnegie*, Harvard University Press, Cambridge, Mass., 1951. Fritz Redlich, in a review of McCloskey's volume, has warned students to beware of accepting books and articles that appear under Carnegie's name as his personal work, noting that James H. Bridge, secretary to Herbert Spencer from 1879 to 1884, served as Carnegie's "literary assistant" from 1884 to 1889, with other assistants doubtless following in his place. These were presumably Carnegie's ghost writers. Redlich maintains, as a consequence, that "access to private correspondence, business records, diaries, drafts of speeches and the like is indispensable for an analysis of a businessman's thinking." The warning is well taken, but this writer, who has had access to correspondence, business records, drafts of newspaper letters, "and the like," finds no noticeable difference in style or emphasis between the Carnegie of this "trustworthy" material and the Carnegie who wrote books and magazine articles. For Redlich's review, see *American Historical Review*, LVII (April, 1952), 707–09.

4. Andrew Carnegie, *Triumphant Democracy or Fifty Years' March of The Republic*, Doubleday, Doran & Company, Inc., Garden City, N.Y., 1933, p. v.

5. Hendrick, *The Life of Andrew Carnegie*, vol. I, pp. 31, 264; Andrew Carnegie, *Round the World*, Charles Scribner's Sons, New York, 1884, p. 23.

6. Carnegie, *Triumphant Democracy*, p. 15.

7. *Ibid.*, p. 32; McCloskey, pp. 137–38. As Edward C. Kirkland has observed, Carnegie had in him "a touch of Henry Ford." *Business in the Gilded*

Age: The Conservatives' Balance Sheet, University of Wisconsin Press, Madison, Wis., 1952, p. 45.

8. Carnegie, *Triumphant Democracy,* pp. 210, 329.

9. Hendrick, *The Life of Andrew Carnegie,* vol. I, pp. 24, 47–48, 66.

10. *Ibid.,* pp. 103, 229; Carnegie, *Round the World,* pp. 14–15, 109–10, 114–15, 345–46.

11. Andrew Carnegie, *Autobiography,* Doubleday, Doran & Company, Inc., Garden City, N.Y., 1933, p. 271; Andrew Carnegie, *An American Four-in-Hand in Britain,* Charles Scribner's Sons, New York, 1884, pp. 15–16; Carnegie, *Triumphant Democracy,* pp. 5, 315; Andrew Carnegie to William E. Gladstone, July 14, 1885, and June 29, 1887, Hendrick, *The Life of Andrew Carnegie,* vol. I, pp. 282, 284 (see also vol. II, pp. 404–06) ; Devere Allen, *The Fight for Peace,* The Macmillan Company, New York, 1930, p. 128; "Mr. Carnegie's Gifts," 1885–1897, Carnegie Papers; A. C. F. Beales, *The History of Peace: A Short Account of the Organised Movements for International Peace,* The Dial Press, New York, 1931, p. 189; and [Burton J. Hendrick], "Andrew Carnegie," *Dictionary of American Biography,* ed. Allan Johnson and Dumas Malone (1928–1936) , vol. III, p. 505.

12. Carnegie, *Round the World,* pp. 224–25, 228, 288, 293–94, 329.

13. Carnegie, *Triumphant Democracy,* pp. 328–29.

14. Andrew Carnegie to James G. Blaine, April 20, 1889, Carnegie Papers; Carnegie, *Autobiography,* pp. 333–34.

15. Andrew Carnegie to Benjamin Harrison, telegram, October 26, 1891, Carnegie Papers; Carnegie, *Autobiography,* pp. 338–40.

16. Andrew Carnegie to George Lauder, Jr., February 24, 1854, Hendrick, *The Life of Andrew Carnegie,* vol. I, p. 80.

17. Andrew Carnegie to James G. Blaine, January 14, 1882, quoted in David S. Muzzey, *James G. Blaine: A Political Idol of Other Days,* Dodd, Mead & Company, New York, 1934, p. 237.

18. Andrew Carnegie to John Patterson, December 1, 1891, and *London Financial Times,* December 19, 1891, clippings, Carnegie Papers.

19. Carnegie, *Triumphant Democracy,* pp. 210, 315.

20. Andrew Carnegie to editor of the *New York Sun* [December, 1895?], to editor of the *London Times,* December 23, 1895, and to the Duke of Devonshire, December 26, 1895, Carnegie Papers; and Andrew Carnegie, "The Venezuelan Question," *North American Review,* CLXII (February, 1896) , 131, 136, 142.

21. Andrew Carnegie to George Lauder, Sr., March 14, 1853, Hendrick, *The Life of Andrew Carnegie,* vol. I, p. 83.

22. Andrew Carnegie to William E. Gladstone, July 14, 1885, June 29, 1887, and March 28, 1891, *ibid.,* pp. 258, 282, 284, 416–17, 420–22.

23. *Ibid.,* p. 270; draft of letter from Andrew Carnegie to unidentified news-

paper, perhaps the *New York Evening Post,* date probably around January 1, 1899, Carnegie Papers (see pp. 11572-K through 11583).

24. Andrew Carnegie to the Duke of Devonshire, December 26, 1895, to S. Theo. Mander, January 16, 1896, to Goldwin Smith, February 6, 1896, to W. T. Stead, January 7, 1898, and to Swire Smith, March 7, 1898, Carnegie Papers; Carnegie, *North American Review,* CLXII, 131, 133.

25. Joseph E. Wisan, *The Cuban Crisis as Reflected in the New York Press (1895–1898),* Columbia University Press, New York, 1934, p. 82; Andrew Carnegie to H. C. Frick, December 15, 1897, Carnegie Papers.

26. Copy, telegram, Andrew Carnegie to William McKinley, undated, but clearly sent shortly before the beginning of the war, Andrew Carnegie to H. C. Frick, April 23, 1898, and to C. M. Schwab, April 23, 1898 (included in "Minutes of Meeting of the Board of Managers of the Carnegie Steel Company," April 26, 1898), Carnegie Papers.

27. Andrew Carnegie to Dr. Adolf Gurlt, June 1, 1898, and telegram to General Nelson A. Miles, undated, but about July 17, 1898, *ibid.*; Nelson A. Miles, *Serving the Republic,* Harper & Brothers Publishers, New York, 1911, p. 274.

28. E. L. Godkin to Andrew Carnegie, November 1, [1898], and Carl Schurz to Andrew Carnegie, November 27, 1898, Carnegie Papers.

29. Erving Winslow to Andrew Carnegie, November 21, 1898, and Edward Atkinson to Andrew Carnegie, November 22, 1898, *ibid.*

30. [Finley Peter Dunne], *Mr. Dooley In the Hearts of His Countrymen,* Small, Maynard & Company, Boston, 1899, pp. 6–7.

31. *New York Times,* October 24, 1898.

32. Andrew Carnegie to Whitelaw Reid, December 1, 1899, Carnegie Papers. The above paragraph is based on a body of sources too large to cite in detail. The interested student, however, will find abundant evidence of Carnegie's attitudes in the Carnegie Papers on file in the Library of Congress. In particular see copies of letters written to various New York newspapers from October, 1898, through January, 1899, letters to John Morley written for the most part in the summer of 1900, and letters to Carl Schurz, October 24, 1898, to John Hay, December 29, 1898, to Stephen B. Elkins, January 2, 1901, and to Arthur Balfour, August 9, 1901. In addition to the Carnegie Papers, see articles by Carnegie that appeared in the *North American Review* in August, 1898, and January, March, and December, 1899.

33. Clipping from *New York Journal,* August 31, 1898, Carnegie Papers.

34. Andrew Carnegie, *Cuba Free!,* leaflet, undated, but evidently written in early December, 1898; draft of letter to *New York Evening Post,* probably written in January, 1899; and letter to the editor of *New York World,* January 29, 1899, all found in Carnegie Papers.

35. Draft of letter to *New York Evening Post,* probably written in January,

1899, to John Hay, July 26, 1900, and to Arthur Balfour, August 9, 1901, Carnegie Papers.

36. Andrew Carnegie, "Americanism *Versus* Imperialism," *North American Review*, CLXVIII (January, 1899) , 12.

37. Andrew Carnegie, "Distant Possessions—The Parting· of the Ways," *ibid.*, CLXVII (August, 1898) , 242; Andrew Carnegie to Stephen B. Elkins, January 2, 1901, Carnegie Papers.

38. Carnegie, *North American Review*, CLXVII, 242–43·

39. *Ibid.*, p. 242; clipping from *New York Journal*, August 31, 1898, Carnegie Papers.

40. See sources cited in footnotes 36–39.

41. Andrew Carnegie to William McKinley, February 2, 1899, McKinley Papers.

42. Garel A. Grunder and William E. Livezey, *The Philippines and the United States*, University of Oklahoma Press, Norman, Okla., 1951, p. 10.

43. Draft, Andrew Carnegie to *New York World*, November 20, 1898, Carnegie Papers.

44. Carnegie, *North American Review*, CLXVII, 241.

45. Andrew Carnegie to *New York World*, November 27, 1898, Carnegie Papers.

46. Draft, Andrew Carnegie to *New York World*, November 20, 1898, *ibid.*

47. See Andrew Carnegie to *New York World*, November 20 and 24, 1898, to John Hay, November 24, 1898, to William McKinley, November 28, 1898, and to *Atlanta Semi-Weekly Journal*, February 2, 1899, Carnegie Papers.

48. Andrew Carnegie to James Wilson, December 3, 1898, *ibid.*

49. Herbert W. Collingwood, editor of *The Rural New Yorker,* "Uncle Sam Talks Turkey," clipping in Herbert W. Collingwood to Herbert Myrick, December 9, 1898, and Andrew Carnegie to James Wilson, December 3, 1898, *ibid.*

50. Andrew Carnegie to E. L. Godkin, November 26, 1898, to *New York World*, January 29, 1899, *ibid.*; Andrew Carnegie to W. J. Bryan, December 26, 1898, January 10, [1899], pencil draft (incorrectly dated 1898) , and Andrew Carnegie to W. J. Bryan, January 11, 1899, telegram, Bryan Papers.

51. Bancroft, vol. V, p. 531.

52. William Merriam Gibson, "Mark Twain and William Dean Howells: Anti-Imperialists," unpublished Ph.D. dissertation, Department of English, University of Chicago, 1940, pp. 94–95·

53. Andrew Carnegie to W. J. Bryan, December 15, 18, 26, and 27, 1898, Bryan Papers; W. J. Bryan to Andrew Carnegie, December 24, 1898, telegram, Carnegie Papers; Joseph Rogers Hollingsworth, "A Study in Party

Division: The Democratic Party, 1893–1900," unpublished Ph.D. dissertation, Department of History, University of Chicago, 1960, p. 199.

54. Andrew Carnegie to Wayne MacVeagh, October 26, 1896, Carnegie Papers; Margaret Leech, *In the Days of McKinley*, Harper & Brothers, New York, 1959, p. 59.

55. Andrew Carnegie to John Hay, November 24, 1898, Carnegie Papers.

56. Andrew Carnegie to William McKinley, November 28, 1898, *ibid.*

57. John Hay to Whitelaw Reid, November 29, 1898, in William Roscoe Thayer, *The Life and Letters of John Hay*, Houghton Mifflin Company, Boston, 1915, vol. II, p. 199.

58. R. F. Pettigrew, *Imperial Washington: The Story of American Public Life from 1870 to 1920*, Charles H. Kerr & Company, Co-operative, Chicago, 1922, p. 273. Pettigrew was the only participant in the Plaza conference to leave an account of what happened.

59. Andrew Carnegie to John Hay, December 27, 1898, and to [John Morley?], May 26, 1899, Carnegie Papers.

60. Andrew Carnegie to John Hay, July 26, 1900, *ibid.*

61. Andrew Carnegie, "The Presidential Election—Our Duty," *North American Review*, CLXXI (October, 1900), 497, 500–502, 504.

62. *The Nation*, October 6, 1898, p. 254.

63. Adams, "Memorabilia," April 4, 1898, Adams Papers.

64. Edward Atkinson to William Fowler, May 10, and May 20, 1898, Atkinson Papers, MHS.

CHAPTER 9/*Old Chiefs and Stalwarts: The Impotent Protest*

1. Benjamin Harrison to James G. Blaine, October 1, 1891, quoted in Walter LaFeber, *The New Empire: An Interpretation of American Expansion, 1860–1898*, Cornell University Press, Ithaca, N.Y., 1963, p. 110.

2. *Ibid.*; A. T. Volwiler, "Harrison, Blaine, and American Foreign Policy, 1889–1893," *Proceedings of the American Philosophical Society*, LXXIX (November, 1938), quoted in William Appleman Williams (ed.), *The Shaping of American Diplomacy*, Rand McNally & Company, Chicago, vol. I, p. 358.

3. William A. Russ, Jr., *The Hawaiian Revolution (1893–94)*, Susquehanna University Press, Selinsgrove, Penna., 1959, p. 187; Calvin DeArmond Davis, *The United States and the First Hague Peace Conference*, Cornell University Press, Ithaca, N.Y., 1962, pp. 26–27.

4. Richard W. Leopold, *The Growth of American Foreign Policy: A History*, Alfred A. Knopf, New York, 1962, p. 158.

5. LaFeber, p. 110.

6. *Ibid.*, p. 149; George W. Baker, Jr., "Benjamin Harrison and Hawaiian Annexation: A Reinterpretation," *Pacific Historical Review*, XXXIII (August, 1964), 295–309.

7. Robert W. Patterson to Benjamin Harrison, March 27, 1898, and Benjamin Harrison to Robert W. Patterson, March 28, 1898, Harrison Papers.

8. "Presentation of Flag to Battery A, May 3, 1898, at Camp Mount, Indianapolis," in Benjamin Harrison, *Views of an Ex-President: Being his Addresses and Writings on Subjects of Public Interest since the Close of his Administration as President of the United States*, The Bowen-Merrill Company, Indianapolis, 1901, pp. 483–84.

9. Record of newspaper interview, enclosed in letter of Morris Ross to Benjamin Harrison, May 20, 1898, Harrison Papers.

10. Benjamin Harrison to R. W. Gilder, May 20, 1898, *ibid.*

11. Benjamin Harrison to N. B. Scott, undated but probably August, 1900, *ibid.* Harrison had been appointed counsel for Venezuela in the arbitration of her boundary dispute with British Guiana. This job kept him busy through much of 1898 and 1899—he was in Paris during the summer of 1899—while the litigation was in progress. Harrison lost the case but received a fee of $100,000. Davis, pp. 63, 204–05.

12. Benjamin Harrison to W. H. H. Miller, September 6, 1900, Harrison Papers. For McKinley's offer and Harrison's acceptance of the post, see William McKinley to Benjamin Harrison, August 24, 1900, *ibid.*, and Benjamin Harrison to William McKinley, August 29, 1900, McKinley Papers.

13. Benjamin Harrison to John Hay, January 22, 1900, Harrison Papers. See also Benjamin Harrison to R. S. Taylor, October 19, 1898, to C. W. Fairbanks, February 2, 1899, to A. W. Soper, February 7, 1899, and to S. B. Elkins, February 8, 1900, *ibid.*

14. Telegram, *New York World* to Benjamin Harrison, February 28, [1898?], *ibid.* The year 1898 written on the telegram is apparently the conjecture of a curator and is in error; the year is probably 1899, although it could also be 1900. See also Claude G. Bowers, *Beveridge and the Progressive Era*, Houghton Mifflin Company, Boston, 1932, p. 93.

15. Harrison, p. 494.

16. Item labeled, "Written Mch 2, 1900. Not given out," is a copy of a statement that Harrison originally intended to release to the public. He did issue a brief statement critical of the Puerto Rican tariff bill on March 3, 1900. See item #38244, vol. 176, Ser. I, Harrison Papers. See also Benjamin Harrison to John W. Foster, March 10, 1900, and to John M. Harlan, March 12, 1900, *ibid.* The quotation is from Ellis P. Oberholtzer, *A History of the United States since the Civil War*, The Macmillan Company, New York, 1917–1937, vol. V, p. 610.

17. Benjamin Harrison to Clarence W. Bowen and to John W. Foster, both March 10, 1900, Harrison Papers.

18. Benjamin Harrison to W. H. H. Miller, September 18, 1900, *ibid.* See Harrison's letters throughout the summer and fall of 1900, including those to N. B. Scott, August 20, 1900, W. H. H. Miller, August 22, 1900, and E. F. Tibbett, September 3, 1900, *ibid.*

19. *Rocky Mountain News* (Denver, Colo.), August 4, 1900, in vol. 51, Scrap-Book, *ibid.*

20. Unidentified newspaper, vol. 51, Scrap-Book, *ibid.*

21. Ser. I, vol. 178, page numbers 28832–4, *ibid.*

22. Benjamin Harrison to John W. Foster, October 17, 1900, and to L. T. Michener, October 17, 1900, Charles W. Fairbanks to Benjamin Harrison (telegram), October 11, 1900, Whitelaw Reid to Benjamin Harrison, October 11, 1900, A. W. Soper to Benjamin Harrison, October 11, 1900, and John W. Foster to Benjamin Harrison, October 17, 1900, *ibid.*

23. Both the headline and "Mr. Dooley's" comments are in vol. 51, Scrap-Book, *ibid.*

24. Harrison, pp. 185–91, 197, 200–201, 210–11, 217, 220–21. The speech was printed in the *North American Review* in January, 1901.

25. Benjamin Harrison to Andrew Carnegie, December 26, 1900, Carnegie Papers. Harrison suggested in this letter that it might be possible to transfer control of the Philippines through some sort of lease arrangement to a minor European power, such as Belgium.

26. Allan Nevins, *Hamilton Fish: The Inner History of the Grant Administration*, Dodd, Mead & Company, New York, 1936, p. 139.

27. Henry Adams, *The Education of Henry Adams: An Autobiography*, Houghton Mifflin Sentry Edition, Boston, 1961, p. 263.

28. For biographical information, see [Henry G. Pearson], "George Sewall Boutwell," *Dictionary of American Biography*, ed. Allan Johnson and Dumas Malone (1928–1936), vol. II, pp. 489–90, and George S. Boutwell, *Reminiscences of Sixty Years in Public Affairs*, McClure, Phillips & Co., New York, 1902, especially the editor's introductory biographical sketch in vol. I, pp. xiii–xxi.

29. Donald Marquand Dozer, "The Opposition to Hawaiian Reciprocity, 1867–1888," *Pacific Historical Review*, XIV (June, 1945), 167, 174–75; David M. Pletcher, *The Awkward Years: American Foreign Relations Under Garfield and Arthur*, University of Missouri Press, Columbia, Mo., 1962, p. 176; and Sylvester K. Stevens, *American Expansion in Hawaii, 1842–1898*, Archives Publishing Company of Pennsylvania, Inc., Harrisburg, Penna., 1945, p. 139.

30. Donald Marquand Dozer, "Anti-Expansionism during the Johnson Administration," *Pacific Historical Review*, XII (September, 1943), 260; Nevins, *Hamilton Fish*, p. 271; LaFeber, p. 128; George S. Boutwell to

Justin Morrill, December 19, 1895, Morrill Papers; Charles Francis Adams, Jr., "Memorabilia," December 25, 1895, Adams Papers; George S. Boutwell, *The Crisis of the Republic*, Dana Estes & Company, Boston, 1900, pp. 7–25; and [George S. Boutwell], *Hawaiian Annexation. Hon. Geo. S. Boutwell's Address Before the Boot and Shoe Club of Boston, December 22, 1897*, J. E. Farwell & Co., Printers, Boston, 1898, pp. 5–12.

31. George S. Boutwell to Justin Morrill, March 27, 1898, Morrill Papers; George S. Boutwell to John D. Long, March 29, 1898, Gardner W. Allen (ed.), *Papers of John Davis Long, 1897–1904*, "Massachusetts Historical Society Collections," vol. LXXVIII, Massachusetts Historical Society, Boston, 1939, pp. 78–79.

32. George S. Boutwell to John D. Long, August 7, 1898, Gardner W. Allen, pp. 180–81; Boutwell, "War, and a Change of our Public Policy," an address delivered at Kingston, Mass., Memorial Day, 1898, in Boutwell, *The Crisis of the Republic*, pp. 57–60, 62.

33. Boutwell, *The Crisis of the Republic, passim.*

34. *Ibid.* The quotation is on p. 101. See also [George S. Boutwell], *The War of Despotism in the Philippine Islands. Address of the Hon. George S. Boutwell, at Springfield, Mass., Sept. 5, 1899*, Anti-Imperialist League, n.p., n.d.; George S. Boutwell, *The President's Policy: War and Conquest Abroad; Degradation of Labor at Home. Address by Hon. George S. Boutwell, President American Anti-Imperialist League at Masonic Hall, Washington, D.C., January 11, 1900*, "Liberty Tracts," No. 7, American Anti-Imperialist League, Chicago, 1900; George S. Boutwell to George F. Hoar, November 14, 1898, Hoar Papers.

35. George S. Boutwell to C. F. Adams, June 7, 1899, Adams Papers.

36. George S. Boutwell to George F. Hoar, December 27, 1899, Hoar Papers.

37. *New York Times*, August 16, 1900.

38. Maria C. Lanzar, "The Anti-Imperialist League," *Philippine Social Science Review*, III (November, 1930), 118.

39. George S. Boutwell to W. A. Croffut, April 11, 1901, Croffut Papers.

40. George S. Boutwell to T. W. Higginson, January 30, 1901, Higginson Papers.

41. W. L. Garrison, "To George S. Boutwell," *Liberty Poems: Inspired by the Crisis of 1898–1900*, The James H. West Co., Boston, 1900, p. 117.

42. As he told Charles Francis Adams. *Charles Francis Adams, 1835–1915: An Autobiography; With a Memorial Address delivered November 17, 1915, by Henry Cabot Lodge*, Houghton Mifflin Company, Boston, 1916, p. 47.

43. Theodore E. Burton, *John Sherman*, Houghton Mifflin Company, Boston, 1907, p. 163.

44. See, for example, his interest during the 1880s in pan-Americanism and the economic penetration of Africa. Pletcher, pp. 341–42; Milton Plesur,

"Looking Outward: American Attitudes toward Foreign Affairs in the Years from Hayes to Harrison," unpublished Ph.D. dissertation, University of Rochester, 1954, pp. 117–18.

45. Nevins, *Hamilton Fish*, p. 319.

46. John Sherman, *Recollections of Forty Years in the House, Senate and Cabinet: an Autobiography*, The Werner Company, Chicago, 1895, vol. II, pp. 974–75, 983, 1020–21; Winfield S. Kerr, *John Sherman: His Life and Public Services*, Sherman, French & Company, Boston, 1908, vol. II, p. 158.

47. Merle Curti, *Peace or War: The American Struggle, 1636–1936*, W. W. Norton & Company, New York, 1936, pp. 145, 149; A. C. F. Beales, *The History of Peace: A Short Account of the Organised Movements for International Peace*, The Dial Press, New York, 1931, pp. 191, 206; Burton, p. 335; U.S., *Congressional Record*, 54th Cong., 1st Sess., 1895, pp. 242–43 (December 19). Sherman was a vice-president of the American Peace Society and of the Universal Peace Union.

48. Sherman, vol. II, p. 1216.

49. Burton, pp. 393–94.

50. Ernest R. May, *Imperial Democracy: The Emergence of America as a Great Power*, Harcourt, Brace & World, Inc., New York, 1961, p. 7.

51. In this speech Sherman made the curious suggestion that Cuba be "attached to Mexico" since "the Mexicans speak the same language, they have the same origin and the same antecedents, and are under many of the same circumstances." The Senate passed the resolution 64-6, with Sherman voting with the majority. U.S., *Congressional Record*, 54th Cong., 1st Sess., 1896, pp. 2244–47, 2257 (February 28) .

52. Quoted in Joseph E. Wisan, *The Cuban Crisis as Reflected in the New York Press (1895–1898)*, Columbia University Press, New York, 1934, p. 120.

53. For McKinley's offer and Sherman's acceptance, see William McKinley to John Sherman, January 4, 1897, and John Sherman to William McKinley, January 7, 1897, John Sherman Papers, Library of Congress, Washington, D.C., cited hereafter as Sherman Papers.

54. Margaret Leech, *In the Days of McKinley*, Harper & Brothers, New York, 1959, pp. 100–102; Kerr, vol. II, p. 376. For other interpretations of the appointment see Thomas Beer, *Hanna*, Alfred A. Knopf, New York, 1929, p. 176; H. Wayne Morgan, *William McKinley and His America*, Syracuse University Press, Syracuse, N.Y., 1963, pp. 250–56.

55. John Sherman to William McKinley, January 7, 1897, to Asa S. Bushnell, January 16, 1897, Sherman Papers; John Sherman to William McKinley, January 16, 1897, and February 10, 1897, McKinley Papers. One of Sherman's letters at this time does hint of some unhappiness with the

arrangement. See John Sherman to Richard Smith, February 9, 1897, Sherman Papers.

56. William McKinley to John Sherman, February 11, 1897, and John Sherman to William McKinley, February 15, 1897, McKinley Papers; Wisan, pp. 279–80.

57. Leech, pp. 102, 151; Lawrence S. Mayo (ed.), *America of Yesterday as Reflected in the Journal of John Davis Long*, The Atlantic Monthly Press, Boston, 1923, p. 186.

58. Louis Martin Sears, "John Sherman," in Samuel Flagg Bemis (ed.), *The American Secretaries of State and their Diplomacy*, Alfred A. Knopf, New York, 1927–1929, vol. IX, pp. 16–17; Albert K. Weinberg, *Manifest Destiny: A Study of Nationalist Expansionism in American History*, The Johns Hopkins Press, Baltimore, 1935, p. 261; Leech, p. 153; and Merze Tate, *The United States and the Hawaiian Kingdom: A Political History*, Yale University Press, New Haven, 1965, pp. 270–71.

59. Morgan, p. 336; John Sherman to William McKinley, August 21, 1897, McKinley Papers.

60. David Starr Jordan, *The Days of a Man: Being Memoirs of a Naturalist, Teacher and Minor Prophet of Democracy*, World Book Company, New York, 1922, vol. I, p. 573; Mayo, p. 153.

61. Leech, pp. 153–54, 191; May, p. 155; John Hay to Henry Adams, May 9, 1898, in William Roscoe Thayer, *The Life and Letters of John Hay*, Houghton Mifflin Company, Boston, 1915, vol. II, p. 173.

62. *The Nation*, April 28, 1898, p. 314; Leech, p. 191.

63. John Sherman to W. S. Ward, April 28, 1898, Sherman Papers.

64. John Sherman to Joseph Foraker, November 8, 1898, quoted in Champ Clark, *My Quarter Century of American Politics*, Harper & Brothers, New York, 1920, vol. I, p. 417; Scrapbook, 1898–1900, vol. 614 of Sherman Papers.

65. Scrapbook, 1897–1898, Sec. of State, mid-May clipping, p. 95, Sherman Papers; William A. Russ, Jr., *The Hawaiian Republic (1894–98) and Its Struggle To Win Annexation*, Susquehanna University Press, Selinsgrove, Penna., 1961, p. 298.

66. Kerr, vol. II, pp. 401–03.

67. *In Freedom's Name No. 3*, Washington Anti-Imperialist League, Washington, D.C., n.d. [probably November, 1899], Croffut Papers; John Sherman to William McKinley, February 16, 1899, McKinley Papers; and *Boston Evening Transcript*, May 22, 1899.

68. For biographical information, see William A. Robinson, *Thomas B. Reed, Parliamentarian*, Dodd, Mead & Company, New York, 1930; Samuel W. McCall, *The Life of Thomas Brackett Reed*, Houghton Mifflin Company, Boston, 1914; and [William A. Robinson], "Thomas Brackett

Reed," *Dictionary of American Biography*, vol. XV, pp. 457–59. The quotation is from Robinson, *Thomas B. Reed*, p. 379.

69. Cecil Spring Rice to Ronald M. Ferguson, March 28, 1890, in Stephen Gwynn (ed.), *The Letters and Friendships of Sir Cecil Spring Rice: A Record*, Houghton Mifflin Company, Boston, 1929, vol. I, p. 104.

70. Champ Clark, vol. I, p. 277; William Allen White, *Masks in a Pageant*, The Macmillan Company, New York, 1929, p. 217.

71. [Robinson], *Dictionary of American Biography*, vol. XV, p. 459; Richard Hofstadter, *The American Political Tradition and the Men Who Made It*, Vintage Books, New York, 1955, p. 197.

72. Cecil Spring Rice to Stephen Spring Rice, April 4, 1890, Gwynn, vol. I, p. 105.

73. Thomas B. Reed to Theodore Roosevelt, August 22, 1891, quoted in Henry F. Pringle, *Theodore Roosevelt: A Biography*, Harcourt, Brace and Company, New York, 1931, p. 130.

74. W. A. White, p. 326; Thomas A. Bailey, "Was the Presidential Election of 1900 a Mandate on Imperialism?" *Mississippi Valley Historical Review*, XXIV (June, 1937), 47; Michael E. Hennessy, *Twenty-Five Years of Massachusetts Politics: From Russell to McCall, 1890–1915*, Practical Politics, Inc., Boston, 1917, p. 32.

75. Arthur Wallace Dunn, *From Harrison to Harding: A Personal Narrative, Covering a Third of a Century, 1888–1921*, G. P. Putnam's Sons, New York, 1922, vol. I, p. 165; Champ Clark, vol. I, p. 284.

76. Henry Adams to Brooks Adams, February 7, 1896, Worthington C. Ford (ed.), *Letters of Henry Adams*, Houghton Mifflin Company, Boston, 1930–1938, vol. II, p. 96; Thomas B. Reed to Theodore Roosevelt, May 29, 1896, quoted in Pringle, pp. 158–59.

77. Robinson, *Thomas B. Reed*, p. 356; John A. Garraty, *Henry Cabot Lodge: A Biography*, Alfred A. Knopf, New York, 1953, p. 149.

78. Robinson, *Thomas B. Reed*, pp. 324, 358; Garraty, p. 184.

79. Thomas B. Reed, "The Safe Pathway of Experience," *North American Review*, CLXIII (October, 1896), 389.

80. Robinson, *Thomas B. Reed*, pp. 358–59; Theodore Roosevelt to John D. Long, February 19, 1898, and to Douglas Robinson, March 30, 1898, Elting E. Morison et al. (eds.), *The Letters of Theodore Roosevelt*, Harvard University Press, Cambridge, Mass., 1951–1954, vol. I, p. 780, vol. II, p. 806; Wisan, p. 409; Morgan, p. 333.

81. Barbara W. Tuchman, "Czar of the House," *American Heritage*, XIV (December, 1962), 101.

82. Bowers, p. 71.

83. Russ, *The Hawaiian Republic*, p. 338.

84. Extraordinary in view of the fact that the speaker has no vote except in

case of a tie. Tate, pp. 285, 300–301; Robinson, *Thomas B. Reed,* pp. 367–68; Dunn, vol. I, p. 291; and U.S., *Congressional Record,* 55th Cong., 2d Sess., 1898, pp. 6018–19 (June 15).

85. Champ Clark, vol. I, p. 288.
86. McCall, pp. 253–59.
87. Leon Wolff, *Little Brown Brother: America's Forgotten Bid for Empire which Cost 250,000 Lives,* Longmans, Green and Co., Ltd., London, 1961, p. 302.
88. Robinson, *Thomas B. Reed,* pp. 369–70, 378.
89. George F. Hoar to Thomas B. Reed, April 21, 1899, quoted in McCall, p. 259; E. L. Godkin to James Bryce, April 23, 1899, Godkin Papers. See Robinson, *Thomas B. Reed,* pp. 377, 380; Dunn, vol. I, p. 308; O. O. Stealey, *Twenty Years in the Press Gallery,* By the author, New York, 1906, pp. 146–47; and Tuchman, *American Heritage,* XIV, 102. Champ Clark wrote in his memoirs (vol. I, p. 300) that Reed earned $500,000 in the three years of his retirement.
90. Fred H. Harrington, "The Anti-Imperialist Movement in the United States, 1898–1900," *Mississippi Valley Historical Review,* XXII (September, 1935), 227. For the interest in Reed as an independent candidate, see Moorfield Storey to George F. Hoar, March 9, 1899, quoted in M. A. DeWolfe Howe, *Portrait of an Independent: Moorfield Storey, 1845–1929,* Houghton Mifflin Company, Boston, 1932, pp. 218–19; George Batchelor to John D. Long, April 20, 1899, Gardner W. Allen, p. 253; Samuel Bowles to Carl Schurz, March 21, 1900, Schurz Papers; Carl Schurz to E. B. Smith, August 7, 1900, and to Moorfield Storey, August 11, 1900, Frederic Bancroft (ed.), *Speeches, Correspondence and Political Papers of Carl Schurz,* G. P. Putnam's Sons, New York, 1913, vol. VI, pp. 201–03.
91. Francis E. Clark, "Thomas B. Reed as a Neighbor," *The Independent,* January 8, 1903, p. 83.
92. McCall, p. 266.

CONCLUSION/*The Anti-Imperialists and America*

1. Claude M. Fuess, *Carl Schurz, Reformer (1829–1906),* Dodd, Mead & Company, New York, 1932, p. 381.
2. Quoted in Robert H. Wiebe, *The Search for Order, 1877–1920,* Hill and Wang, New York, 1967, p. 228.
3. Quoted in William A. Russ, Jr., *The Hawaiian Republic (1894–98) and Its Struggle To Win Annexation,* Susquehanna University Press, Selinsgrove, Penna., 1959, pp. 315–16.

4. William Vaughn Moody, *Gloucester Moors and Other Poems*, Houghton Mifflin Company, Boston, 1901, p. 19. The ode was first printed in the May, 1900, issue of *The Atlantic Monthly*.

5. Daniel J. Boorstin, *America and the Image of Europe: Reflections on American Thought*, Meridian Books, Inc., New York, 1960, pp. 121–22.

6. Maria C. Lanzar, "The Anti-Imperialist League," *Philippine Social Science Review*, V (October, 1933), 268; Fred H. Harrington, "The Anti-Imperialist Movement in the United States, 1898–1900," *Mississippi Valley Historical Review*, XXII (September, 1935), 223.

7. Quoted in Howard K. Beale, *Theodore Roosevelt and the Rise of America to World Power*, Collier Books, New York, 1962, p. 33.

8. Theodore Friend, *Between Two Empires: The Ordeal of the Philippines, 1929–1946*, Yale University Press, New Haven, 1965, pp. 81, 107–08.

9. Walter Lippmann, "A Compact Plan for Puerto Rico," *Chicago Sun-Times*, June 18, 1963.

10. Whitney T. Perkins, *Denial of Empire: The United States and Its Dependencies*, A. W. Sythoff, Leyden, Netherlands, 1962, pp. 195, 197; William Appleman Williams, *The Contours of American History*, The World Publishing Company, Cleveland, 1961, p. 368.

11. George F. Kennan, *Russia and the West under Lenin and Stalin*, Mentor Books, New York, 1962, p. 247. See also Whitney T. Perkins, p. 26; Christopher Lasch, "The Anti-Imperialists, the Philippines, and the Inequality of Man," *Journal of Southern History*, XXIV (August, 1958), 329–30; Richard W. Leopold, *The Growth of American Foreign Policy: A History*, Alfred A. Knopf, New York, 1962, pp. 187–88; Thomas A. Bailey, *A Diplomatic History of the American People*, 4th ed., Appleton-Century-Crofts, Inc., New York, 1950, pp. 517–18; and A. Whitney Griswold, *The Far Eastern Policy of the United States*, Harcourt, Brace and Company, New York, 1938, p. 33.

12. See Whitney T. Perkins, *passim.*; Friend, pp. 8–9, 264–65; Julius W. Pratt, *America's Colonial Experiment: How the United States Gained, Governed, and In Part Gave Away a Colonial Empire*, Prentice-Hall, Inc., New York, 1950; and Garel A. Grunder and William E. Livezey, *The Philippines and the United States*, University of Oklahoma Press, Norman, Okla., 1951.

13. Lasch, *Journal of Southern History*, XXIV, 329–30.

14. See fn. 54, Chapter 5.

15. George F. Kennan, *American Diplomacy, 1900–1950*, A Mentor Book, New York, 1951, pp. 21–22.

16. See Charles Francis Adams, *"Imperialism" and "The Tracks of our Forefathers," A Paper Read by Charles Francis Adams Before the Lexington,*

Massachusetts, Historical Society, Tuesday, December 20, 1898, Dana Estes & Company, Boston, 1899, p. 10; Adams, "Memorabilia," October 27, 1898, and May 15, 1900, Adams Papers.

17. [Finley Peter Dunne], *Mr. Dooley In the Hearts of His Countrymen,* Small, Maynard & Company, Boston, 1899, pp. 3–4.

18. Quoted in Leon Wolff, *Little Brown Brother: America's Forgotten Bid for Empire which Cost 250,000 Lives,* Longmans, Green and Co., Ltd., London, 1961, p. 228.

19. Quoted in Wallace E. Davies, *Patriotism on Parade: The Story of Veterans' and Hereditary Organizations in America, 1783–1900,* Harvard University Press, Cambridge, Mass., 1955, p. 335.

20. Kermit Vanderbilt, *Charles Eliot Norton: Apostle of Culture in a Democracy,* The Belknap Press of Harvard University Press, Cambridge, Mass., 1959, pp. 213–14.

21. Theodore Roosevelt to Leonard Wood, April 17, 1901, Elting E. Morison et al. (eds.), *The Letters of Theodore Roosevelt,* Harvard University Press, Cambridge, Mass., 1951–1954, vol. III, p. 60.

Index

Abstractness, 45-46

Adams, Brooks, 107

Adams, Charles Francis, Jr., xi, xiii, 5, 107-132, 141-142, 154, 215, 228, 256n, 269n, 270-271n, 280n
  anti-imperialist views, 87, 107-132, 221
  attack on anti-imperialist movement, 113-120, 226
  business and writing career, 108-110
  businessmen disapproved by, 12-13
  on Cuban question, 184
  dissenting viewpoint, 109, 112, 221
  election of 1900, 120-132, 183
  family background, 107-108
  historical writings, 108, 111
  mugwumpery, 9, 107, 109, 112
  on race, 235
  social and political views, 108-132, 238-239
  on Spanish-American War, 112-120, 238-239
  on town-meeting government, 14-15

Adams, Henry, 107, 110, 129, 158, 194, 205, 272n, 278n

Adams, John, 69

Adams, John Quincy, ix

Adams, John Quincy, II, 109

Addams, Jane, xi, xii

Adirondacks, preservation of, 67

Africa, Portuguese bases, 188

Aguinaldo, Emilio, 231-232
  capture of, 83
  leader of guerrilla war, 31-32, 46, 78
  suppression of rebellion, 101-102
  sympathy of anti-imperialists for, 160-161, 202-203

Alabama case, 70-72

Alaska, annexation of, xiii, 72, 194

Aldrich, Nelson, 147n, 186

Aldrich, Thomas Bailey, xii, 5, 10, 12
  "Unguarded Gates," 12

Allison, William, 147n

American Antiquarian Society, 141

American Experiment, 81
  failure of, 54, 69-70, 81

American Historical Association, 141, 142

American life, decline in quality of, 59-61
  effect of imperialist policies on, 28-30, 54-69
  Godkin on, 53-54, 59-69, 78-79
  homogeneity of, 23

American life, James on, 39-40
  mugwumps' criticism of, 28-30, 39, 43, 48
  Norton's view of, 58
  uniqueness of, 223-225
American Peace Society, 93
American traits corrupted by imperialism, 22-23, 28-29, 48-51, 70, 233
Americanism, 74-75
Angell, James Burrill, xi, 9
Anti-Imperialist, The, 87, 100, 103
Anti-Imperialist League, xiii, 5, 98-100, 130, 136, 159, 202, 236
  Boutwell president of, 193-197
  contributions to, 174, 180
  criticism of, 236
  founding of, 98
  "Liberty Congress," 128, 196
  membership, 5, 225
  third party plans, 130
Anti-imperialist movement, x, xii-xv, 5, 186, 215-239
  Adams and, 107-108, 113-120
  Atkinson and, 99-101
  appraisal of, 215-225, 230-237
  Carnegie and, 173-174, 180-181
  composed of old men, 9-10, 186, 196, 228
  criticism of, 236-237
  critique of America, xiv
  economic expansion and, 234
  failure of, 215, 226-230
  foreign trade policies, 84-88, 234
  Harrison and, 193
  heritage of, 238-239
  Hoar and, 159
  impact of, 225-230
  informal empire, 87
  James and, 52
  leaders, x-xiii, 5, 215
    age of, 9, 186, 228
    disunity among, 226-227
  meaning of, 216-225

Anti-imperialist movement, moral nature, 13-15, 85, 87, 154, 218, 232
  mugwumps and, xiii, 5, 17
  See also Mugwumps
  political independence, 5-6
  political nature, 5-6, 85, 87
  precedents, xiii, xiv
  preoccupation with past, 13-15, 154
  in Republican Party, 135-137
  Sherman and, 203
  trade-without-territory policy, 85-88
  views of Godkin, 71
Art and literature, 60
  decline in morality and, 57-58, 60
Arthur, Chester, 73
Ashfield (Mass.) "Academy Dinners," 57
Asia, American intervention, 155, 218
  trade relations, 93-94, 102, 105-106
Atkinson, Edward, xi, xiii, 84-106, 203*n*, 215, 221, 228, 266*n*
  anti-colonialist program, 84-106, 217-218, 234
  anti-imperialist writings, 87, 98
  attacks on, 98-101
  business activities, 89-90
  criticism by Adams, 89, 115, 116, 119
  on Cuban question, 93-95
  economic expansionism, 87-88
  edited *Anti-Imperialist,* 87, 100, 103
  family background, 88-89
  favored Anglo-American relations, 175, 184
  founded Anti-Imperialist League, 98-100
  free trade proposals, 84-106
    with Europe and Canada, 101-102, 105
  on Hawaii annexation, 90-91, 93-94
  informal empire approach, 87-106

Atkinson, Edward, inventions, 89-90
  mugwumpery, 5, 7, 9, 67, 90, 103
  neutralization of new territories,
    95-97, 101
  optimism and self-esteem, 89
  on Philippine annexation, 94-101,
    184
  political beliefs, 89-106, 129
  on Puerto Rico, 94-95
  on Spanish-American War, 93-94
  suppression of pamphlets, 23, 33,
    98-101
  on Venezuela crisis, 90, 92
Atlantic Monthly, 57

Bacon, Augustus, 157
Bacon, Theodore Woolsey, 131
Bacon Amendment, 157
Bailey, Thomas A., 120
Baltimore incident (1891), 187
Bancroft, George, 56
Barnum, P. T., 10
Beveridge, Albert J., 186, 207, 230
Bierce, Ambrose, xii
Bigness, 46-47
Birney, Gen. William, 127
Birney, James, xi, 127
Blaine, James G., 21, 73, 169, 181, 187,
    255n
  criticism of, 13, 145, 204-205
  mugwumps' opposition to, 5, 15, 36
Bonaparte, Charles J., 226, 280n
Boorstin, Daniel, 224
Boston, Mass., 11, 110-111
  social changes, 11, 37
Boston Evening Transcript, 100n
Boston Herald, 122
Boston Journal, 100n
Boutelle, Charles, 136
Boutwell, George S., xi, xiii, 10n, 158,
    187, 193-197, 211, 215, 228
  on Hawaii annexation, 194-195
  political career, 194-195

Bowles, Samuel, 118, 130
Bradford, Gamaliel, xi, 5, 9, 115, 119,
    130-131
Bridge, James H., 281n
British Guiana, xiv, 75, 286n
British West Indies, 176
Brook Farm circle, 36
Brooks, Van Wyck, 58
Bryan, William Jennings, x, xii, 131,
    255n, 272n, 279n
  anti-imperialist opposition to, 37,
    59, 190-191
  election of 1900, 122-123, 181, 204
  supported Treaty of Paris, xii, 155,
    157-158, 180-181, 196, 203, 227
Bryce, James, 79-80
Burke, Edmund, 115
Businessmen, 53-54, 60, 222
  disliked by mugwumps, 12-13, 108
Butler, Ben, 10

Cable, George Washington, xii, 67
Cambridge, Mass., 60-61
Canada, 170-171, 178, 218
  expanding trade with, 101-102, 105
Caribbean, United States influence,
    xiv, xv, 33-34, 229, 232
Carlyle, Thomas, 57
Carnegie, Andrew, xi, xiii, 100, 165-
    186, 217, 228
  on Anglo-American relations, 170-
    172, 175-176
  anti-imperialism of, 10n, 87, 135,
    165, 173-185, 215, 226, 228
  authorship of writings, 281n
  pacificism, 167-168, 183-184
  Philippine annexation, 174-180,
    183-185, 226
  protests, 165-166
  "race imperialism," 172, 175
  republicanism of, 167
  role in election of 1900, 181-183,
    211

Carnegie, Andrew, social and political ideas, 165-167, 222
  Triumphant Democracy, 166-167, 171
Carnegie Endowment for International Peace, 168
Censorship, 33
Century Magazine, 27
Chamberlin, Fred C., 98*n*
Chicago Tribune, 237
Chile, xiv, 72-73, 170, 187-188, 205-206
China, Open Door policy, 106
  trade relations, 93-94, 102, 105-106, 218
Chinese immigrants, 65, 146, 160, 235
Cities, problems of, 223-224
Civic Federation, 26
Civil rights legislation, 141
Civil service reform, 36, 67, 108, 141, 197
Civil War, xiii, 62, 71
  Alabama claims, 70-72
  reconstruction policies, 6, 77
Civilization, 82
  dangers to, 63-64
  effect of war and imperialism, 40-43, 73-74
Clark, Champ, x, 204-205, 208
Clay, Henry, 59
Clayton-Bulwer Treaty, 170
Cleveland, Grover, x, 9, 122, 131, 142
  campaign of 1884, 9, 59
  foreign policies, 188, 198-199
  mugwump support for, 9, 131, 145-146
  trade policies, 92
  Venezuela crisis, 40-42, 45, 75, 92, 198, 206
Codman, Charles R., 5, 9, 119, 130
Colonialism, 77, 218
  "anti-colonial imperialists," 84-88, 94-95

Colonialism, attitude of Harrison, 187-190, 192-193
  attitude of Schurz, 22-24, 26-28, 30
  British, 84-85, 91-92
  checks on, 225-230
  effect on American ideals, 231-235
  effect on U.S. security, 218
  Godkin on, 71, 77
  inconsistent with American traditions, 77, 231-235
  moral and constitutional implications, 85
  trade and, 84-88
  views of Adams, 117-118
  views of Carnegie, 168-169
  views of James, 44
  See also Expansionism; Imperialism
Congo, Berlin Conference on, 72-73
Conservation of natural resources, 20
Conservatism, 222-223, 233, 238
  of mugwumps, 10-11
Constitution, 29, 77, 160, 216
Croker, Richard, 124
Croffut, William, 10, 130
Cuba, xiii, 25-26, 30, 153, 256*n*
  anti-imperialist views, 25-26, 30, 153, 195, 209, 236
  crusade to liberate, 219
  nationalist revolution, 78
  proposed annexation, 93-95, 113, 188-189
  rebels in, 172
  Roosevelt's policies, 30, 132
  views of Atkinson, 93-95
  views of Carnegie, 172-173, 176-177, 184
  views of Godkin and Norton, 70, 72-73, 76-78, 80
  views of Schurz, 30
  views of Sherman, 198-200
  See also Spanish-American War
Cullom, Shelby, 136

Curtis, George W., 67
Cuyler, Theodore, xi, 131

Danish West Indies, purchase of, 70, 72, 188
Day, William, 135, 201
Debs, Eugene, 11
Declaration of Independence, 29, 51-52, 140, 155, 163, 208
Democracy, 34, 54
    anti-imperialists' distrust of, 54, 62-65, 68-69, 75-78
    detrimental effects of, 54, 62-65, 68-69, 75-78
    effect of imperialist policies on, 28-30, 33
    mass, 54, 222
    mediocrity encouraged, 37-38
    mistrust of the masses, 65, 222
Democratic Party, xii, 7-8, 142-143, 227, 271-272n
    election of 1900, 120-132
Dewey, Admiral George, ix, xiv, 25, 99, 136, 179, 185, 207, 227, 232
Diaz, Porfirio, 31
Domestic problems, 238
    effect of colonialism on, 218-219
Dunne, Finley Peter, xii, 192, 236

Economic expansionism, 30, 84-87, 93, 101, 103, 105, 198
    free trade and, 104-106
    imperialism and, 216-217, 234
Edmunds, George F., xi, 10n, 136
Education, 60
    Charles Francis Adams on, 110-111
Egalitarianism, results of, 64
Election of 1900, x, 107-132
    Boutwell in, 196
    Carnegie in, 181-182
    Harrison in, 190-192
    Hoar in, 161
    mugwumps' policies, 120-132

Election of 1900, Reed in, 210
    Sherman in, 203
    splitting of anti-imperialist vote, 120-130
Electoral reforms, 108
Eliot, Charles W., xi, 5, 6, 9, 131, 142, 280n
    on political independence, 6
Élites, 54, 222-223
Elkins, Stephen B., 147n
Ellis, Havelock, 36-37
Emerson, Ralph Waldo, xi, 10, 57
Endicott, William, Jr., 5, 9
England, 92-93
    Carnegie's views, 167, 172
    opinions of James concerning, 39
    See also Great Britain–United States relations
Equality, 62, 64
    fear of, 222
Europe, 15, 224
    expanding trade with, 101-102, 105, 218
Everett, Edward, 111
Expansionism, 71-73, 76, 78, 113-114
    constitutional objections to, 216
    diplomatic objections to, 218
    economic, 84-88, 93, 101, 105, 198
    economic objections to, 216-218
    effect on American ideals, 28-29
    effect of annexing tropical people, 23
    historical objections to, 220
    McKinley administration, xii, 210-211
    moral objections to, 219
    objections of anti-imperialists, 216
    political objections to, 220
    racial objections to, 219
    trade-without-territory policy, 85-88
    See also Colonialism; Imperialism

Far East, trade relations, 102, 105
  U.S. involvement, xv, 231-234
Fisk, Jim, 194
Ford, Henry, 281n
Foreign policy, 70-72
  American security and expansion-
    ism, 148-149, 218, 233-234
Foreign trade, Atkinson's view, 84-
    106
  economic development and, 101-
    106
  effect of imperialism, 216-218
  with Europe and Canada, 101-103,
    105
  expansion through, 84-106, 188
  favored by anti-imperialists, 84-88
  Open Door policy, 89-106
  "permeation" policy, 104
  with Philippines, 178-179
France—United States relations,
    xiii
"Free security," end of, xv
Free silver, 37, 122-123, 127, 181
Free Soil party, 6
Free trade, 86-87, 92, 178, 217
  Adams advocate of, 269n
  advocated by anti-imperialists, 85-
    88, 105
  Atkinson on, 91-93
  doctrine of comparative advantage,
    86
  views of Schurz, 30, 85, 87, 103, 217
  views of William G. Sumner, 104-
    105
French Revolution, 45
Friend, Theodore, 179n
Fuller, Henry Blake, xi

Garfield, James A., 59
Garland, Hamlin, xi
Garrison, Wendell Phillips, xi

Garrison, William Lloyd, xi
Garrison, William Lloyd, Jr., xi, 5, 10,
    130
Gary, James A., 135
Gilded Age, 110
Gilder, Richard Watson, 10, 189
Gladstone, William E., 172
Godkin, E. L., xi, xiii, 37, 53-83, 194,
    215, 228, 257n, 258n, 264n
  anti-imperialist ideas, 71-77, 87,
    210
  businessmen disapproved by, 12-13
  characteristics, 35, 55-56
  critics of, 56-57
  Cuba annexation, 73, 76-77, 184,
    199
  decline in quality of American life,
    53-54, 59-69, 78-79
  disliked by Roosevelt, 57
  editor of *The Nation*, 20, 55-56,
    130, 173, 199
  family background, 54-55
  on future of America, 82-83
  Hawaii annexation, 73
  influence of, 55-56
  on jingoism, 74-76
  on Mexican intervention, 71, 73
  mugwumpery, 8-9, 12-14, 59
  objections to expansion, 76-77
  opposition to immigration, 65
  pessimism of, 35, 53-54, 66-67, 69-
    70, 79, 82
  on Philippine annexation, 77-79
  on Puerto Rico annexation, 77
  racist ideas, 66
  return to England, 39, 79-80
  on Santo Domingo annexation, 72
  on socialism, 66
  on Spanish-American war, 76-80
  on Venezuela crisis, 75
Gold standard, 125, 128
Gompers, Samuel, xi, xii

"Good government" movement, 20

Gorman, Arthur, x

Gould, Jay, 194

Grand Army of the Republic, 39, 236-237

Granger Associations, 99

Grant, U.S., xiii, 6, 21, 53, 59, 72, 194

Great Britain–United States relations, xiii, 70-71, 75
  Atkinson's proposal for *entente*, 92-93, 101
  Carnegie's views of, 170-172, 175-176
  colonial policies, 168-169, 175
  Harrison on, 188-189

Greece, ancient, 57-58
  decline of, 62-63
  nationalist revolution, 78

Greeley, Horace, 6, 21, 59, 272n

Griggs, John W., 99-100

Guatemala, 73

Guizot, François, 15

Hague International Court, 189

Haiti, 30, 72, 188, 194, 256n

Hale, Edward Everett, xi, 10n, 151, 277n

Hale, Edward Everett, Jr., 277n

Hale, Eugene, x, 10n, 136, 147n, 156, 193

Hanna, Mark, 147n, 186, 199, 202

Harmon, Judson, 122

Harper's Weekly, 20, 25, 30, 99

Harrison, Benjamin, x, xiii, 8, 10n, 24, 132, 136, 145, 170, 198, 204-205, 211, 215-216, 227-228, 286n, 287n
  appointed to Hague Court, 189
  expansionist policies, 188
  opposition to McKinley's policies, 187-193

Harrison, Benjamin, party loyalty, 193

Hartford Times, 119

Harvard College, 9, 11, 36, 110, 140-141, 162, 280n
  Charles Eliot Norton at, 57-58

Haskins, David G., 130, 151

Hawaii annexation, xiv, 104, 145-150, 221, 276n
  Boutwell's views of, 194-195
  Carnegie's views of, 176, 184
  Godkin's opposition, 73, 76
  Harrison's attempt, 24, 145, 188
  Hoar's views, 145-150, 275n
  by joint resolution of Congress, 148
  opposed by Reed, 207-208
  opposed by Schurz, 26, 31
  petition of Hawaiians opposing, 147
  for security reasons, 148-149
  Senate debate over, 76, 148-150
  Sherman and, 198, 200
  Sumner's free trade proposals, 104-105
  views of Atkinson, 90-91, 93-94

Hawthorne, Nathaniel, 111

Hay, John, 19, 158, 175, 182, 190, 230
  on Adams–Schurz dialogue, 129
  ambassador to Great Britain, 153
  Secretary of State, 129, 158
  sympathy with Carnegie's views, 135

Hayes, Rutherford B., 20, 59, 197

Haymarket Riot, 11, 37

Henderson, John B., xi, 10n, 127, 136

Higginson, Henry L., 56

Higginson, Thomas Wentworth, xi, 5, 7, 9, 87, 117-119, 130, 196-197
  appraisal of Hoar, 163-164
  on Atkinson's *Anti-Imperialist*, 87

Hill, Gov. David B., 55-56, 124

Historical Studies of Church Build-ing in the Middle Ages (Norton), 57

Hoar, George Frisbie, x, xiii, 139-164, 196, 226-228, 237, 276n, 278n, 280n
  anti-imperialist views, 10n, 87, 184, 215
  anti-mugwump stand, 139-145, 159, 163-164
  attacks on imperialism, 159-160
  attack on Norton, 80n, 150-151, 164, 237, 277n
  autobiography, 162-163
  on Bryan, 279n
  character, 141-142, 164
  criticism of, 150, 163-164
  family background, 140
  on Hawaiian annexation, 148-150, 226-228, 275n
  Higginson's appraisal, 163-164
  party loyalty, 139-145, 156-159, 162, 186, 193, 211
  political career, 140-164
  racial views, 160, 219, 232-233
  relationship with President McKin-ley, 152-153, 158-159, 161-162, 228
  views on Spanish-American War, 136, 146-151, 276n

Hobart, Garret, 157
Hofstadter, Richard, 9
Homestead Strike, 182
Honduras, 73
Housing for underprivileged, 67
Howells, William Dean, xi, 10, 67
Hungary, nationalist revolution, 78

Idealism of anti-imperialists, xiv, 82, 222-223, 238-239

Idealism of anti-imperialists, aban-donment of national ideals, 28-30, 48
  American traits corrupted by im-perialism, 22-23, 28-29, 48-51, 70, 233
  effect of colonialism on, 231-235

Immigration policy, 10-12, 108-109, 223
  Godkin's opposition to, 53, 65
  mugwumps' attitude, 10-12, 14-15, 17, 37
  rising influence of immigrants, 15

Immorality, 69; *see also* Morality

Imperialism, 82
  American traits corrupted by, 22-23, 28-29, 48-51, 70, 233
  based on economic power, 84-106
  contrary to American traditions, 33
  economic implications, 86-87, 216-217, 234
  free trade policy vs., 30, 85, 87, 103, 217
  informal empire approach, 84-106
  rise of new "orthodoxy," 44
  Adam Smith's condemnation of, 84-85
  trade and, 84-88, 103, 217
  See also Colonialism; Expan-sionism

India, British policy, 168-169
Indianapolis, Liberty Congress, 196
Indians, American, 20, 52, 77, 160, 235
Individuality, 38, 64
Industrialism, 10, 54, 59, 61, 223-224
Ingalls, John J., 16
Intellectuals' role in democratic sys-tem, 38
Interstate Commerce Act of 1887, 90
Ireland, immigrants from, 65, 108
  nationalist revolution, 78

Isolationism, 229
Italy, 57, 63
  nationalist revolution, 78

James, Henry (brother), 39
James, Henry (father), 35-36
James, William, xi, xiii, 8, 35-52, 67,
    215, 228, 257n, 258n
  anti-imperialist, 10-11, 70, 184
  appreciation of American traits,
    35-38, 50-52, 81, 87
  end of innocence in America, 47-
    52
  family background, 35-36
  mugwumpery, 8, 11, 35-39
  opposition to imperialism, 40-52
  opposition to McKinley, 43, 46, 48,
    131
  optimism, 35, 112
  Philippine annexation opposed by,
    43-46
  psychologist and philosopher, 36
  on Theodore Roosevelt, 42-43, 236
  on savage instincts, 40-43
  on Spanish-American War, 41-42,
    44, 49
Japanese-American relations, 178,
    200-201, 234, 276n
Jefferson, Thomas, 51
Jewish immigrants, 65
Jingoism, 35, 41, 73, 74-76, 92, 206
Johnson, Andrew, xiii, 20, 127, 194
Johnson, Henry U., 127, 136
Jordan, David Starr, xi, 201
  anti-imperialist views, 87-88, 104
  election of 1900, 131
  free trade proposals, 104-105

Kasson, John, 85
Kennan, George F., 231, 234-235
Kirkland, Edward C., 66, 281n
Knights of Labor, 90

Know-Nothing Party, 65
Korea, 178

Labor conditions, 11, 37, 224
  Atkinson and, 90
  strikes, 66
Labor unions, rising influence of, 15
LaFeber, Walter, 276n
Laissez-faire economics, 66, 84
Lasch, Christopher, 232
Latin America, 71, 78
  nationalist revolutions, 78
  trade relations, 85, 94, 105, 218, 234
  U.S. policies, 169-171
Leech, Margaret, 46n
Liberty, 82, 220
Lincoln, Abraham, 19, 20, 29
Lindsay, William, 149
Lippmann, Walter, 55, 229
Literature, 53, 60
Lloyd, Henry Demarest, xi, xii
Lodge, Henry Cabot, 141, 145, 161,
    205-206, 256n
  McKinley's expansionist policies,
    135
  on Philippine annexation, 32, 157-
    158
London Daily News, 55
Long, John D., 135, 137, 141, 201
Longfellow, Henry Wadsworth, 56
Lowell, James Russell, 15, 57, 59-60,
    64, 66-67
Lower classes, rise of, 67-68

McCall, Samuel, 136
McEnery Resolution, 156-158
McKinley, William, 37, 46, 59, 205,
    208, 255n, 280n
  annexation policies, 94-95, 97, 103
  assassination, 162
  Andrew Carnegie and, 181-183
  election of 1900, 123-132, 203, 226

McKinley, William, expansionist ventures, 94-95, 97, 103, 210-211

Harrison's opposition to, 189-192

honorary degree at Harvard, 162, 280n

opposition of James, 37, 43, 46, 48, 131

opposition of Reed, 205, 208

opposition of Schurz, 24-28, 30

opposition to, 59, 205, 227

Philippine policy, 78-79, 88, 93-97, 135-137

relationship with Sen. Hoar, 152-153, 158-159, 161-162

revolt against expansionist policies, 186-193, 210-211

trade policies, 87

war policy, 48

Mahan, Alfred T., 135, 147

Maine, 206

"Manifest destiny" expansionism, 70

Manila Bay, Dewey's victory, ix, xiv, 25, 207, 227, 232

Mann, Arthur, 11

Manufactures Record, 102

Mason, William, 136

Massachusetts Historical Society, 111

Massachusetts Reform Club, 114, 116-117

Masses, influences of, 74-75

mistrust of, 54, 65, 222

Masters, Edgar Lee, xi

Materialism, 36, 61-63

disastrous effects of, 63

Maximilian, Emperor of Mexico, 71

Mencken, H. L., 16, 55

Mexican-American relations, 31, 71

Miles, Gen. Nelson A., 173

Monroe Doctrine, 45, 154, 162, 189, 218

Moody, Dwight L., 10

Moody, William Vaughn, xi, 224

Moody, William Vaughn, "An Ode in Time of Hesitation," 224

Moral critique of anti-imperialists, 13-15, 85, 87, 154, 218, 232

"The Moral Equivalent of War" (James), 258n

Moralistic view of history, 50

Morality, decline of, 53-54, 59-61, 79

relationship between art and, 57-58, 60

Morrill, Justin, x, xiii, 10n, 136, 139, 147-150, 277n

Morton, J. Sterling, x

Morton, Oliver, 19

Mugwumps, 5-17, 252n

anti-imperialists, xii, 5, 10, 17, 130-132

attitude toward businessmen, 12-13

attitude toward immigration, 10-13

characteristics of, 9

conservativism of, 10-11

against corruption and machine politics, 13-14, 16

criticism of, 15-17

criticism of American life, 39, 43

culture, 9

effect of social conflict and change, 11

election of 1900, 120-132

favored break-up of old parties, 59

Godkin, 59

Hoar's rejection of, 139-145

"independent voters," 5-9

industrialism, 14

"informal" imperialism, 103-106

interests and causes, 6-14, 67

James on, 38-39

leaders, 5, 9-10, 14

negativeness of, 16

in New England, 5, 9-10

in New York State, 9

Norton, 59

Mugwumps, origin of term, 6
  on party loyalty, xv, 5, 14
  plans for third party, 127, 130
  political beliefs, 6-7, 10-15
  political independence, 5-9, 143
  power in party politics, 14-15
  preoccupation with past, 13-15
  principles, 5-6
  reform activities, 7-8, 17
  social and political problems avoid-
     ed by, 17
  voting according to moral princi-
     ples, 8-9
     See also Anti-imperialist move-
        ment
Myths, national, 51

Nation, The, 35, 57, 150-151, 201
  edited by Godkin, 55-56, 75-76, 78,
     80
  influence of, 35
  Norton contributor to, 57, 60
National character, xv, 63
National Civil Service Reform
     League, 20
National homogeneity, 32
Nationalist revolutions, 78
Naval stations, acquisition of, 86,
     103, 105, 148, 188-189
Negroes, policy toward, 67, 160, 235
Neutralization policies, 95-96, 101
New England, mugwumps, 5, 9
New York, mugwumps, 9
New York Evening Post, 20, 55, 130,
     173, 199
New York Times, The, 236
New York World, 219
Newspapers, yellow press, 54, 74-76
Niagara Falls, preservation of, 67
Nicaragua, rights for canal, 70, 73,
     256n

North American Review, 57, 60, 74,
     91, 102, 180-183, 206
Northampton, Mass., 60
Norton, Andrews, 56
Norton, Charles Eliot, xi, xiii, 39, 53-
     83, 110, 130, 215, 228, 280n
  accomplishments, 67
  on Anglo-American relations, 70-72
  anti-imperialist ideas, 70-77, 80-81,
     87, 225
  Ashfield "Academy Dinners," 67
  on decline in quality of American
     life, 13, 53-54, 60-69, 222
  family background, 56-57
  on future of America, 83
  Hoar's attack on, 80, 150-151, 164,
     237, 277n
  on immigration, 65
  on labor troubles, 11, 66
  literary works, 57
  mugwumpery of, 9, 59
  pessimism of, 53-54, 60-65, 68-69
  on rise of lower classes, 67-68
  on Santo Domingo annexation, 70,
     72
  on Spanish-American War, 80-81,
     237-238
  teaching career, 57-58
  on Venezuela crisis, 75
Nouveaux riches, 65

Olney, Richard, x, 171
Open Door policy, 89, 104-106, 179
Orthodoxy, 43-44

Paine, Thomas, 223
Palmer, George Herbert, 49
Palmer, John McCauley, 59, 128
Pan-American Conference (1889-90),
     169, 187
Panama Canal Zone, 33
Parker, Theodore, 10

Parkhurst, Charles H., xi

Parkman, Francis, 56

Past, mugwumps' preoccupation with, 13-15

Peabody, George F., xi

Peabody, Josephine, 61

Peace, 198
  Atkinson's plans for, 93

Pennsylvania, boss rule, 31

Perkins, George W., 207

Perry, Bliss, xi

Perry, Ralph Barton, 36

Peru, 72-73, 188

Pettigrew, Richard, 149, 182

Philippine Islands
  American role, 32-33, 43-47
  American trade policy, 101-106, 178-179, 217-218
  American troops sent to, 227
  annexation of, 26, 30-31, 77-78, 83, 120
    anti-imperialists and, 230-232
    Congressional opposition, 136
    McKinley's policy, 88, 93-100, 135-137
    opposition of Atkinson, 94-101
    opposition of Carnegie, 165, 174-180, 183-185
    opposition of James, 43-47, 49
    opposition of Reed, 208-210
    opposition of Schurz, 26-28, 30-32
    opposition to, 136, 151-159, 219, 230-232
  Atkinson's pamphlets, 97-101
  Atkinson's plan to neutralize, 94-97
  colonial government, 33
  effect on U.S. security, 233-234
  guerrilla insurrection, ix, xv, 28, 31, 78-79, 83, 99, 101-102, 116-121, 156, 160-161, 209, 236
  independent status, 103, 106, 229

Philippine Islands, independent status, Treaty of Paris; *see* Treaty of Paris
  United States Commission, 99, 230
  value of trade with, 101-106

Pierce, Franklin, 59

Platt, Orville H., 147n

Platt, Thomas C., 147n

Platt Amendment, 162

Poland, nationalist revolution, 78

Political independence of anti-imperialists, 5-6

Political parties, 7
  control of, 38-39
  corruption and machine control, 13-14, 38-39, 59, 69, 124
  lack of good men, 53, 59
  loyalty, 14
  reforms, 132
  role of intellectuals, 38-39

Politicians, 13-14, 38, 224

Populist movement, xiv

Portugal, 188

Potter, Henry Codman, xi

Poverty programs, 90

Pratt, Julius, 105

Progressive Era, xiv, 33

Prosperity, 54, 61-63
  detrimental effect of, 70
  effect of imperialistic policies on, 192-193

Public opinion, effect of anti-imperialists on, 225-228, 236

Puerto Rico, 26-27, 30, 195, 219, 256n
  acquisition of, 26-27, 30, 33, 77, 83, 94-95, 153, 173, 176, 195, 219
  opposed by anti-imperialists, 221
  question of statehood, 229
  tariff question, 190, 216
  views of Atkinson, 94-95
  views of Carnegie, 173, 176
  views of Godkin, 77-83

Puerto Rico, views of Harrison, 188
  views of Hoar, 153
  views of Schurz, 26-27, 30, 33
Pullman Strike of 1894, 11, 66

Quay, Matthew, 157
Quincy, Mass., 14-15, 109

"Race imperialism," 172, 175
Racial views, xv, 27, 70, 160, 232-233,
  235
  attitudes of anti-imperialists, 219-
    220
  of Adams, 235
  of Godkin, 66
  of Hoar, 160, 219, 232-233
  of James, 47, 49
  of Schurz, 22-24, 28, 32, 219
  superiority of Americans, 47-49
Radicalism, 36, 65, 218
Railroads, 108
Redlich, Fritz, 281n
Reed, Thomas B., x, xiii, 10n, 127,
  136, 139, 203-211, 215, 227-228
  anti-imperialism, 187
  opposed annexation of Hawaii,
    207-208
  opposed Philippine annexation,
    208-210
  opposed war with Spain, 206-207
  party loyalty, 203-204
  political career, 203-204
  resentment toward McKinley, 205,
    208-209
  retirement, 209-210
  Speaker of the House, 203-204, 209
  wit, 204-205
Reid, Whitelaw, 174-175, 182
Representative government, 48
Republican government, 220
Republican Party, 6-7, 142-144, 271-
  272n

Republican Party, anti-imperialists,
  135-137, 210-211, 228
  election of 1884, 8, 16, 21
  election of 1900, 121, 124-129
  founding of, 7-8
  influence of Harrison, 193
  inner councils, 186
  mugwumps' desire for reform, 7,
    16
  revolt against McKinley, 186-193,
    210-211
  Schurz and, 18-21
Rizal, José, 161
Robinson, Edwin Arlington, xi
Rogers, Henry Wade, xi
Roosevelt, Franklin D., 234
Roosevelt, Theodore, 126-127, 204-
  205, 207, 230, 233-237, 256n
  campaign for governor of New
    York, 126-127, 161
  criticism of mugwumps, 15, 57
  expansionist policy, 42-43, 132, 147,
    186, 236
  Godkin and, 56
  Philippine policy, 157, 226, 233
Root, Elihu, 216
Ruskin, John, 57
Russ, William A., Jr., 276n
Russia, 93, 175

Samoa, xiv, 73, 145, 187, 198
Santayana, George, 44, 49-51, 58n
Santo Domingo, proposed annexa-
    tion, xiii, 146, 188, 194, 198
  opposed by Boutwell, 194
  opposed by Hoar, 146
  opposed by Norton, 70, 72
  Sherman's opposition, 198
  views of Godkin, 72
  views of Schurz, 22-23, 30
Savage instincts, 40-43

Schurman, Jacob G., xi, 230
Schurz, Carl, xi, xiii, 9, 18-34, 115-
    116, 173, 180, 184, 215, 228-229,
    255n, 256n, 265n, 272n
  advocated free trade policy, 30,
    85, 87, 103, 217
  anti-imperialistic views, 22-27, 47-
    48
  attacks on McKinley administra-
    tion, 24-28, 30
  censorship opposed by, 33, 112
  character of, 19, 35
  criticisms of, 31-32
  Cuban annexation, 30
  edited newspapers, 20, 180
  election of 1900, 124-129, 272n
  exile from Germany, 18-19
  Hawaii annexation, 24, 26
  Law of, 22-24, 28, 30, 32, 195, 219
  mugwumpery of, 19-22
  Philippine annexation, 26-28, 30-
    32, 88
  political career, 18-21
  political theory, 20, 32, 226
  Puerto Rico annexation, 26-27, 30,
    33
  Santo Domingo annexation, 22-23,
    30
  Spanish-American War, 25
  speeches, 19
Science, effect of new, 61
Security, effect of expansionism on,
    148-149, 218, 233-234
Self-determination, rights of, 78
Sherman, John, x-xi, xiii, 10n, 135,
    193-203, 211, 215, 228, 289n
  anti-imperialism, 187, 193-203
  appointed Secretary of State, 187,
    197-202
  political career, 197-198
  Republicanism, 197
Sherman, Roger, 140, 155

Sherman Anti-Trust Act, 141, 197
Sherman Silver Purchase Act, 197
Slums, 82
Smith, Adam, 84-85
Smith, Charles Emory, 100
Smith, Edwin Burritt, 130
Social conflict and change, 11, 61,
    222-223
  attitude of mugwumps, 14-15, 17
  progress and, 238-239
Socialism, 66, 166
South Africa, 175, 190
Spain, 199-200
  American relations with, 199-200
  colonial methods, 104
Spalding, John Lancaster, xi, 10n
Spanish-American War, 22, 30, 33,
    76, 80
  effect on American character, 40-
    43
  opposition of Adams, 112-120
  opposition of anti-imperialists, 221
  opposition of Godkin, 76, 264n
  opposition of Norton, 80-81
  opposition of Reed, 206
  outbreak of, 146-147, 201
  views of Atkinson, 93-94
  views of Boutwell, 195
  views of Carnegie, 172-173
  views of Harrison, 189
  views of Hoar, 147-151, 276n
  views of James, 35, 40-44
  views of Schurz, 25
  views of Sherman, 201
Spencer, Herbert, 166, 281n
Spooner, John C., 136, 147n
Springfield Daily Republican, 117-
    118, 130
Steffens, Lincoln, 56
Storey, Moorfield, xi, 5, 10, 67, 118,
    125, 130, 280n
Suffrage for women, 67

Sumner, William Graham, xi, 10, 87-88, 104, 129, 229
 case for informal imperialism, 87-88
 free trade proposals, 105
Supreme Court, 162, 216

Taft, William Howard, 230
Tammany Hall, New York City, 124-125, 127
Tariff reform, 36, 67, 108, 197, 216-217
 McKinley Tariff of 1890, 165
Taylor, Graham, xi
Teller Amendment, 4, 95
Terms, definition of, xv-xvi*n*
Texas, 114
Third parties, plans for, 127, 130, 182
Ticknor, George, 56
Tilden, Samuel J., 59
Tillman, Ben, x
Town-meeting government, 14-15
Trade, anti-imperialists' view of, 84-88
 See also Foreign trade; Free trade
Trade-without-territory policy, 85-88
Treaty of Paris, xii, 5, 95, 121, 131, 174, 209
 opposition to, 151-159, 164, 180
 ratification of, 202-203, 225
 Senate debate, 156-159
 views of Hoar, 151-159, 164
Triumphant Democracy (Carnegie), 166-167, 171
Tropical territories, Schurz's opposition to annexing, 22-26, 219
Turkey, 146
Turner, Frederick Jackson, 261*n*
Twain, Mark, xi, 10, 129, 180-181
 on independent voting, 8-9
Tyranny, 32

Union Pacific Railroad, 108
Universal suffrage, 67
 Godkin and Norton on, 64-65
University of Michigan, 192-193

Van Dyke, Henry, xi
Veblen, Thorstein, xi
Venezuela crisis of 1895-96, xiv, 24, 75, 90, 92, 194, 198, 206, 286*n*
 views of Atkinson, 90, 92
 views of Boutwell, 194
 views of Carnegie, 171-172
 views of Godkin, 75
 views of Harrison, 188
 views of Hoar, 145
 views of James, 35, 40-41, 45, 48
 views of Norton, 75-76
 views of Reed, 206
 views of Schurz, 24
 views of Sherman, 198
Vest, George C., 154
Villard, Henry, xi
von Hengelmüller, Baron, 201
von Holst, Hermann, xi, 10*n*
Voting of mugwumps, 8-9, 126-128, 131-132
Vulgarity, age of, 54, 60-61, 63, 82

Wallace, Lew, 127
War, Carnegie's views, 167-168
 Godkin on, 73-74
 views of James, 40-42
Warren, Winslow, 5, 119, 131, 280*n*
Washington, Booker T., 67
Wealth, detrimental effects of, 54, 60-63, 65
Webb, Beatrice, 6
Webster, Daniel, 10, 15, 59
Welch, Richard E., Jr., 257*n*
Wellington, George, 136
Welsh, Herbert, 130
Western Hemisphere, 51, 170-172

Westward expansion, effects of, 61

White, Horace, xi, 9, 20, 130

White, William Allen, 17, 85, 204

Williams, William A., interpretation
 of anti-imperialists, 85, 265n

Winslow, Erving, 5, 119, 130-131,
 203n

Wolcott, Edward O., 141

World power, America as, 50, 218,
 229, 233

World War I, xv, 215

World War II, xv

Yale Review, 86